the HOLY
SPIRIT
in
the NEW
TESTAMENT

the HOLY SPIRIT in the NEW TESTAMENT

David Ewert

Foreword by
Willard M. Swartley

HERALD PRESS
Kitchener, Ontario
Scottdale, Pennsylvania
1983

Canadian Cataloguing in Publication Data

Ewert, David, 1922-
  The Holy Spirit in the New Testament

Includes bibliographical references and index.

ISBN 0-8361-3309-9

1. Holy Spirit. 2. Bible. N.T.—Criticism,
interpretation, etc. 3. Spiritual life.
I. Title.

BT121.2.E92   231'.3   C82-095089-0

Scripture quotations are from the Revised Standard Version of the Bible,
copyrighted 1946, 1952, © 1971, 1973.

THE HOLY SPIRIT IN THE NEW TESTAMENT
Copyright © 1983 by Herald Press, Kitchener, Ont. N2G 4M5
  Published simultaneously in the United States by
  Herald Press, Scottdale, Pa. 15683
Library of Congress Catalog Card Number: 82-81340
International Standard Book Number: 0-8361-3309-9
Printed in the United States of America
Design by Alice B. Shetler

83 84 85 86 87 88 89 10 9 8 7 6 5 4 3 2 1

To our children,
Eleanor Ruth, Marianne Esther, Ernest James,
Grace Arlene, Doreen Elizabeth (and their spouses),
in whose lives
the Spirit of God has begun a good work.

Contents

Foreword

The Holy Spirit's role and work in both the Christian's personal life and in the church need clarification today as much as ever. Many Christians pay too little attention to the distinctive place of the Holy Spirit; some Christians, on the other hand, major on a few biblical teachings about the Holy Spirit and turn both Christian theology and life into an experiential reductionism. All that seems to matter is a specific (usually *my*) experience of the Spirit, whether it be tongue-speaking, the second work of grace, or faith-healing. Because Christians today tend to fall too easily into one of these extremes, David Ewert's book on the Holy Spirit makes a timely contribution.

Ewert's treatment of the subject is broad and comprehensive. Prefaced by a chapter on the role of the Spirit in the Old Testament, it discusses all the New Testament texts which mention the Holy Spirit. Arranged topically, the study systematically follows the canonical order of the New Testament: part one, the Gospels; part two, Acts; and part three, the Epistles. At times the discussion is cross-referenced so that one part of the study illumines another.

This book is theological exposition at its best, supported by extensive exegetical commentary and spiced by inspirational applications. Further, Ewert helpfully draws on the studies of other important writers on the topic: James D. G. Dunn, Michael Green, George Lampe, F. D. Bruner, F. F. Bruce, Ralph Martin, and John R. W. Stott, to mention only those more prominent. His frequent quotations from such writers are often gems to be treasured. In his exegetical investigations, Ewert neither awoids difficult problems nor presents the more tenable positions in doctrinaire fashion. This is especially evident in his treatment of the difficult problem of the differences between the accounts in John and in Acts regarding the giving of the Holy Spirit (ch. 4). Similarly, his treatment of the relationship between Pentecost (Acts 2) and tongue-speaking (1 Cor. 12—14) is most helpful (ch. 5), as well as his discussion of the difference between baptism with the Holy Spirit and filling with the Spirit (chs. 7 and 11).

His biblical exposition sometimes conveys special inspirational power. Having noted how the Spirit engineered the spread of the gospel to the Samaritans, the Gentiles, and the followers of John the Baptist (ch. 6), Ewert climaxes his discussion of Acts by showing how the Spirit aids the mission of the church in power, practice, and program (ch. 8). Or, more personally, the Spirit's work in us frees us from sin, law, and death (ch. 10). Quoting Burton, he observes that life in the Spirit is not simply a middle road between legalism and lawlessness, but a highway above them both.

Within the context of his comprehensive theological exposition, Ewert's discussion of the gifts of the Spirit is convincing (ch. 14). His perception that the accent falls upon service and edification of the body and not upon personal gratification nor even the discovery of one's own gifts is on target. The Spirit is about Jesus' kingdom business and the gifts of the Spirit serve its cause. As Howard Charles has observed, detached from Jesus and his kingdom purpose, claims to experiences of the Spirit are like a waxed nose, pushed in any direction that satisfies the whim and fancy of the situation. Ewert's exposition in its thoroughness and faithfulness to the biblical text helps prevent us from such wax-play with the Spirit.

Two more commendable features of this book merit mention. Ewert writes clearly, enabling lay persons to read and study the book with profit. At the same time, college and seminary students will learn much from the study as well. For this reason it can and should be used in congregational settings—by Sunday school classes, by midweek Bible study groups, and other such groups seeking serious study of the Holy Spirit, whose work, gifts, and power can and will unleash new resources for God's people to live out their calling more fully.

Finally, and perhaps most essential, Ewert's treatment of this important topic creates in the reader a yearning to be more open and submissive to the Holy Spirit. We want to bear the fruit of the Spirit. Our voices join the cry of the early believers, *Abba*. Filled with the hope of the Spirit as our *arrabōn* (down payment) and the *aparchē* (firstfruits), we cry *Marantha*—Come, Lord Jesus!

Willard M. Swartley
Elkhart, Indiana

Author's Preface

To add another book on the Holy Spirit to the great number available is a daunting undertaking. One can only hope that by ordering the biblical materials in a new way, familiar truths will shine with new luster. Blaise Pascal explained to the readers of his *Pensées:* "Let no one say that I have said nothing new; the arrangement of the subject is new." Certainly when one undertakes a biblical study of the Holy Spirit, one cannot create new materials; one is "bound" by the Word of God. But perhaps, by ordering the materials in a new way and bringing the relevant biblical passages to bear on the life of the church in our day, old truths can be seen in a new light.

My interest in this subject reaches back many years. Repeated requests to lecture and to write articles on various aspects of the biblical doctrine of the Holy Spirit stimulated my interest in this important area of theology. A doctoral dissertation on the eschatological significance of the Holy Spirit in the writings of Paul called for further study and reflection. In 1979, the German mission society Licht dem Osten published a Russian version of a shorter manuscript I had been asked to prepare on this topic. These, and other occasions, led to the conclusion that there is room for yet another volume on the Holy Spirit.

Whenever one picks up a major strand in the theology of the New Testament, however, a number of others tend to be drawn into the discussion. Perhaps this indicates that with all its diversity there is an underlying unity in the New Testament writings. Christology, the doctrine of salvation, the church and its ministries, as well as the blessed hope of the believer are all closely intertwined with the apostolic teachings on the Holy Spirit. A conscious effort has been made in the following pages to avoid any detailed study of these related subjects. Brief forays into ancillary fields, however, are unavoidable if one wants to place a major theme into the broader context of New Testament theology.

Many have instinctively sensed that the teaching of the New Testament on the Holy Spirit is a key that unlocks many doors. As Dunn suggests,[1] they have taken up the haunting words of Bob Dylan, with their unconscious echo of John 3:8, "The answer, my friend, is blowing in the wind" [wind=*pneuma*=Spirit]. But they have not spelled this out in fuller terms. In fact, many Christians suspect that when theologians write on the Holy Spirit, they can at best offer the reader the bare bones of academic knowledge. If theological sophistication becomes a substitute for an understanding of Christian reality, such suspicions are warranted. However, religious experiences and emotions, like theological ideas, can also become ends to themselves, thereby becoming idolatrous.[2]

If we had to choose between academic "knowledge" about the Holy Spirit and personal "experience" of the Spirit's presence and power in our lives, obviously we would choose experience. But fortunately we do not have to make that kind of choice. Every believer should be concerned about the reality of his or her faith; but it is hard to believe that such a person would not also be vitally interested in what the New Testament teaches on the important subject of the Holy Spirit.

William Barclay claims in his autobiography that God gave him the gift of making difficult things simple.[3] Those who have read his writings have no reason to doubt that claim. This is also my hope in preparing the following chapters. The reader must judge whether I have succeeded.

The chapters fall into three larger areas. The first major section deals with "The Promise of the Spirit." After an introductory chapter on the Spirit in the Old Testament, Part I concentrates on the Holy Spirit in the Gospels. Part II focuses on Acts under the topic "The Coming of the Spirit." The third section, and the longest, is given to the study of the Holy Spirit in the New Testament epistles under the topic "The Spirit in the Life of the Believer."

I pray that this study shall prove to be a helpful handbook for those who wish to become better acquainted with this vital subject. The notes at the end of each chapter point the reader to some of the literature in this field of study.

Since we are dealing with the third member of the Trinity, an element of profound mystery and awe must always attend the study of the Holy Spirit. Jesus likened the Spirit to the wind, with its mysterious and numinous character. But just as we can hear and feel the blowing of the wind, by God's grace we can experience the presence and power of the Spirit, if we are willing to get in the path of God's wind.

David Ewert
Winnipeg, Manitoba

PART ONE
The Promise of the Spirit

CHAPTER 1

The Prophetic Hopes of the Coming of the Spirit

The Holy Spirit's presence can be observed everywhere in the documents of the New Testament. All the books of the New Testament were written after Pentecost and bear the stamp of the pervasive presence of the Spirit in the early church. The apostles firmly believed that the risen and exalted Lord was active in the world and, above all, in the new community which had been created by the outpouring of the Spirit at Pentecost.

Although there are always surprises in the way God acts in salvation history, the coming of the Spirit at Pentecost had been anticipated by Old Testament prophets hundreds of years in advance. We are not surprised, then, to find that the Holy Spirit is called a "promised" Spirit (Lk. 24:49; Acts 14:4; 2:33; Gal. 3:14; Eph. 1:13).

Before his ascension the risen Christ assured his disciples that he would send them "the promise of my Father" (Lk. 24:49). Whereas the Holy Spirit is not mentioned specifically in this verse, it is clearly implicit in Acts 1:4, 5, where Jesus asks his disciples to wait for "the promise of the Father," which is described as the baptism with the Spirit. Pentecost, as Peter explains later, was the fulfillment of "the promise of the Holy Spirit" (Acts 2:33).

In order to witness the fulfillment of the promise of the Father, the disciples are urged by the risen Lord to remain in Jerusalem (Lk. 24:49; Acts 1:4). To wait for the "promise of the Father" does not mean to wait for the Father to promise something, but to wait for the Father's promise (of the Spirit) to be fulfilled.

For Paul the promise of the Holy Spirit was implicit in the Abrahamic covenant. Writing to the Galatians, he explains "that in Christ Jesus the blessing of Abraham might come upon the Gentiles, that we might receive the promise of the Spirit through faith" (Gal. 3:14). Clearly no mention is made of the Holy Spirit in the covenant promises to Abraham, but God did promise to bless all the tribes of the earth through Abraham. This promise to bless all the nations, explains Paul, was fulfilled through the death of Jesus Christ on the cross (Gal. 3:13) by which the way was opened for even the Gentiles to "receive the promise of the Spirit" through faith (Gal. 3:14).[1]

Once again Paul speaks of the Holy Spirit as the "promised Holy Spirit" in Ephesians 1:13. He reminds his readers that when they heard and believed the gospel of salvation, they were "sealed with the promised Holy Spirit" (Eph. 1:13). One reason the Spirit is called "the Holy Spirit of promise" is that he was promised from days of old by the prophets and more recently by Jesus. However, in the light of the next verse (Eph. 1:14), "the Holy Spirit of promise" also points forward to the final consummation when we shall enjoy fully what in this life is but a foretaste. The Spirit, then, was not only promised in the past, but holds great promise for the present, as well as for the future.

Before we ask how the promise of the Spirit was fulfilled at Pentecost, or how it will be fully realized at the end of this present age, let us look at the prophetic hopes of the coming of the Spirit in the Old Testament. These anticipations of the coming of the Spirit should, however, be seen in a somewhat broader context, and so we begin with some observations on the activity of the Spirit of God under the old covenant.

A. The Activity of God's Spirit Under the Old Covenant

From the dawn of human history, God's Spirit has been at work in the world. In fact several Old Testament writers suggest that the world was created by the Spirit of God (Gen. 1:2; 2:7; Job 33:4; Ps. 104:30). Since the Hebrew word for spirit *(ruach)* also has the meaning of "breath" and "wind," it is not always clear which of these meanings should be given to *ruach*. (In the New Testament the Spirit is nowhere said to have been the agent in God's creative activity; this role is ascribed rather to Jesus Christ; see Colossians 1:16.) In spite of the ambiguity in the meaning of *ruach*, we would not be wide of the mark if we said that God's Spirit is seen in the Old Testament as, among other things, that power by which man and the cosmos as a whole is created and sustained.

The Spirit of God, however, is much more prominent in the history of the people of God than in the creation of the world. God's Spirit enabled Israel's heroes to perform acts for the salvation of God's people. When the *ruach* of God came upon Othniel (Judg. 3:10) or upon Jephthah (11:29), when he took possession of Gideon (6:34), and rushed upon Saul (1 Sam. 11:6), these otherwise obscure men became endowed with unusual powers. When the Spirit of the Lord came upon that strong man, Samson, he tore a lion asunder (Judg. 14:6), and struck terror into the hearts of the Philistines with his acts of valor. But when he disobeyed God, upon the suggestion of Delilah, he lost his strength (Judg. 16:20)—a clear sign that he had received his strength from the Spirit of God.

The sudden infusions of divine power were often quite violent and overwhelming. The action of the Spirit taking possession of a person can be described dramatically as "clothing himself" with the person, putting him on like a garment, and energizing him or her (e.g., Judg. 6:34). Such unexpected invasions of God's Spirit alert us to the fact that God's Spirit is not under human control. Like the wind of which Jesus spoke to Nicodemus, the Spirit of God invades people's lives even today in sovereign freedom. Some of us may prefer the more gentle whisper of the Spirit to the roaring wind; Elijah, in fact, had to learn that God could work through silence just as he could in lightning and thunder (1 Kings 19:12). But it should not be forgotten that we cannot organize the work of God's Spirit and we cannot determine his manner of working. If God's *ruach* breaks into people's lives more violently at times than we can appreciate, we must remember that it is not for us to say how the Spirit is to work.

God's Spirit also enlightened and inspired Israel's rulers. Moses was full of the Spirit of God so that he might lead Israel through forty years of life in the wilderness. When the work got too heavy for him, God gave him seventy helpers and promised that he would take some of the Spirit which was on Moses and put it upon them (Num. 11:16, 17). Moses' successor, Joshua, upon whom he later laid his hands (Deut. 34:9), is described as a man in whom the Spirit was present (Num. 27:18-23). Joseph was set over Egypt by Pharaoh because he recognized that God's Spirit was in him (Gen. 41:38-51). The judges of Israel were able to perform their duties because the Spirit of the Lord had come upon them (e.g., Judg. 3:10). Saul was similarly endowed with power to lead Israel (1 Sam. 11:6). And after Samuel had anointed David, God's Spirit came upon him to enable him to be king (1 Sam. 16:13).[2]

Sometimes God's Spirit gave people special insights which could not be attributed to their own ingenuity or intelligence. For example, Joseph was given the ability to interpret Pharaoh's dreams because God's Spirit was in him (Gen. 41:38f.; cf. also Dan. 5:14). At times God's Spirit equipped people with skills to enable them to fulfill a special calling. The artisan Bezalel, for example, was filled with the Spirit of God to fashion the furnishings of the tabernacle (Ex. 31:3). Believers living in the present post-Pentecostal era need to remember that they, too, are completely dependent on God's Spirit for illumination and insight into the will and ways of God (cf. 1 Cor. 2:6-16). Even where human skills are required, we still need the help of the Spirit of God.

Thus far we have mentioned the activity and presence of the Spirit of God upon chosen individuals only; this remains a characteristic of the Old Testament period. There is also a sense in which

God's Spirit is active among Israel as a whole, however. Isaiah explains that the exodus and God's guidance of Israel in the wilderness is to be attributed to the activity of the Spirit of God. "The Spirit of the Lord gave them rest" (Is. 63:14). In retrospect, he complains that Israel rebelled and grieved God's Holy Spirit (63:10; see Eph. 4:30 for Paul's exhortation not to grieve God's Holy Spirit), which led Israel to ask: "Where is he who put in the midst of them his holy Spirit?" (Is. 63:11). In the postexilic period, God assures his distressed people with the words of Haggai: "My Spirit abides among you; fear not" (2:5). And Zechariah gives Zerubbabel Yahweh's assurance: "Not by might, nor by power, but by my Spirit, says the Lord" (4:6).

Even the ordinary Israelite knows of the presence of God's Spirit in his life. The godly person might pray for God's Spirit to lead him aright (Ps. 143:10). When David fell into sin, he prayed that God would not take his Holy Spirit away from him (Ps. 51:11). Only here and in Isaiah 63:10, 11 does the Old Testament speak explicitly of the Holy Spirit, and in both passages the moral and ethical aspects of the Spirit's activity are stressed. In this respect the Qumran literature is very different from the Old Testament, for here the expression "Holy Spirit" occurs frequently (e.g., 1 QS 4:20f.; 1 QH 7:6f.; 16:12). In the New Testament, of course, the writers speak very freely of the "Holy Spirit."

The pervasive presence of God's Spirit is everywhere assumed in the Old Testament. The psalmist asks: "Whither shall I go from thy Spirit?" (Ps. 139:7). God's Spirit stands in parallel construction to the "presence" of God in this passage. It is by his Spirit that God makes his presence known.

Yet nowhere is the activity of the Spirit of God so prominent as in prophecy. God's Spirit gives insights to the prophet which the ordinary person does not have, empowering the prophet to speak God's words to his people. When the Spirit of the Lord came upon Eldad and Medad, they prophesied—much to the consternation of those who thought that only duly-appointed elders had the right to prophesy (Num. 11:24-30). Similarly, when the Spirit of Yahweh came upon Saul, he began to prophesy (1 Sam. 10:6, 10), as did his messengers when they met Samuel's prophetic band (1 Sam. 19:20ff.). Sometimes the Spirit of God would even pick up the prophet and whisk him away, as he did in the case of Elijah (1 Kings 18:12). Perhaps we have reminders here that we cannot prescribe to the Spirit the manner of his working.

In the earlier period ecstatic elements often attend the invasion of the prophet's life by the Spirit of God. As time goes on these features seem to recede into the background. The great preexilic prophets of Israel prefer to attribute their prophetic call and endowment to the Word of Yahweh rather than to his Spirit. Some scholars have even suggested that the literary prophets stood in reaction to the earlier nonliterary prophetic movement.[3]

Not all agree, however. It is true the preexilic prophets speak more often of the *dabar* (word) of the Lord coming to them than of the Spirit, but we should not drive the wedge too sharply between these two concepts. God's Spirit and his Word are often found in parallel construction. David, for example, says: "The Spirit of the Lord speaks by me, his word is upon my tongue" (2 Sam. 23:2). When Saul disobeyed God's Word, the Spirit of the Lord left him (1 Sam. 15:26; 16:14).

In this regard it should not be overlooked that the "hand" of Yahweh may seize the prophet (Is. 8:11; Ezek. 1:3); and the experience can be just as overwhelming as when the "Spirit" takes hold of him (Ezek. 3:12). (In Ezekiel 37:1 the "hand" of the Lord and the "Spirit" of the Lord stand in parallel construction.)

Moreover, even in the preexilic prophets we have clear references to the illuminating and inspirational work of the Spirit of God. Micah, for example, claims the Spirit to declare God's message to Israel: "But as for me, I am filled with power, with the Spirit of the Lord" (3:8). And a prophet is still known as "the man of the Spirit" (Hos. 9:7). The "word" presupposes the "Spirit."[4] Also, some of the physical expressions of the power of the Spirit from earlier times come to the fore in the exilic prophet Ezekiel (Ezek. 2:2; 3:12, 24; 11:24).

Be that as it may, there is no question in the minds of the biblical writers that all true prophecy is inspired by God's Spirit. Nehemiah recalls: "Thou didst bear with them, and didst warn them by thy Spirit through the prophets" (9:30). Zechariah complains about Israel's disobedience in the past to "the law and the words which the Lord of hosts had sent by his Spirit through the former prophets" (7:12).

This close connection between the Spirit and the Word of God has often been overlooked in the history of the Christian church. By elevating the Spirit over the Word of God, or vice versa, churches have fallen into unfortunate extremes. One might mention, for example, the conflict that developed between Luther and Thomas Muenzer in this regard. Muenzer, who emphasized the Spirit at the expense of the Word, called Luther the "Pope of the Lutheran Scripture Perverters." Luther rejected Muenzer, on the other hand, even if, as he put it, he had "swallowed the Holy Spirit, feathers and all." The Bible nowhere puts the Spirit and the Word over against each other. A "spiritualism" that is not kept within scriptural bounds can be just as devastating as a rigid and mechanical spirit-less use of the Bible.

The activity of God's Spirit in the Old Testament, whether in a moment of inspiration or in its more permanent presence in the lives of God's people, is never viewed as a natural, human quality. The work of the Spirit in persons is always God's gift. Michael Green expresses it well when he says, "Though *ruach* may be found in man, it is always so to speak, on loan, and not a possession; a resident alien, not a native."[5]

From this brief résumé of the activity of God's Spirit in general, we turn now to those passages in which a special outpouring of God's Spirit is anticipated in the age to come.

B. The Spirit of God in the Hopes of the Prophets

In spite of the presence of God's Spirit in the world, the history of Israel, the life of godly individuals, and particularly the prophets, ancient Israel by and large refused to obey God's Spirit. Her recurring apostasy from Yahweh inspired the hope of a better day in the future. This new age was to be attended by an unusual activity of the Spirit of God.

Since the days of the monarchy, when God entered into a covenant with David (2 Sam. 7:12-17), this hope for a new age expressed itself in terms of an ideal king, a messianic prince from the house of David. The fallen booth of David (Amos 9:11) was to be rebuilt by a ruler who would be endowed in a special way with the Spirit of God. "There shall come forth a shoot from the stump of Jesse, and a branch shall grow out of his roots. And the Spirit of the Lord shall rest upon him, the spirit of wisdom and understanding, the spirit of counsel and might, the spirit of knowledge and the fear of the Lord" (Is. 11:1, 2). The prophet then goes on to describe the age of peace and righteousness which this eschatological ruler, endowed with this unusual measure of God's Spirit, will bring about in this world.

This hope that the ideal future king would be full of the Spirit of God is found also in Jewish literature of the intertestamental period. The Psalms of Solomon, for example, say that "God will make him mighty in the Holy Spirit" (17:37) and his subjects shall share in this gift (18:8).

This hope ultimately found fulfillment in the greater son of David, Jesus Christ, on whom the Spirit descended and remained (Jn. 1:32), and who received the Spirit from God in rich measure (Jn. 3:34).

But there was yet another form in which this hope for the coming age of the Spirit was expressed. The Spirit was promised also to the servant of Yahweh. "Behold my servant, whom I uphold, my chosen, in whom my soul delights; I have put my Spirit upon him, he will bring forth justice to the nations" (Is. 42:1).

There has been much debate on who the servant is in this and other passages of Isaiah. The figure of the servant seems to be rather fluid. He does not always represent the same person or persons. There is fluctuation between the individual and the group. In some instances the servant is simply Israel (e.g., Is. 41:8; 43:10; 44:21; 45:4); in other places he is clearly something other than Israel, for his duty is to restore Israel (Is. 49:5, 6). At times he seems to be identified with the true Israel, the righteous remnant (e.g., 44:1; 51:1, 7). However, there are also passages in which the servant is an ideal figure, the coming redeemer who in his suffering atones for the sins of many (Is. 53).[6]

This suffering servant, who brings redemption to the world, does so by the enablement of God's Spirit. As in Isaiah 42:1, so also in 61:1, 2, the prophet takes up this theme: "The Spirit of the Lord God is upon me, because the Lord has anointed me to bring good tidings to the afflicted; he has sent me to bind up the brokenhearted, to proclaim liberty to the captives, and the opening of the prison to those who are bound; to proclaim the year of the Lord's favor, and the day of vengeance of our God; to comfort all who mourn."

These two strands of hope—that of the anointed son of David and of the servant endowed with God's Spirit—were combined in Jesus' own person and ministry. When God acknowledged Jesus as his Son through a voice from heaven, the language was reminiscent of the enthronement of the Davidic king (Ps. 2:7); and when he added, "in whom I am well pleased," he used language which described the suffering servant (Is. 42:1). The New Testament opens with the affirmation that Jesus was the son of David (Mt. 1:1); and when Jesus preached his first sermon in Nazareth, he applied to himself the words which Isaiah spoke of the servant of Yahweh: "The Spirit of the Lord is upon me, because he has anointed me" (Lk. 4:18).

It is of special interest to us at this point not only that Jesus fulfilled in his person the hopes of an ideal king of David and that of the suffering servant, but that both of these strands of expectation are connected with a special effusion of God's Spirit upon the people of God. It is the hope of the prophets that in the age to come the Spirit will be poured out on all flesh.

Isaiah foresees a new age which will be characterized by an abundance of vegetation, prosperity, and peace. This glorious future will be inaugurated with the outpouring of God's Spirit from on high (Is. 32:15). "For I will pour water on the thirsty land, and streams on the dry ground; I will pour my Spirit upon your descendants, and my blessing on your offspring" (Is. 44:3).

Better known is the prophecy of Joel, for Peter quotes it in his Pentecost address:

> And it shall come to pass afterward,
> that I will pour out my Spirit on all flesh;
> your sons and your daughters shall prophesy,
> your old men shall dream dreams,
> and your young men shall see visions.
> Even upon the menservants and maidservants
> in those days, I will pour out my spirit.
>
> —*Joel 2:28, 29*

This promise, too, stands in the context of the hope of renewed material blessings. It is the spiritual counterpart to the rain and the crops. The recipients of this future blessing are said to be "all flesh"—an expression which is probably limited to Judah in the context of Joel 2. How Peter understood the phrase when he quoted this passage on the first Christian Pentecost is hard to say; as he himself was to discover, however, "all flesh" transcended national boundaries and included all those who would call on the name of the Lord for salvation—both Jews and Gentiles. One might say, then, that this promise takes up the wistful longing of Moses, expressed in Numbers 11:29, "Would that all the Lord's people were prophets, that the Lord would put his spirit upon them!" and stamps it as a definite part of Yahweh's program for the future.

The promise that God's Spirit will be given to men and women, both slave and free, recalls another promise of God which, according to the prophets, is to be fulfilled in the future. Joel's prophecy is reminiscent of Jeremiah's promise of a new covenant which will bring about an intimate knowledge of the Lord on the part of the people of God (Jer. 31:33).

> The days are coming, says the Lord, when I will make a new covenant with the house of Israel. . . . I will put my law within them, and I will write it upon their hearts; and I will be their God, and they shall be my people. And no longer shall each man teach his neighbor and each his brother, saying,

"Know the Lord," for they shall all know me, from the least of them to the greatest, says the Lord; for I will forgive their iniquity, and I will remember their sin no more.
　　　　　　　　　　　　　　　　—Jer. 31:31-34

Whereas Jeremiah foresees the establishment of a new covenant—a covenant based on the forgiveness of sins, one in which all will know God intimately and will obey his commandments readily—he says nothing about the place of the Spirit in this transformation of the human heart. If we turn to Ezekiel, however, we find that the outpouring of God's Spirit will not only bring about the renewal of the heart, of which Jeremiah speaks, but that this renewal shall be brought about by God's Spirit.

I will sprinkle clean water upon you, and you shall be clean from all your uncleannesses, and from all your idols I will cleanse you. A new heart I will give you, and a new spirit I will put within you; and I will take out of your flesh the heart of stone and give you a heart of flesh. And I will put my spirit within you, and cause you to walk in my statutes and be careful to observe my ordinances.
　　　　　　　　　　　　　　　　—Ezek. 36:25-27

It is the hope of Old Testament prophets, therefore, that a new age will be inaugurated through the suffering of God's anointed servant and through the Davidic king upon whom God's Spirit will rest in an unusual way. This new age will be initiated with an outpouring of God's Spirit, giving birth to a new people of God and the establishment of a new covenant. This rich effusion of God's Spirit will signal a rebirth of prophetic activity and, above all, lead to a transformation of the lives of all those who receive the gift of the Spirit.

The intertestamental literature has little to contribute as far as new understandings of the Holy Spirit are concerned. Generally the Apocrypha and Pseudepigrapha stand in the tradition of the Old Testament and define the Spirit's activity primarily in terms of prophecy.[7] Rabbinic Judaism has little to say about the Holy Spirit; when it does, the Spirit's activity is related primarily to prophecy: "For this reason it should be assumed without further proof, that rabbinic scholars everywhere (except where the context makes it necessary to think of the Spirit inspiring Scripture) understood by the Holy Spirit 'the Spirit of prophecy' of 'prophetic endowment.' "[8]

Sectarian Judaism, however, as represented in the Qumran community, has much to say about the Holy Spirit.[9] Indeed the Qumran literature has considerable affinity with the language of the New Testament. We have already mentioned that the phrase "Holy Spirit," which is relatively infrequent in the Old Testament, is a common expression in the Dead Sea Scrolls. On the other hand, Qumran, like the Old Testament, anticipated the outpouring of the Spirit at the beginning of the new age.[10] A few lines from the Manual of Discipline remind us also of the close connection between the new covenant and the eschatological outpouring of the Spirit:

> God will purify by his truth all the deeds of man, and will cleanse for himself some of mankind, so as to destroy every evil spirit from the midst of his flesh and cleanse him by the holy spirit from all his wicked deeds. He will sprinkle the spirit of truth upon him like water of purification from every false abomination.
>
> —1 QS 4:20f.

With this cursory overview of the Spirit in the Old Testament and the intertestamental period, we move on to the New Testament, where we are struck by a fresh outburst of prophecy through the renewed activity of the Spirit of God, particularly in the infancy narratives of Luke's Gospel.

C. The Spirit and Prophecy at the Dawn of the New Era

Whereas Matthew begins his Gospel with the infancy narratives of Jesus, Luke steps back further and intertwines the nativity of John the Baptist with that of Jesus. He begins his account of the good news with the promise of a son given by a heavenly messenger to a childless couple, Zechariah and Elizabeth. Abraham and Sarah, like Zechariah and Elizabeth, were also childless until their old age, but by a gracious intervention on the part of God they were given a son. Elkanah and Hannah were also promised a son, Samuel, who was one of the famous Old Testament prophets, just as John, the forerunner of Messiah, was to be. This parallelism puts the Baptist in continuity with the births of famous figures in sacred history.[11] His name, John, was given before his birth to signify that God had a special role for him.

This son to be born was to be great before the Lord, to drink no wine or strong drink, and to be "filled with the Holy Spirit, even from his mother's womb" (Lk. 1:15).[12] This fullness of the Spirit was to enable John to carry out his prophetic ministry in the tradition of Elijah (vv. 16, 17). Here clearly the Spirit of prophecy that turned Saul into a prophet (1 Sam. 10:10), the Spirit that spoke through David (2 Sam. 23:2), and above all the Spirit that filled Elijah and Elisha (2 Kings 2:9-16) is in Luke's mind. The Gospels present John the Baptist as a prophet—indeed, as greater than other prophets (Lk. 7:28; 20:6), and one cannot conceive of a prophet who does not have the Holy Spirit.

As we have pointed out earlier, there is no substantial difference between the coming of the Spirit of God upon the prophets (e.g., Is. 61:1) and the coming of the Word of God to them (Ezek. 1:3). Similarly in the case of the Baptist, the angel declares that he will be filled with the Holy Spirit from the womb, and then, later, the Word of God comes to John (Lk. 3:1, 2). These are alternate ways of describing the beginning of his prophetic ministry; they remind us once again of the close connection between the Spirit and the Word of God.

During Elizabeth's pregnancy, Mary, who was to be the mother of Jesus, visited her. As Mary entered the house and greeted her host, the child in Elizabeth's womb leaped for joy (Lk. 1:44)—a gladness that hailed the advent of the messianic age. Momentarily she "was filled with the Holy Spirit and she exclaimed with a loud cry, 'Blessed are you among women, and blessed is the fruit of your womb!'" (Lk. 1:41, 42). This joyful outburst was the result of prophetic inspiration by the Holy Spirit, which gave Elizabeth insights hidden to others. She not only perceived that Mary was with child, but also that her child was the Messiah.[13] Elizabeth's canticle makes it plain that God had done much more for Mary than for her and Zechariah. Be that as it may, the close connection between prophecy and the fullness of the Spirit is again obvious.

After the birth of John, "his father Zechariah was filled with the Holy Spirit, and prophesied" (Lk. 1:67). Friends and neighbors ask: "What then will this child be?" (v. 66), for God's favor so obviously rested upon it. But Zechariah knew through the illumination of the Spirit of God that the newborn infant had a divine vocation, and broke out in his famous *Benedictus* (vv. 68-79). "Zechariah's words must be understood as the result of the Holy Spirit's coming upon him. They are words of prophecy, words which express God's revelation." [14]

Whereas in the preceding scene Elizabeth is filled with the Holy Spirit (Lk. 1:41) and she was enlightened by the Spirit to perceive the blessedness of Mary, now Zechariah is "filled with the Holy Spirit" (1:67) and praises God for John. In his canticle of praise he is enabled by the Spirit to give a commentary on the salvatory events which were beginning to take place by the birth of the Messiah's forerunner. Both his insights and his utterances indicate that a new day is dawning, for the Holy Spirit is once again equipping both men and women to prophesy as the Old Testament prophets had predicted.

A fourth passage in the Lucan infancy narratives in which the Holy Spirit is said to inspire prophetic utterances is Luke 2:25-27. Luke reports that the Holy Spirit was upon the godly Simeon (v. 25). Through the Holy Spirit it was disclosed to him (v. 26) that he should not die before he had seen the Lord's Christ (v. 27). Led by the Spirit (v. 28), he came to the temple court where he met the parents of Jesus with the Christ-child and, taking the baby up in his arms, he blessed it and spoke his famous *Nunc Dimittis* (Lk. 2:29-32).

As the giving of the forerunner's name was followed by a prophetic statement indicating the child's destiny, so the naming and dedication of Jesus is followed by prophetic utterances inspired by the Holy Spirit. Not only did Simeon recognize that the child he took in his arms was the Messiah, but the Holy Spirit also enabled him to foretell the saving acts of Christ.

The vocabulary of Simeon's canticle seems to have its primary source in the prophecies of Isaiah (40:5; 42:6; 46:13; 49:7; 52:9, 10), but the Holy Spirit illuminated Simeon so that he could interpret these Old Testament texts and show that they were about to be fulfilled through the Messiah, who had come to bring salvation to the world.

One might compare the first two chapters of Luke to an Old Testament island surrounded by the waters of the New Testament. Zechariah, Elizabeth, and Simeon, whose prophetic utterances Luke reports, stand, as it were, at the turning point of the ages. The language of their oracles is borrowed from the Old Testament, but by the Holy Spirit they are given to see that the days of fulfillment have arrived, and that God is about to do something new for the salvation of his people.

This renewed activity of the Spirit of God was anticipated by the prophets; the infancy narratives of both John and Jesus are characterized by "fillings" with the Holy Spirit, giving birth once again to prophecy. In spite of the renewed activity of the Spirit surrounding the birth of the forerunner, John belongs to the period of the preparation. All he can claim for himself is that he baptizes with water; the greater one will baptize with the Holy Spirit. In our next chapter we shall seek to clarify what this meant.

CHAPTER 2

The Baptism of the Spirit Anticipated by John the Baptist

All four of the canonical Gospels preface their account of Jesus' ministry with a brief summary of the prophetic ministry of John the Baptist. Luke intertwines the infancy narrative of John with that of Jesus; but he does so in a way that leaves no doubt about John's preparatory role. "He was not the light, but came to bear witness to the light," as John the evangelist put it (Jn. 1:8). Nevertheless, he was a "man sent from God," and he made a deep impression on others as forerunner of the Messiah.

No better evaluation of John's significance can be found than the saying of Jesus: "I tell you, among those born of women none is greater than John; yet he who is least in the kingdom of God is greater than he" (Lk. 7:28). John was given the unique privilege of preparing the way for the Messiah. There was nothing greater than that prior to the Messiah's coming. But now that the kingdom of God which John anticipated has arrived in the person of Jesus, those who have the privilege of entering this kingdom are greater even than John. Of those who belong to the age of promise, John is the greatest; those who enter the kingdom in the age of fulfillment are even more privileged.

What marks the dividing line between the age of promise and that of fulfillment is the coming of the Spirit on Jesus and through Jesus on all those who belong to him. John baptized with water only, Jesus was to baptize with the Holy Spirit. However, the oracles attending the birth narratives of John, and his prophetic activity, clearly indicate that the age of the Spirit had begun to dawn. Before we look more closely at John's prediction of the coming baptism with the Spirit, let us say a few words about the Baptist's ministry.

A. The "Baptist" Movement[1]

Whereas we know John as a great preacher and prophet, no epithet fits him better than that of "the Baptist" (usually in the participial form, "the Baptizer"). John's calls to repentance and to baptism in the Jordan were two aspects of the call to covenant renewal.

Although there were antecedents to John's baptism in the lustrations and ablutions practiced in Judaism and in the baptizing of proselytes who wanted to become members of the Jewish community, John's baptism was unique. Quite aside from the fact that John himself did the baptizing (in contrast to self-baptism, as in Judaism), John baptized Jews. Moreover, his baptism had eschatological significance; it prepared people for the coming of the greater one.

The response to his call to repent and to be baptized was overwhelming: "All the country of Judea, and all the people of Jerusalem" went out to him to be baptized, confessing their sins (Mk. 1:5). Baptism was a symbolic act by which John's converts dramatized their decision to turn from their sinful ways.[2] It was an expression of their hope that they would escape the eschatological judgment that was about to begin.

Those who responded to John's message and publicly confessed their desire to return to God's ways by being baptized represented an identifiable community, known as "disciples of John." They were known, for example, by their prayers (Lk. 11:1) and their fasting (Mk. 2:18). No doubt many went home after being baptized to wait for the coming one, and when he appeared upon the scene, many of John's disciples recognized him as the greater one and went over to him. Some, to be sure, were hesitant and needed a bit of prodding from the Baptist himself, who explained that he was not the bridegroom but only his friend; having heard the bridegroom's voice, he could only rejoice to see his followers go over to Jesus (Jn. 3:27-29). "He must increase, but I must decrease," was John's way of succinctly describing the purpose of his calling (Jn. 3:30). To have prepared a people for the coming one was all that John was concerned about, for he thought of himself only as the forerunner of the coming one.

Very central to John's message was his prophecy concerning the greater one for whom he was preparing the way. John's coming signaled the beginning of the joyful tidings of salvation and the inbreaking of the rule of God (Mk. 1:1). As in the days of the first exodus when God promised to send his messenger before the people (Ex. 23:2) to lead them through the wilderness, and as in the days of the prophet Isaiah, who announced a second exodus from Babylon through the wilderness, so John was to prepare the way in the wilderness for the great deliverance that God was about to effect. And just as the first covenant was made in the wilderness, so the wilderness again becomes the place of covenant renewal.

The appearance of a prophet at the turning point of the ages was to be a decisive event in the history of salvation. John is not important simply for his own sake, but he stands at the beginning of the unfolding drama of redemption which centers in Jesus of Nazareth.[3] His message is telescoped to focus upon a single theme: the coming of the greater one. In comparison to the coming one, John is insignificant, so insignificant that he is not worthy to perform the most menial task for him. "After me comes he who is mightier than I, the thong of whose sandals I am not worthy to stoop down and untie" (Mk. 1:7).

The precise identity of the coming one—a formulation which echoes Malachi 3:1f.; 4:5f.—was not yet revealed to John. But as the first exodus was under the leadership of God's Spirit (Is.

63:11, 14), so John announced that the coming exodus would be characterized by a fresh outpouring of the Spirit. "I have baptized you with water," he explains, "but he will baptize you with the Holy Spirit" (Mk. 1:8 and parallel passages).

This prophecy of the coming Spirit baptism is of utmost significance for our study, so we turn now to this promise of the baptism of the Spirit.

B. The Baptism of the Greater One
1. The Promise

Two of the synoptic writers, Matthew and Luke, give the promise of the Spirit baptism in somewhat fuller form: "He will baptize you with the Holy Spirit and with fire" (Mt. 3:11; Lk. 3:16). Mark omits "and with fire," as does the writer of the fourth Gospel.[4]

It has been argued that Mark's version is the original and that "and with fire" was added later after the Pentecost event, when the Spirit's coming was attended by tongues of fire (Acts 2:1ff.). Quite the opposite approach has been taken by others who hold that John's prediction that the greater one would baptize with the Holy Spirit was added after Pentecost. In support of the latter, it has been pointed out that the disciples of John in Ephesus evidently knew nothing of a Holy Spirit (Acts 19:1-7), and so this saying about the coming Spirit baptism can hardly go back to John. Actually the disciples of John could not have been totally ignorant of the Holy Spirit; they did not know, however, that the Spirit had been poured out at Pentecost.

We do best to take both the promise of the coming Spirit baptism and the baptism with fire as genuine predictions of the Baptist. The question remains as to how this dual prediction is to be understood. Of the two coming baptisms the baptism with (or "by" or "in") the Holy Spirit is less strange. We have seen earlier that the Spirit is frequently compared to water (Is. 32:15; 44:3; Ezek. 36:25-27); therefore verbs like "pouring," "filling," and "baptizing" are quite naturally associated with the coming of the Spirit in its richness and profusion.

A baptism with fire seems somewhat more foreign to our way of thinking, but fire was a common Old Testament symbol for the presence of God, in particular his judgments (Is. 29:6; 31:9; Ezek. 38:22; Amos 7:4; Zeph. 1:18; 3:8). Even a river of fire is mentioned in Daniel 7:10 and in extracanonical Jewish literature (Sib. 3:44; 1 QH 3:29-32). Since fire is spoken of as a lake or river (see "lake of fire," Rev. 20:15), it is not at all strange that John should speak of God's judgment as a baptism with fire.

We do not need to speculate on what baptism with the Spirit means, for our Lord himself has given us the interpretation of that phrase. It is clearly a reference to the coming of the Spirit at Pentecost (Acts 1:5). The question remains, however, how the baptism with fire is related to this Pentecostal baptism with the Spirit, and the answers vary greatly.

To identify the baptism with fire with the fiery tongues that appeared on the disciples in the upper room when the Spirit was poured out, is hardly an acceptable solution. To say simply that the coming Holy Spirit will purify people's hearts, and that the baptism with fire is a way of describing this process, does not take us far enough either.

A. M. Hunter seems to be of the opinion that the Holy Spirit is the fire that Jesus had come to bring. In one of Jesus' memorable sayings, he expressed the wish that this fire were already kindled, but he knew this was not possible until he had undergone the baptism of his own death (Lk. 12:49f.). Hunter comments, "The purpose of Jesus' mission is to unloose in the world the pentecostal fire of the Spirit, which must, initially, be a fire of judgment."[5] Just how the Spirit functions as judgment, he does not explain.

James Dunn seems to take a similar line of interpretation and explains the dual baptism in this way: "The most probable interpretation is that Spirit-and-fire together describe the one purgative act of messianic judgment which both repentant and unrepentant would experience, the former as a blessing, the latter as destruction."[6]

In both Matthew and Luke the baptism with fire seems to be

understood in terms of God's final judgment, for John is reported to have spoken of the separation of the righteous from the wicked and the destruction of the latter in the eschatological judgment (Mt. 3:12; Lk. 3:7).

This would lead us to understand the dual baptism—with the Holy Spirit and with fire—as a reference to God's gracious visitation at Pentecost, on the one hand, and to his judgment on the wicked at the end of the age. That this eschatological judgment began with the separation of those who repented and received the gift of the Spirit from those who remained in their sins, is thereby not denied. Joel, in his prediction of the future outpouring of the Spirit (2:28), also spoke of "blood and fire and columns of smoke" (2:30). Peter quotes the entire passage in his Pentecost speech, but that does not mean that he thought that every detail of the prophecy was being fulfilled at that very moment (Acts 2:17-21). Just as the day of the Lord in the Old Testament brings judgment on the wicked and salvation to the people of God, so the baptism of the Spirit marked the beginning of the new age of salvation, and the baptism with fire will take place when God, in the words of the Baptist, "will clear his threshing floor and gather his wheat into the granary, but the chaff he will burn with unquenchable fire" (Mt. 3:12).

The coming baptism with the Holy Spirit stands in marked distinction to the water baptism of John. This did not mean, however, that the baptism with water would be done away with by the coming one. The fact is Jesus also baptized with water, although, as the fourth Gospel informs us (Jn. 3:22; 4:1, 2), Jesus' disciples did the actual baptizing. Nevertheless, prior to Pentecost, water baptism was not yet connected with Spirit baptism. There is no evidence, however, that those who were baptized with water into the messianic community were rebaptized after the coming of the Spirit at Pentecost (with the exception of the Ephesian disciples, who were unaware of the Pentecost event, Acts 19:1-7). Presumably the gift of the Spirit transmitted their former water baptism into Christian baptism in which water and Spirit are but two aspects of the same experience.

2. *The Fulfillment*

In the fourth Gospel the Baptist's promise that the one upon whom the Spirit had descended would baptize with the Holy Spirit (Jn. 1:33), is bordered by the identification of Jesus as the lamb of God (Jn. 1:29, 37). The evangelist evidently wanted to underscore that the baptism with the Spirit lay beyond the cross and the resurrection, when God's lamb would take away the sin of the world. And that, in fact, is what happened.

After his glorious resurrection our Lord instructed his disciples to wait in Jerusalem for the promise of the Father about which they had heard earlier. This promise, Jesus explained, was now about to be fulfilled: "For John baptized with water, but before many days you shall be baptized with the Holy Spirit" (Acts 1:5). Here Jesus clearly points to the Pentecostal outpouring of the Spirit as the fulfillment of John's prediction about the baptism with the Spirit which the greater one would bring.

Later, when Peter reported to the Jerusalem community on the coming of the Spirit upon the Gentiles, he said that it had reminded him of Jesus' words just quoted: "John baptized with water, but you shall be baptized with the Holy Spirit" (Acts 11:15, 16). What had happened to Jews at Pentecost also happened to Gentiles; they too experience the baptism with the Spirit.

John's promise, therefore, was fulfilled on the day of Pentecost, when all those who repented and believed the gospel were baptized with the Spirit (Acts 1:5). That the fulfillment of the promised Spirit baptism was not exhausted by the Pentecostal outpouring of the Spirit can be seen from the experience of the household of Cornelius, upon whom the Holy Spirit fell as Peter preached the gospel. Both the Pentecost believers and the Gentile converts in the house of Cornelius were baptized with water after they had received the gift of the Holy Spirit. The only condition for receiving the Spirit was repentance and faith (Acts 2:28; 11:17, 18).

From the fourfold promise of the baptism with the Spirit in the Gospels, and from the two passages in Acts, it is obvious that Spirit baptism refers to an initiatory experience. The founding of the church at Pentecost and the incorporation of new believers following Pentecost are both described as a baptism with the Holy Spirit.

Outside of these six passages there is only one other reference to the baptism with the Spirit which is quite in keeping with what has just been said (1 Cor. 12:13), and we shall have more to say on that when we come to Paul.

By a strange hermeneutical principle it is often argued today that since the disciples of Jesus were "Christians" before Pentecost, the baptism of the Spirit for them must therefore be understood as a "second work of grace," and that this should be the experience of all believers. Such a view betrays a complete lack of historical perspective. One cannot force the experience of believers in the post-Pentecost era into the mold of the experience of the followers of Jesus prior to the cross and the outpouring of the Spirit by the exalted Lord.

It is unfortunate that there is so much confusion on this point today; it may be of significance to explain why the baptism with the Spirit is understood by many Christians to describe not the beginning of their new life in Christ, but rather a post-conversion experience, a second work of grace.

C. The Baptism of the Spirit Today

From second-century Montanism on to the present there have been those who wondered whether they had received all that there was available to them in Christ when they came to him in repentance and faith and received the assurance of the forgiveness of their sins. Was there not "something more"? That growth and maturation in the Christian life is constantly encouraged by the apostles in their writings is, of course, obvious to all who know the New Testament. But the question is whether there is not yet another experience, perhaps not unlike conversion, by which the believer is lifted from the level of spiritual ordinariness to a higher plane.

Historically speaking the teaching of a second work of grace, often called Spirit baptism, received strong impetus from the

Methodist-holiness quest for instantaneous sanctification, subsequent to conversion.[7]

Charles Finney, a great leader in American revivalism and
education in the mid-nineteenth century, also taught an
experience subsequent to conversion which he called the baptism
of the Holy Spirit. He understood this, however, to be an
experience in which the believer was empowered in a special way
for some ministry in God's kingdom. This represented a shift from
sanctification to enablement for service.

Toward the end of the nineteenth century churches in
Anglo-Saxon countries in particular were strongly affected by the
deeper life movements in which it was held that a "second blessing" should follow upon conversion. Some called it "complete
sanctification," others "endowment with power," and still others
"Spirit baptism."

The Keswick movement in Britain furthered this doctrine of
the second work of grace. Through the ministry of the American
P. R. Pearsal Smith the holiness teaching of Keswick was taken to
Germany, where it gave impetus to the *Gemeinschaftsbewegung,*
where this teaching was, however, rejected eventually.[8]

A great many outstanding Christian leaders at the end of the
nineteenth and the beginning of the twentieth centuries, such as
A. J. Gordon, F. B. Meyer, A. B. Simpson, and others, testified to
and advocated a "second experience." The American revivalist
R. A. Torrey, president of Moody Bible Institute at the beginning
of this century, was very influential in his advocacy of a second
work of grace. Torrey understood the baptism with the Spirit
along the lines advocated by Finney as a special endowment with
power for service and witness.

Suffice it to say, the baptism with the Spirit has been understood in different ways in the past. There have also been those
who have thought of salvation as occurring in two stages of Christian experience, yet without using the term "baptism of the
Spirit" to describe the second work of grace.

In current "charismatic" circles, which have their spiritual
roots in the holiness movements, the theology of the "second

blessing" has found unique expression. The baptism of the Spirit is understood as a second stage in one's Christian experience in which one receives the gift of speaking in tongues.

It should be clearly understood that believers experience Christ in different ways; any experience which helps to make Christ and his gracious gifts more meaningful and real can hardly be condemned. In fact it would be a pity if a believer never experienced anything new after conversion. John R. Stott sums it up rather well:

> Although I believe we must insist that, according to the New Testament, God's *norm* is one initiatory "baptism" with the Spirit, followed by a continuous and increasing appropriation of his fullness which involves a steady growth in holiness and into Christian maturity, yet it must be added that within this process of growth there may be many deeper experiences and that sometimes the Spirit works more abnormally still.[9]

Professor Dunn adds to that: "The religious man should neither *expect* any particular experience simply because it is usual, nor *suspect* any particular experience because it is unusual; he must rather *respect* the whole range of spiritual experience as possibly valid."[10]

Therefore, we should not reject or question the claims of devout followers of Christ who have had a significant second or third profound experience since their conversion. Nevertheless, one searches in vain in the New Testament for a description of a second work of grace (the experience of the Samaritans [Acts 8] and the Ephesian disciples [Acts 19] will be discussed later). For that reason, one should be careful not to use New Testament terminology which speaks of the beginning of the Christian life to describe one's Christian experience following conversion. Otherwise, we fall into the error of Humpty Dumpty, who explained to mystified Alice, "When I use a word, it means just what I choose it to mean." "The New Testament confines talk of Spirit-baptism to the experience of the Spirit at conversion-initiation, and speaks of *all* later experiences of empowering as a being filled with the Spirit."[11]

Returning for a moment to John the Baptist, who anticipated the baptism of the Spirit, we should add that he did not live to see the fulfillment of his prediction. The one coming after him, the Messiah, was to be the one who would baptize with the Holy Spirit. This greater one, however, first came upon the scene at the turning point of the ages as the bearer of the Spirit, and to that topic we turn next.

CHAPTER 3

The Messiah, the Bearer of the Spirit

Two strands of expectation seem to be discernible in the prophetic hopes of the coming age of the Spirit. On the one hand, there is the hope that the Spirit will be poured out upon all flesh (Joel 2:28f.); on the other hand, the activity of the Spirit in the new age is associated with the coming of a unique personage, depicted either as a king in the line of David (Is. 11:1ff.) or as a suffering servant (Is. 42:1ff.) who is to be anointed with the Spirit of God to carry out his vocation.

In the New Testament these two strands of prophetic expectation are brought together in the person of Jesus, the Messiah. Jesus first received a special endowment of the Spirit of God and then imparted it to others.[1] Not only was Jesus conceived of the Holy Spirit, not only was he anointed with the Spirit at his baptism, but, as John the Baptist predicted, he would also baptize others with the Spirit.

Jesus was supremely the man of the Spirit. Of John the Baptist it was said that he would be filled with the Spirit even from his mother's womb (Lk. 1:15); of Jesus it is reported that he was conceived of the Spirit.

A. Jesus' Conception by the Spirit

1. Affirmations

The narratives of Jesus' birth found in Matthew and Luke are very dissimilar, but they have one thing in common: that Joseph did not "know" Mary (a Hebrew euphemism for sexual relations) before Jesus' birth. Jesus was conceived without a human father (Mt. 1:18; Lk. 1:34, 35). When Mary asked the angelic messenger, Gabriel, how this could possibly be, he answered: "The Holy Spirit will come upon you, and the power of the Most High will overshadow you" (Lk. 1:35). In the Matthean account we read: "When his mother Mary had been betrothed to Joseph, before they came together she was found to be with child of the Holy Spirit" (Mt. 1:18).

The Holy Spirit (equated in the Lucan version in poetic parallelism with the power of God) was to be the agent. Beyond that nothing is said about Mary's conception of Jesus. It is stated in a simple, unargumentative way, offering no hints as to why it should have happened as it did. There have always been skeptics who thought the Gospel writers invented the stories of the virgin birth since in a Hellenistic environment many heroes were said to have been divinely conceived. But such pagan myths offer no real parallels to the virginal conception of Jesus, for always they are born out of the sexual union of some "divine" father and a human mother.

Others have suggested that the stories of the virginal conception of Jesus are based on the miraculous births of the Old Testament. Sarah, for example, bore Isaac when she was ninety. But while there are *miraculous* births in the Old Testament, there are no *virgin* births. Michael Green writes, "The birth stories . . . are without analogy in pagan or Jewish literature."[2] The conception of Jesus by the Holy Spirit must then be understood as unique. Although only two New Testament writers mention it specifically, it is an integral part of New Testament teaching.

It is only to be expected that the birth of Christ, who stands at the head of a new humanity, should be singularly different from any other births.

2. Objections

In liberal theology the conception of Jesus by the Holy Spirit has been largely denied. For some this doctrine is nothing more than an attempt by the early church to confess the miracle of the incarnation—a confession of faith, but not a statement of fact.

Some have objected to the doctrine of the virgin birth on rationalistic grounds; they do not believe in miracles. Others think they must object to it on exegetical grounds, since the New Testament generally is silent on this doctrine. Still others do so on dogmatic grounds, for they argue that it detracts from the incarnation by making Christ's conception different from ours.

But why should our Lord be less human just because he was born of Mary without the cooperation of a human father? The New Testament nowhere suggests that Jesus was half divine and half human just because he was conceived by the Holy Spirit and born of Mary. That other writers besides Matthew and Luke fail to mention the virgin birth means simply that this doctrine was not germane to the purposes of their accounts. Paul, for example, nowhere mentions the virgin birth (he does say that Jesus was born of a woman, Gal. 4:4); this does not mean that he rejected this teaching, but evidently it was not a doctrine about which the churches to whom he wrote had questions. If we can believe in the miracle of the resurrection, we should have no difficulty in believing in the virginal conception of Jesus.

3. Significance

The virgin birth proclaims the great truth that God, not man, brought the Savior into the world. The coming of Jesus into the flesh did not occur upon Joseph's initiative, but upon God's. For early Christians the coming of the Spirit was the sign of the new age; therefore, the conception of Jesus by the Spirit was clear evidence that the new creation had begun, just as the Spirit of God was active at the beginning of the new creation.

To be conceived of the Holy Spirit makes the Savior unique. Whereas God might have chosen to bring in the redeemer by the normal processes of conception, he chose this unique way. The virgin birth holds the once-only place in human history reserved for the coming of Christ at the turning point of the ages.

The activity of the Holy Spirit in the conception of Jesus remains a mystery. All the efforts on the part of some theologians and scientists to find analogies in nature to this miracle of parthenogenesis are less than helpful. The virgin birth teaches us in a profound way that God, in his infinite grace, became one of us, and that the Messiah is his gift to humanity.

Whereas Jesus was conceived in a miraculous way by the Holy Spirit, he was born of a woman like every other person. Of his infancy and boyhood, next to nothing is known; the thirty years from birth to the beginning of his ministry are passed over in almost total silence by the Gospel writers. But when the sound of John the Baptist's voice was heard in the Jordan Valley and multitudes were responding to his call to repent and be baptized, Jesus also went out from Galilee to be baptized by John in the Jordan. It was at this occasion that the heavens were opened and the Spirit of God came upon him to equip him for his ministry.

B. Jesus' Endowment with the Spirit
1. The Baptism of Jesus

The climax of John the Baptist's ministry was his baptism of Jesus. Although this did not mark the end of John's activity, it signaled the beginning of our Lord's ministry. It has never been easy to explain why Jesus was baptized, particularly since our Lord had no need to confess sins as did others who came to John for baptism. Somehow Jesus recognized in the prophetic preaching of John that the hour had come for him to begin his mission (that Jesus had an earlier mission in Judea is thereby not denied), and when John hesitated to honor Jesus' request for baptism, Jesus gave that rather cryptic answer: "For thus it is fitting for us to fulfil all righteousness" (Mt. 3:15).

With his baptism Jesus stepped into the eyes of the public and entered upon his vocation. Identifying with sinners in their need, he proclaimed his solidarity with fallen humanity. Standing in the dirty waters of Jordan, Jesus began to go the way of humiliation that would lead to the cross. The Gospel writers give no explanation of the meaning of Christ's baptism. The opening of the heavens, the coming of the Spirit on Jesus, and the voice from heaven were evidence enough that his baptism was part of God's plan. Probably no one but Jesus himself understood the deep significance of his baptism by John. Only from the standpoint of the cross and the resurrection are we able to enter into its meaning.[3]

All three Synoptics report that when Jesus was baptized and came up out of the water the heavens were opened (Mark has "torn open")—an indication that God was about to reveal himself (Mk. 1:10; Mt. 3:16; Lk. 3:21). Luke adds that as Jesus prayed the heavens were opened (Lk. 3:21) and the Holy Spirit came down upon him like a dove. He explains that the Spirit came down bodily, indicating that his experience was real and not a figment of someone's imagination.

Why the Holy Spirit is likened to a dove is not quite clear. There is some rabbinic evidence that the sound of the *bath quol* (the divine echo) was likened to the cooing of a dove. Moreover, some rabbis interpreted the moving of the Spirit of God over the waters of creation (Gen. 1:2) in terms of a bird fluttering over its young. Since 1 Peter 3:20, 21 relates baptism to the flood, it has been suggested that Noah's dove—as a sign that judgment was past and God's day of grace had begun—lies behind the symbolism here. Others associate the dove with Israel and link Jesus to the new Israel (or is it that Jesus at the moment was regarded as the true, ideal Israelite when he received the Spirit as a dove?).[4]

What we do know is that with the coming of the Spirit upon Jesus, the promise of God to put his Spirit upon his servant was fulfilled (Is. 42:1). This is explicitly stated in Matthew 12:18. Or, to touch upon another strand of prophetic hope, the Spirit now rests upon the son of David (Is. 11:1ff.). In Jerome's commentary on Isaiah 11:1ff., there is a quotation from the lost *Gospel According to the Hebrews* in which it is stated:

It came to pass that when the Lord had ascended from the water the whole fountain of the Holy Spirit descended and rested upon him, and said to

him, "My Son, in all the prophets I looked for thee, that thou mightest
come and I might rest in thee; for thou art my rest, thou art my Son, my
first-born, who art king for evermore."[5]

The coming of the Spirit on Jesus, however, cannot be
understood apart from the voice from heaven: "Thou art my
beloved Son; with thee I am well pleased" (Mk. 1:11). In this
word from the Father there is an allusion to both Psalm 2:7 and
Isaiah 42:1. Psalm 2:7 points to the Davidic king who is God's representative on earth; Isaiah 42:1 speaks of the suffering servant
who gives his life for others.

That the coming of the Spirit upon Jesus was designed to
equip him for his messianic mission is clearly stated by our Lord
himself (Lk. 4:18) and by Peter in his message to the Gentiles in
the house of Cornelius. He recalls "how God anointed Jesus of
Nazareth with the Holy Spirit and with power; how he went
about doing good and healing all that were oppressed by the
devil, for God was with him" (Acts 10:38). Without being equipped
with the Holy Spirit, the messianic activity of our Lord would
have been inconceivable.

According to the fourth Gospel the baptism of Jesus and the
coming of the Spirit upon him was not only to equip Jesus for his
ministry, but it was also to reveal him to Israel (Jn. 1:31). John
confessed later that he had not known that Jesus was the coming
one, but when he saw the Spirit descend as a dove from heaven
and remain upon him, he recognized him as the one. Whether he
knew Jesus at all prior to this event is hard to say. Though they
were related they may never have met before, since Jesus grew up
in Galilee and John in Judea. Be that as it may, John did not at
first know that Jesus was the coming one.

Moreover, John does not claim to have gained this special
insight on his own. He got it by divine revelation. "He who sent
me to baptize with water said to me, 'He on whom you see the
Spirit descend and remain, this is he who baptizes with the Holy
Spirit' " (Jn. 1:34). When he saw the Spirit descending on Jesus,
he knew that he was the coming one. Having recognized this,
John understood that his baptism in water was not only a way in

which people signified their repentance and their return to God's way of righteousness, but also it was designed to make Christ "manifest to Israel" (Jn. 1:31).

The descent of the Spirit on Jesus at the moment of his baptism, however, signified not only that Jesus was the coming one; nor was it only an endowment with power from above but, with the descent of the Spirit, Jesus initiated the new age. In the words of Dunn: "Only with the descent of the Spirit does the new covenant and the new epoch enter, and only thus does Jesus himself enter the new covenant and epoch. He entered as representative man—representing in himself Israel and even mankind."[6]

In contrast to the Synoptics, John's Gospel adds that when the Spirit came upon Jesus, "it remained on him" (1:32). The verb "remain" denotes the beginning of the Spirit's permanent dwelling in Jesus.[7] Jesus is henceforth the bearer of the Spirit. This is underscored by John the evangelist when he explains that God—at least God appears to be the subject—did not give his Spirit to Jesus by measure.[8] And because he possesses the Spirit in fullest measure, he will effect the eschatological outpouring of the Spirit at Pentecost. The one who is uniquely the bearer of the Spirit will be the dispenser of the Spirit.

The baptism of Jesus is sometimes taken to be a prototype of the second work of grace—the baptism with the Spirit. This thesis breaks down in its failure to grasp the fact that we are dealing here with events whose significance, at least for those who recorded them, lies almost totally in the part they play in salvation history. In other words, we are dealing not so much with stages in Jesus' spiritual life, which form a permanent pattern which all believers are to imitate in their Christian experience, but we are dealing rather with stages in salvation history itself. In the words of Dunn:

> The experience of Jesus at Jordan is far more than something merely personal—it is a *unique* moment in history: the beginning of a new epoch in salvation-history—the beginning, albeit in a restricted sense of the End-time,

the messianic age, the new covenant. This means that although Jesus'
anointing with the Spirit may possibly be described as a second experience
of the Spirit for Jesus, it is not a second experience of the new covenant, or
of Jesus within the new covenant. It is in fact the event which begins the
new covenant for Jesus—it initiates the messianic age and initiates Jesus
into the messianic age.[9]

We should not fail to grasp the fundamental truth, however,
that, just as Jesus was endowed with God's Spirit for his messianic
mission, so we must be endowed with the Spirit if we are to fulfill
our calling and ministry in the kingdom of God.

One might have expected that Jesus should now immediately begin to proclaim the imminence of the kingdom of
God. But this is not the case. The Spirit with which he had been
endowed at his baptism first drives him into the wilderness where
his sonship and messianic calling was to be put to the test.

2. The Temptation of Jesus

The opening verse in all three synoptic accounts of Jesus'
temptation clearly links the temptation of Jesus with his baptism.
"Jesus' expulsion into the desert is the necessary consequence of
his baptism; it is the same Spirit who descended upon Jesus at his
baptism who now forces him to penetrate more deeply into the
wilderness."[10]

Just as Yahweh, after making the covenant with Israel, tested
his people and disciplined them as a father his son (Deut. 8:5), so
Jesus, the founder of the new covenant, is led by the Spirit into
the wilderness to be tested as God's Son ("If you are the Son of
God," said the tempter, Mt. 4:3, 6).[11]

Luke reports that "Jesus, full of the Holy Spirit, returned
from the Jordan, and was led by the Spirit for forty days in the
wilderness, tempted by the devil" (Lk. 4:1, 2). Mark stresses that
Jesus' departure into the wilderness took place immediately upon
his baptism and he uses a more forceful expression than either
Luke or Matthew: "The Spirit . . . drove him out [ekballo] into
the wilderness" (Mk. 1:12).

It is of interest that Luke inserts a long genealogy of Jesus between the story of his baptism and his temptation. There are parallels to this in the Old Testament. For example, before the call of Abraham, his genealogy is recorded (Gen. 11). In the case of Moses, his genealogy is given after his call (Ex. 6:14-25). Since Luke traces Jesus' genealogy back to Adam, it seems to be his way of linking Jesus, who was called to his messianic task at his baptism, with all of humanity. The sinners with whom he stood in the waters of Jordan were but representatives of fallen humanity as a whole.

Having been guided into the wilderness by the Spirit, Jesus is then tempted by the devil. The verb "tempt" *(peirazo)* often means to test, and is used in the Old Testament for God testing his people in order "to assess the reality of their faith and obedience."[12]

The forty days may recall Israel's forty years of testing in the wilderness. But there are other Old Testament parallels. Moses, for example, stayed on the mountain for forty days when Israel was constituted a people of God in the wilderness (Ex. 24:18). Elijah walked for forty days in the wilderness back to Sinai, where God renewed his prophetic calling (1 Kings 19:8).

Both Mark and Luke indicate that Jesus was tempted throughout the forty-day period, but the three recorded temptations in Luke and Matthew come only at the end of the forty days. Besides, these temptations were not the end of the devil's attempt to defeat Jesus. In fact, Luke reports that after completing these temptations, the devil "departed from him until an opportune time" (Lk. 4:13). It would not be wide of the mark to say that during the passion of our Lord, Satan launched his final and most violent attack on the Son of Man, only to be defeated when the grave gave up the crucified Christ on Easter morning. It should not be overlooked, however, that the entire ministry of Jesus was characterized by fierce conflict with the enemy of humanity, Satan.

Mark gives an interesting detail about Jesus' dwelling in the wilderness, namely, that "he was with the wild beasts" (Mk. 1:13). Whereas this may have been mentioned simply to underscore the loneliness of Jesus (when God brought the beasts to Adam, he could not find a companion among them for himself, Gen. 2), these beasts also symbolize evil powers (Ps. 22:11f.; 91:11-13). It is even possible that the reference to the beasts is reminiscent of the new covenant that God promises to make not only with humanity but also with the beasts (Hos. 2:18).

Like Old Testament prophets and like the forerunner, John, Jesus went into the wilderness under the direction of the Holy Spirit to have his calling tested and clarified. The three specific temptations mentioned in Matthew and Luke all seem to indicate that Jesus had to decide whether he would be a Messiah according to the popular expectations of Judaism, or whether he would be the suffering servant who redeems humanity by the cross.

The temptation to make bread out of stones was, among other things, a temptation to use his power as Son of God for his own ends instead of being obedient to the Father. It struck at the relationship of Jesus to his Father.[13] Following Matthew's order, the second temptation was to jump down from the "wing" of the temple—a temptation made even sharper by the quotation from Psalm 91 which promised protection to the godly. This may have been a temptation to proclaim himself as a Messiah with a dazzling sign. The last temptation was Satan's offer of the kingdoms of the world to Jesus, if Jesus would fall down and worship him and thus receive his lordship from Satan rather than from God.

It is interesting that Jesus' answers to the tempter are all taken from Deuteronomy—a book which records Israel's wilderness experience. But quite in contrast to Israel's many defeats in the wilderness, our Lord came through his temptations victoriously. He went into this battle with the evil one in the fullness of the Spirit (Lk. 4:1), and when the temptations were over, he came out of the wilderness into Galilee "in the power of the Spirit" (Lk. 4:14).

John Taylor writes:

> For him the descent of the dove was a moment of seeing and hearing, in which he realized in a deeper, clearer recognition, his own role both as Son of God and as Suffering Servant, and the identity of those two Old Testa-

ment images. He had to go into the wilderness to wrestle with the meaning of this vision for himself and for the world. Then, with the Spirit of the Lord upon him, he was ready to begin his mission.[14]

C. Jesus' Ministry by the Spirit
1. The Proclamation of Good News

Equipped by the Spirit of God, with the nature of his messiahship tested and affirmed, Jesus began his ministry in Galilee both in word and in deed. Rumors that a mighty prophet of God had appeared began to spread over all the province. Luke reports: "And Jesus returned in the power of the Spirit into Galilee, and a report concerning went out through all the surrounding country" (4:14). In the power of the Spirit he went to his hometown, Nazareth, where he attended the synagogue, as was his custom. When he was asked to read the selection from the prophets, he opened the scroll at Isaiah 61:1f., and read: "The Spirit of the Lord is upon me, because he has anointed me to preach good news to the poor ..." (Lk. 4:18). After the reading he closed the book and commented: "Today this scripture has been fulfilled in your hearing" (Lk. 4:21). The anointed prophet of Isaiah 61 is now the Messiah who proclaims good news. "Could anything stress more strongly the concentration of the Spirit in the person of the Messiah for mission?"[15]

Jesus' message that day contained all the great themes of the gospel: to bring healing to those who are brokenhearted, release to prisoners of war, the recovery of sight for the blind, to set at liberty the oppressed. The good news was that the year of the Lord's favor had arrived. The Old Testament year of jubilee, the year of liberation and forgiveness of debt appointed by Yahweh (Lev. 25), symbolized for Jesus the day of salvation which he was announcing (Lk. 4:18, 19).[16] Taylor writes, "Under the compulsion of the Spirit he goes to his combat with the devil and emerges victorious; he has bound the strong man. Now armed with the same Spirit he comes to unbind the prisoners and let the broken victims go free."[17] The new era of salvation had begun. Before their very eyes that which was said of the anointed servant of

Yahweh long ago was being fulfilled in the person and ministry of Jesus.

The words of our Lord were spoken with such grace that the audience was initially quite overwhelmed, but in the end they were ready to kill him. Indeed the experience of Isaiah the prophet, from whom he had quoted, was being repeated in our Lord's experience in that the hearts of the hearers were sluggish and their ears heavy and their eyes closed (Is. 6:9, 10), so that they failed to grasp the message of salvation which God had sent through Jesus.

2. Deeds of Power

Not only did Jesus preach in the power of the Spirit, but his mighty works were also done in the Spirit's power. According to Matthew 12:28, Jesus made the claim that he was casting out demons by the Spirit of God, and that this was a sign that the kingdom of God had come. The presence of the Spirit in Jesus' ministry explains why he thought of the kingdom of God as already present while at the same time expecting a future consummation. The Spirit was the sign that the eschatological kingdom had arrived. That Luke refers to the "finger of God" instead of "Spirit of God" does not change the meaning of Jesus' saying. Whether Jesus said that he cast out demons with the "finger" or the "Spirit" of God is an academic question; both describe the powerful working of God.

The claim that he was casting out demons by the Spirit of God is related to that vivid metaphor of binding the strong man (Mt. 12:29; Mk. 3:27). By casting out demons Jesus takes up the struggle with the strong man, the devil, who stands at the head of all evil powers which oppress humanity and oppose the coming of the rule of God. And since Jesus is the stronger one, the evil one is defeated in this struggle.

However we may interpret the details of the cosmic conflict in which Jesus was engaged throughout his life, one matter is clear: Jesus' mission was an invasion of Satan's kingdom; by the power of the Holy Spirit, Jesus overcame the evil one and robbed him of his goods. "The exorcisms are a sign of the defeat of Satan. Thus the eschatological defeat of Satan is seen to take place in the ministry of Jesus and his disciples." In the words of Michael Green, "The man endued with the Holy Spirit is more than a match for the unclean spirits."[18]

Jesus' awareness of being uniquely possessed and used by the divine Spirit to speak with authority the words of God, and to perform deeds of power, was the mainspring of his mission and the key to its effectiveness. His consciousness of a spiritual power so real, so effective, so new, was the wellspring of both his proclamation of the presence of the future kingdom and his authority in deed and word. His messianic consciousness is summed up in the word "Spirit."

The failure to recognize God's Spirit at work in delivering souls from the bondage of Satan, and the rejection of the message of Jesus, is consequently described as the sin against the Holy Spirit. The Holy Spirit was believed to be the only source of revelation and prophetic inspiration. Also, it was by the Holy Spirit alone that a person's mind could be illuminated so that he or she could understand and obey God's message. The deliberate rejection of Christ's message, and the accusation that Jesus was in fact doing his mighty deeds by the power of Beelzebul, put his critics in mortal danger.

All three Synoptics report Jesus' assurance that all sins and all blasphemies a person may commit can be forgiven (Mt. 12:31, 32; Mk. 3:28, 29; Lk. 12:10), but he made one fearful exception. Blasphemy against the Holy Spirit makes it impossible for a person to be forgiven. "Therefore I tell you, every sin and blasphemy will be forgiven men, but the blasphemy against the Spirit will not be forgiven. And whoever says a word against the Son of man will be forgiven; but whoever speaks against the Holy Spirit will not be forgiven, either in this age or in the age to come" (Mt. 12:31, 32, and para.). For the rabbis to speak against the Holy Spirit would mean to speak against the Torah. Jesus, however, puts his own inspiration above that of the Torah.

The sin against the Holy Spirit is much more serious than the commission of even vile sins such as murder, immorality, or idolatry—to mention the three which were considered most grievous in Judaism. Conscious and deliberate rejection of the work of God's Spirit in the powerful deeds of Jesus was an expression of defiant hostility to God which betrayed a hardening of the heart.

The question may be asked why the sin against the Holy Spirit is more serious than the sin against the Son of Man which, according to Jesus, can be forgiven. Perhaps the answer is that Jesus' messiahship was still veiled. If people did not yet recognize that he was God's Messiah, there were extenuating circumstances. "The failure of the scribes to recognize him as the Bearer of the Spirit ... could be forgiven," says Lane, because Jesus' true dignity was still hidden.[19] However, the refusal to see in the words and deeds of Jesus signs of the inbreaking of the kingdom put his contemporaries in mortal danger, for Jesus acted and spoke by the power of the Spirit of God. Michael Green agrees:

> It is one thing to mistake and misrepresent Jesus, clothed in all his humility as Son of Man; it is one thing to misread his parabolic teachings coming as it does in riddles. But it is quite another thing to ascribe the power of the Holy Spirit to the devil—which is what the scribes were doing.[20]

Jesus' critics might be forgiven if they failed to recognize the source of Jesus' power, but when they willfully refused to recognize that the power of God was at work in Jesus, they were putting themselves in a position where forgiveness could not reach them.

In Matthew's Gospel we have an additional comment which may be helpful in understanding the sin against the Holy Spirit. "Either make the tree good, and its fruit good; or make the tree bad, and its fruit bad; for the tree is known by its fruit" (Mt. 12:33). Professor Tasker points out that Peter spoke a word against the Son of Man when he denied him, but he was not a bad tree; he was not deliberately speaking against the Holy Spirit. He blasphemed, but he repented deeply. His was not the sin against the Holy Spirit. Quite different was the sin of Judas, who began to serve the devil while professing to be a disciple of Jesus. The root of his nature was bad, as was the fruit of his character.[21]

Beyer says wisely that the sin against the Holy Spirit "can hardly refer to the mere utterance of a formula in which the word *pneuma* appears. It denotes the conscious and wicked rejection of the saving power and grace of God towards man. Only the man who sets himself against forgiveness is excluded from it."[22]

For those who are called upon to deal pastorally with people who fear that they have committed the unforgivable sin, Cranfield makes the observation: "It is a matter of great importance pastorally that we can say with absolute confidence to anyone who is overwhelmed by the fear that he has committed this sin, that the fact that he is troubled is itself a sure proof that he has not committed it."[23]

In this chapter, then, we have underscored the fact that Jesus is presented by the Gospel writers as the bearer of the Spirit. The presence of the Spirit in his life is a sign that the new age, the age of salvation, has dawned. By the power of the Spirit, he takes up battle with the forces of evil and brings in the rule of God. Those who close their hearts to the message of Jesus and who in their blindness and obduracy fail to see God's Spirit at work in the words and the mighty deeds of Jesus, commit the unforgivable sin against the Holy Spirit.

CHAPTER 4

The Promised Spirit in the Message of Jesus

There are relatively few references to the future activity of the Spirit in the synoptic Gospels. The emphasis lies rather on the Spirit's inspiration of prophetic utterances at the turning point of the ages and on the conception of Jesus by the Holy Spirit and to his subsequent endowment for his messianic mission. There are, however, a few passages (besides the Baptist's prediction of the coming Spirit-baptism) that do point to the future. We want to mention them only briefly before we move on to John's Gospel, where the future activity of the Spirit is very much in focus.

Jesus' promise that the heavenly Father will give "good gifts" to his children who ask (Mt. 7:11) is given by Luke in this form: "If you then, who are evil, know how to give good gifts to your children, how much more will the heavenly Father give the Holy Spirit to those who ask him!" (11:13). Matthew and Luke do not differ in meaning, only that the "good things" in Matthew are understood in the spiritual sense.[1] The gift of the Holy Spirit epitomizes, as it were, the Father's many other good gifts. In Pentecostal circles this promise of Jesus to give the Holy Spirit to those who earnestly desire and ask for it is understood as giving ground for teaching a post-conversion baptism of the Spirit.[2] But, as Leon Morris puts it, "the reference is rather to the Spirit's work in the Christian's life generally, as in Romans 8."[3] Not only does the believer need the help of the Spirit to perform his Christian service, but also he needs to pray constantly for the gift of the Spirit in his daily walk with God. Jesus promises that such prayers will not go unanswered.

Another promise of Jesus concerning the activity of the Holy Spirit in the future, which the Synoptic writers record, is found in different settings and in somewhat different forms in the three synoptic Gospels. In its Marcan form it reads: "And when they bring you to trial and deliver you up, do not be anxious beforehand what you are to say; but say whatever is given you in that hour, for it is not you who speak, but the Holy Spirit" (Mk. 13:11; cf. Mt. 10:19, 20; Lk. 12:11, 12; 21:14f.).

Jesus foresees the many situations in which his followers will have to answer for their faith before hostile human courts. They will not be able to rehearse their defense in advance; unanticipated questions will be asked and unexpected charges will be hurled at them. However, they are not to worry, for the promise is that the Spirit will give Christ's faithful witnesses the right words in the moment of crisis.

Almost immediately after the Spirit was poured out at Pentecost, Jesus' promise found fulfillment in Peter's inspired defense before the Sanhedrin in Jerusalem (Acts 4:8). Persecuted saints throughout the centuries have found Jesus' promise to be trustworthy. Preachers, however, who fail to prepare their sermons properly and then trust in the Holy Spirit's help to proclaim God's truth, can hardly claim this promise of Jesus to cover up their neglect.

We turn now to the fourth Gospel, where the references to the future activity of the Holy Spirit are found in greater number than in the Synoptics. From the beginning of the Bible to the end of the third Gospel there are 126 references to the Spirit, while from the Gospel of John onwards (one eighth of the Bible) there are 196.[4]

John, of course, like the Synoptic writers, knows also of the endowment of Jesus with the Spirit (Jn. 1:32, 33). Indeed, to use a phrase from the *Gospel According to the Hebrews,* "the whole fountain of the Spirit" came upon our Lord at his baptism and rested upon him.[5] "For he whom God has sent utters the words of God, for it is not by measure that he gives the Spirit" (Jn. 3:34). Of the prophets it was said that the Holy Spirit rested on them "by measure,"[6] and John may be contrasting Jesus, who received the Spirit in boundless measure, with the prophets of old. Or he may be saying that the day anticipated by the prophets, when the Spirit would be poured out, has begun to dawn in the person of Jesus.

While there is some debate on whether the one who gives the Spirit so bountifully is the Father or the Son, the difference in meaning is not great. Finally, it is through the incarnation, death, and resurrection that the rich gift of the Spirit is made available to Christ's followers through Jesus Christ, who possessed the Spirit in its fullness.

The possessor of the Spirit, in turn, becomes the dispenser. But before Christ can baptize with the Spirit (Jn. 1:33), he must take away the sin of the world (Jn. 1:29). The future activity of the Spirit lies beyond the cross and the exaltation of Jesus. This must be taken into account as we look at the "promised Spirit" in the message of Jesus.

A. The New Birth by the Spirit

In one of the best known Gospel stories, Jesus confronts a Jewish rabbi with words that took this "ruler of the Jews" off his feet: "Truly, truly, I say to you, unless one is born of water and the Spirit, he cannot enter the kingdom of God" (Jn. 3:5).

Nicodemus had called on Jesus at night. Perhaps he was afraid to come by day, lest his fellow Pharisees suspect that the message of this Galilean troubler had grabbed him. According to some rabbinic teachers, the night was a good time to study the Torah.[7] Nicodemus knew that the night was a good time to converse with Jesus; at night he had him all to himself. Since John has a tendency to use words with a double meaning, however, it is possible that the word "night" suggests also the spiritual darkness in which Nicodemus lived in spite of his religious scrupulosity.

Nicodemus was a man in high position, a ruler of the Jews. Very likely he was a member of the Sanhedrin, the high court of Israel, composed of Sadducees (priests) and Pharisees (scribes) and lay elders of the aristocracy.[8] He represented the religion of Judaism at its best, for he was a Pharisee. No doubt he was longing for the kingdom and he may have wanted to talk to Jesus precisely about that subject, for Jesus' answer suggests that Nicodemus may have asked how one might enter the kingdom (Jn. 3:3).

He opens the conversation with some kind words about Jesus. He acknowledges him as a teacher come from God. No doubt he had heard an authentic prophetic note in the message of Jesus. Moreover, he had been struck by the signs Jesus did. Popular rabbinic thought had it that a prophet who did a sign was to be listened to. Perhaps Nicodemus was one of those mentioned in John 2:23-25 who believed in Jesus because of the signs they had witnessed. Jesus, however, read Nicodemus' heart like an open book and transposed his spiritual quest into a higher key. There is only one way into the kingdom of God, explains Jesus, and that is by the new birth. This new birth is made possible by the Spirit of God.

1. The Fact of the New Birth (Jn. 3:3, 5)

Among New Testament writers the term "new birth" is peculiarly Johannine. That is not to say, however, that other writers do not use the concept. Peter speaks of being "born anew to a living hope" (1 Pet. 1:3). According to James, God begat us by the word of truth (1:18). Paul in his letter to Titus speaks of a rebirth and renewal which comes from the Holy Spirit (3:5).

The writers of the New Testament, in fact, are not alone in speaking of a new birth. The term was well-known both in the Hellenistic and the Jewish world. When Gentiles became members of the Jewish synagogue by circumcision and baptism, they were described as newborn children. Some rabbis theorized on whether a proselyte could legitimately marry his own sister, since he was born again and was a completely new person. The term "born again" was found also in the mystery religions, where the initiates were said to be reborn. In Mithraism this new birth was effected by the use of animal blood. So it was not the novelty of the term that struck Nicodemus; it was its meaning, and its application.

Perhaps there is no metaphor in the New Testament that stresses the radicalness of conversion as does the "new birth." The Old Testament anticipated such a thoroughgoing renewal of persons when God promised his people that he would take the stony heart out of them and give them a heart of flesh (Ezek. 36:25-29). "Are you a teacher of Israel," asks Jesus, "and yet you do not understand this?"

But Nicodemus, for all his theological acumen, lacked spiritual insight. He failed to see that Jesus was speaking of a supernatural birth. He understood the word *anothen* (which can mean either "again" or "from above") in the sense of "a second time," whereas Jesus spoke of a birth "from above," from heaven. Of course, to be born "from above" means also to be born "again," but not in the way Nicodemus understood this. He knew that it was absurd to suggest that a person could enter a second time into his mother's womb and be born again; he was right, Jesus spoke of a spiritual birth.

Without this new birth, Jesus explained, a person cannot see the kingdom of God (v. 3). To "see" is to participate in it, to accept God's reign, and this is not different from "entering" into the kingdom (v. 5). God's kingdom is his rule over the hearts and lives of men and women. This rule was breaking into human history in a powerful way through the coming of Jesus. Today it is being extended by the proclamation of the gospel, and in God's time will come to a glorious climax when Christ returns. To participate in the kingdom which was present in the person of Jesus and in the eternal kingdom in the age to come, one had to be born again, said Jesus, and he explains why this is so.

2. The Necessity of the New Birth (Jn. 3:6, 7)

Jesus explains to Nicodemus that what is born of the flesh is flesh; it is for this reason that a new birth by water and Spirit is necessary. Every person is born of the flesh—a word which in this context is very similar to "humanity." Often the word "flesh" is used to designate the evil power which is at work in fallen humanity, but here it refers to humans as they are born into this world. Physical birth as such is not an evil thing, as some Gnostics thought. It does mean, of course, that we participate in human weakness, frailty, and morality. Schnackenburg writes: "The Johannine contrast between 'flesh' and 'spirit' differs from the Pauline, in so far as it does not envisage the propensity of the flesh to sin, but concentrates on its creaturely impotence."[9] To enter God's kingdom, however, one has to be born from above.

To enter a second time into one's mother's womb, if this were possible, would mean to be born of the flesh a second time. Another birth on the horizontal plane would not bring us closer to the kingdom. Flesh and Spirit are two different orders of existence.

3. The Means of the New Birth (Jn. 3:5)

It may be that Nicodemus misunderstood Jesus deliberately in order to draw out of him a clearer and more explicit answer. "How can a man be born when he is old?" asked Nicodemus. Jesus' answer: "Unless one is born of water and the Spirit, he cannot enter the kingdom of God." Just as the Spirit of God exercised his creative powers at the dawn of the first creation (Gen. 1:2), so the Spirit of God can create a new life even in one who is old. But why is water combined with Spirit as an agent of this new creation?

It would hardly be sufficient to answer that Jesus simply borrowed the language of Genesis 1, where God's Spirit hovers over the face of the waters. Some rabbis spoke of the natural birth as a birth by water.[10] By adding the word Spirit, Jesus would be saying that a natural birth does not automatically bring people into the kingdom; they must have a spiritual birth.

Others suggest that John, who wrote his Gospel long after the church had been established, has Christian baptism in mind, where the receipt of the Spirit and the baptism with water are closely connected. Only in the baptism of John the Baptist is baptism with water and baptism with the Spirit set in juxtaposition; in Christian baptism they go together. That the later church took John 3:5 to refer to Christian baptism can be seen, for example, from the fourth-century *Apostolic Constitutions*, where it is stated: "Unless a man is baptized of water and Spirit, he shall not enter the kingdom of heaven."[11] This meaning, however, could not possibly have made any sense to Nicodemus. Boer writes: "There is no need, however, to refer the expression 'water and spirit' to the later rite of Christian baptism or to suggest that Jesus did not actually speak these words. John's baptism in the waters of Jordan was well known, as was also his prophecy of the baptism by the Spirit which the Messiah would confer."[12]

Since Jesus was speaking to a Jewish rabbi who presumably knew his Old Testament, it is much more likely that Jesus had passages from the Jewish Scriptures in mind in which the age to come is described not only as a day in which the Spirit will be poured out but also a day when fresh waters will flow from the presence of the Lord (Is. 32:15). Moreover, the Spirit that was to be poured out was to have a cleansing effect on those who would repent of their sins. "I will sprinkle clean water upon you, and you shall be clean. . . . A new heart I will give you, and a new spirit I will put within you" (Ezek. 36:25f.). F. F. Bruce writes: "It is probably this promise that underlies the words in John 3:5 about the new birth 'of water and spirit'—words in which their original context may have borne some relation to John's Baptism."[13] According to the Qumran literature Jesus' words may have been understood by Nicodemus in this way. In the *Manual of Discipline* we read: "He will cleanse him of all wicked deeds by means of a holy spirit; like purifying waters He will sprinkle upon him the spirit of truth."[14] Whether Nicodemus understood Jesus to say that the eschatological outpouring of the Spirit was at hand in the coming of Jesus or not, that seems to be the meaning of

Jesus' words. The new birth involves an inner cleansing, and that is possible only by the work of the Holy Spirit. Paul later put these elements in apposition when he wrote: "He saved us, not because of deeds done by us in righteousness, but in virtue of his own mercy, by the washing of regeneration and renewal in the Holy Spirit" (Titus 3:5—notice: water and Spirit).

It is by the Spirit that our consciences are awakened so that we see the need of a new life. The Spirit convicts us of sin. The Spirit brings home the message of the gospel to our hearts. By the Spirit we are assured that the good news is trustworthy. The Spirit enables us to cast ourselves totally upon God's mercy and to accept his pardon for our offenses. And that is how we enter God's kingdom. But, like everything else that comes from God, the birth by the Spirit has an element of mystery about it.

4. The Mystery of the New Birth (Jn. 3:8)

"The wind blows where it wills, and you hear the sound of it, but you do not know whence it comes or whither it goes; so it is with every one who is born of the Spirit."[15] The charge that this statement is not true scientifically is perverse; such an illustration from nature makes perfectly good sense in any generation. Equally perverse was the resistance on the part of some saints to the introduction of fanning mills, on the grounds that Jesus had said that the wind blew where it willed (not where man makes it blow).

For all we know a gust of wind may have swept through the narrow streets of Jerusalem at the very moment when Jesus and Nicodemus were closeted together and Jesus may have said: "You hear that wind, Nicodemus, don't you? But you can't explain where it comes from nor where it goes. The birth from the Spirit is just as mysterious."

The Spirit of God, in its recreating, regenerating activity, is beyond the control and comprehension of humans. It breathes into this world from another realm and gives new life to persons. Our inability to understand the mysterious nature of the wind does not mean that we do not experience its effects, its power.

Similarly the one born of the Spirit can be identified, even though the process is inexplicable to us. The skeptic may say there are natural powers: the energy of life, the energy of the atom, the energy of the human spirit by which one gains control of nature. Jesus spoke to Nicodemus of another power: the energy of God which comes from another world and creates new people. It blows into the valley of dead bones and they begin to live. No one can fathom the mysterious operations of the Spirit. We stand in constant amazement at the miracle of a physical birth; the miracle of a birth "from above," which is effected by the Spirit of God, is no less miraculous.

Some regard Jesus' words about the birth from the Spirit as anachronistic, since the Spirit had not yet been given. Inasmuch as Nicodemus must have been familiar with the concept of "rebirth," and should have known of the eschatological outpouring of the Spirit from the Scriptures, there is nothing anachronistic about Jesus' words. Moreover, there are other occasions where Jesus' hearers were unable to understand fully what he was saying; but he did not withhold truth from them which they would understand later on account of it. That is not to deny, however, that the saying of Jesus about the birth from the Spirit has a post-Pentecostal reference.

Notice that when Jesus promises abundant life (Jn. 7:37, 38), John adds: "For as yet the Spirit had not been given" (v. 39). Here we have at least one occasion in which Jesus spoke of the Spirit as a present reality, yet an editorial insertion makes it clear that the promise would be fulfilled only after Jesus "was glorified." "It is entirely conceivable that in 3:5 John quotes Jesus after a similar fashion without adding an editorial comment upon the futuristic reference of the Lord's teaching," writes Boer.[16] Similarly Raymond Brown remarks: "The begetting through Spirit of which verse 5 speaks seems to be a reference to the outpouring of the Spirit through Jesus when he has been lifted up in crucifixion and resurrection."[17]

We should read John 3:5, therefore, in the light of 7:39. The "lifting up" of the Son of Man mentioned in John 3:14, and the "glorification" of which John speaks in 7:39, refer to the same event: the death and exaltation of our Lord. F. F. Bruce writes: "Even if earlier he had impressed on Nicodemus the necessity of the new birth 'of water and the Spirit,' this new birth, with the eternal life to which it was the gateway, could not be experienced until the Son of Man had been 'lifted up' (Jn. 3:5, 14f.)."[18]

That John would not hesitate to write in the present tense should not surprise us, for he wrote long after the Spirit was poured out. The promise of Jesus that the Holy Spirit would bring about a new birth has been fulfilled in the lives of countless millions from the day of Pentecost up to the present hour; and we can be sure of the Spirit's life-changing activity until Christ returns. The Spirit holds promise, however, not only for the beginning of the new life, but also for its continuance. The Spirit makes possible the worship of the Father.

B. Worship in the Spirit

In his dialogue with the Samaritan woman at the well in Sychar, Jesus offered this troubled soul living water which, in contrast to the water from the well, would slake her thirst forever (Jn. 4:11-15). While Jesus does not say what he means by the gift of living water, the conversation quickly moves to the coming of the Spirit. The new birth, as Jesus explained to Nicodemus, was possible only by water and Spirit (Jn. 3:5). Presently we shall hear Jesus call the thirsty to come and drink, followed by John's comment that Jesus spoke of the coming Spirit (Jn. 7:37-39). One might also mention a line from Qumran: "Like purifying water He will sprinkle upon him the spirit of truth" (1 QS iv. 21).

From the dialogue on living water, the conversation moves to the proper place of worship. The Samaritans had built a rival temple of Yahweh on Mt. Gerizim. This temple was destroyed by the Jew, John Hyrcanus, in 128 BC. The Samaritans, however, refused to give up their place of worship in favor of Jerusalem. Jesus, nevertheless, reminds the woman that the true knowledge of God was given to Israel and that salvation for the world comes through Israel. This eschatological salvation was dawning in the person of the Messiah, as Jesus goes on to explain: "But the hour is coming, and now is, when the true worshipers will worship the Father in spirit and truth, for such the Father seeks to worship him. God is spirit, and those who worship him must worship in spirit and truth" (Jn. 4:23, 24).

As is typical in John's Gospel, this saying reflects the tension between the "already" and "not yet." While worship in the Spirit lies beyond Pentecost, the presence of Jesus as the bringer of salvation and the bearer of the Spirit anticipates that coming hour. But what did Jesus mean when he predicted the worship in Spirit and truth?

Some exegetes take *pneuma* (spirit) to be a reference to the human spirit and not to the Holy Spirit. "A man must worship, not simply outwardly by being in the right place and taking up the right attitude, but in his spirit."[19] "Truth" in that event refers to sincerity and reality in a person's approach to God. In contrast to the "external" worship of Jews and Samaritans, often carried out routinely, God's genuine worshipers in the future will worship "inwardly" with sincerity of heart.

That is not likely the meaning of Jesus' words, and it certainly does not square with the worship of the early church, where bread was broken, hymns were sung, and so forth. Schnackenburg writes:

> A spiritualistic understanding, as though Jesus was contrasting the material place of worship with a purely interior worship of God in the mind of man, is excluded by the concept of *pneuma*, which according to verse 24 can only mean the Spirit of God, as it mostly does in the Johannine writings.[20]

Similarly Brown: "His statement has nothing to do with worshiping God in the inner recesses of one's own spirit; for the Spirit is the Spirit of God, not the spirit of man, as verse 24 makes clear."[21]

How then are we to understand worship in Spirit and truth? Brown suggests that the expression "Spirit and truth" is almost hendiadys.[22] The pair of words, with the emphasis on "Spirit," seems to mean the same thing in both of its elements.[23] The "truth" is the revelation of God in Jesus Christ (Jn. 14:6), made real by the Spirit poured out at Pentecost. By the Spirit which the Father will give to those who believe in the Son, true worship will be made possible.

The reason people need the help of the Spirit to worship is that he is Spirit. This is not a comment on the essence of God's nature, but a reference to his otherness, his transcendence and holiness. "The proposition, 'God is Spirit' means that he is invisible and unknowable."[24] God belongs to a world that is different from ours. As creatures, born of the flesh, we are not capable of worshiping such a God. In fact, because of our sinfulness, we do not even want to worship him as our Father, and so he must "seek" people to worship him. We need to have our hearts cleansed by his Spirit; we need to become new creatures; we must be taught to pray. And this is made possible only by his Spirit.

This means that only those who have the Spirit of God can worship him as Father. "God can be worshiped as Father only by those who possess the Spirit that makes them God's children."[25] After the conversation with Nicodemus, it is clear that the genuine worshipers are those who are "born of the Spirit."

Also, true worship of God is no longer tied to a specific place. While this is not the major emphasis in Spirit-worship, Jesus does speak of this kind of worship in contrast to "this mountain" or Jerusalem as the place of worship (Jn. 4:20, 21). "With the person of Jesus, this day is already dawning, and a new type of worship is signalled in which the place where it is offered is unimportant."[26] In a day when some churches are manifesting an "edifice complex," it is well to remember these words of Jesus.

Moreover, since all those who worship God in the Spirit are bound together by the same Spirit, the worship in Spirit and truth, while it allows for private worship, is basically corporate. And since the Spirit transcends all social, racial, and religious barriers, the true worshipers—be they Jews, Samaritans, or Gentiles—can worship together without anger and quarreling.

Those who are "born of the Spirit" and who worship the Father "in Spirit and in truth" have the promise of an abundant life.

C. The Abundant Life Through the Spirit

It was at the Feast of Tabernacles—a festival rich in symbolism and popular appeal—that our Lord proclaimed to the festal crowds: "If any one thirst, let him come to me and drink. He who believes in me, as the scripture has said, 'Out of his heart shall flow rivers of living water.' Now this he said about the Spirit, which those who believed in him were to receive; for as yet the Spirit had not been given, because Jesus was not yet glorified" (Jn. 7:37-39).

1. The Historical Setting (Jn. 7:37)

In later September or early October, Israel celebrated the Feast of Tabernacles, known also as the Feast of Booths—reminiscent of the huts Israel had lived in during their wanderings in the wilderness following the exodus.[27] The festival lasted a week (Deut. 16:13). Since Leviticus 23:36 mentions an additional solemn day of rest, it is not quite certain whether "the last day" in our passage is the seventh or the eighth day. If the latter, then Jesus' words were spoken on the one day when the traditional water-rites were not performed. Whether the seventh or eighth day, his words would have caught the attention of his hearers.[28] On this last day Jesus stood up in the temple precincts, where he had very likely sat and taught, and loudly proclaimed: "If any one thirst, let him come to me and drink."

This marvelous invitation takes on added meaning if one recalls some of the circumstances which attended the Jewish Festival of Booths. This last festival of the year was a harvest festival, and it became the occasion to pray for rain. If rain fell during Tabernacles, it was looked upon as an assurance of abundant early rains, so necessary for the crops the following year. Even today, the Jordanian Arabs, despite their hate for the Jews, watch carefully to see if rain falls during the Israeli celebration of Tabernacles as a sign of the weather to come.

During the Feast of Tabernacles in Jesus' day, a procession went down to the fountain of Gihon on the southeast side of the temple hill. This fountain supplied the waters of the Pool of

Siloam. While the priest filled a golden pitcher with water, the choir repeated Isaiah 12:3, "With joy you will draw water from the wells of salvation." Then the procession went up to the temple through the water gate.

The accompanying crowds carried the symbols of Tabernacles. In their right hand they had the *lulab*—a bunch of myrtle and willow twigs tied with palm, reminiscent of the branches used to construct huts in the wilderness. In their left hand they carried the *ethrog*—a lemon or citron serving as a sign of the harvest. Singing and swinging the *lulabs*, they proceeded around the altar of holocausts in the temple court. The priest then went up to the ramp to the altar to pour water into a silver funnel through which it flowed to the ground.[29]

We can readily see how the prayers for rain, the ceremonial of carrying water, and the water libations provided our Lord with a most appropriate setting for his offer of living waters. Jesus, as it were, takes the water symbolism of the feast and presses it into his service. The people were thinking of rain and of their physical needs; Jesus turns their attention to the deeper needs of the heart and promises to meet these needs.

Quite aside from the use of water in the celebration of Tabernacles, however, Jesus' words have rich Old Testament overtones. Many Old Testament passages expressed the hope for a new age in pictures of fresh waters which rejuvenate the parched land; Zechariah 9—14 is particularly apropos to our text, for it describes the new age in the context of a Tabernacle festival. The messianic king comes to Jerusalem, triumphant and riding on an ass (9:9). God then gives instructions to pray for rain (10:1). A fountain is opened for the house of David for the cleansing of Jerusalem (13:1). When that day comes living waters will flow from Jerusalem to the Mediterranean and the Dead Sea (14:8). And after all enemies are destroyed, people will come up year after year to Jerusalem to keep Tabernacles properly (14:16). The striking similarity of Jesus' words, spoken on that memorable last day of the feast, to these promises of Zechariah are too close to be coincidental.

So when Jesus shouted loudly into the temple halls: "If any one thirst, let him come to me and drink," his words evoked a great many sacred memories.[30] Obviously Jesus did not mean that he had a secret source of H_2O, or that he was offering the many tabernacle visitors a drink of water. He was telling the crowds what he had already told the Samaritan woman at the well by Sychar, that he had water to give that would quench the deepest thirst of human persons. In our passage, the Evangelist, who wrote long after the day of Pentecost, gives us the interpretation of what Jesus meant when he offered his listeners water to drink.

2. The Evangelist's Explanation (Jn. 7:39)

"Now this he said about the Spirit, which those who believed in him were to receive; for as yet the Spirit had not been given, because Jesus was not yet glorified."

That water was a symbol of God's Spirit is well attested in the Old Testament promises of the outpouring of God's Spirit. For example, Isaiah anticipates the inauguration of the new age in these words: "For I will pour water on the thirsty land, and streams on the dry ground; I will pour my Spirit upon your descendants." Ezekiel said: "I will sprinkle clean water upon you, and you shall be clean. . . . A new heart I will give you, and a new spirit I will put within you."

What the prophets anticipated, Jesus promises to fulfill: His Spirit shall be like fresh water poured on parched land, making the wilderness to blossom like a rose. John, however, is careful to explain that "the Spirit was not yet." Pentecost had not yet occurred when Jesus spoke these words. John, of course, writing after Pentecost, puts Jesus' words into perspective. Since the observation of the Evangelist ("the Spirit was not yet") could be misconstrued to mean that there was as yet no Holy Spirit (when in fact God's Spirit was active throughout the Old Testament, not to mention the Spirit's activity in Jesus' ministry), some copyists have added words to make the statement less categorical.[31] But John is not denying the existence of the Spirit prior to Pentecost; he is simply explaining that the Holy Spirit had not yet been

given in the characteristically Christian manner and measure.
Taylor writes:

> In a disturbing flash of insight the Gospel of John says with reference to the
> death and resurrection of Jesus: "The Spirit had not yet been given, be-
> cause Jesus had not yet been glorified," which R. P. C. Hanson suggests
> might be better rendered: "It was not yet Spirit," as one might say, "It was
> not yet spring." That is exactly how it must have appeared to anyone look-
> ing back from the end of that prodigious first century. There had never
> been anything like it before, and it had all stemmed from Jesus.[32]

As in John 1:29-34, where the bearer of the Spirit is the lamb
of God that takes away the sin of the world; and as in John
3:1-15, where the new birth from the Spirit is connected with the
"lifting up" of the Son of Man; so here John explains that the
Spirit was not yet "because Jesus was not yet glorified" (7:39).
This is John's way of speaking of the cross and the exaltation that
was to follow Christ's death.

"The departure of Jesus in death would also make possible
that baptism of the Spirit, which was to be the supreme gift of
Jesus to all who believed in him."[33] Before the Spirit could come,
Jesus had to die. "If I do not go away," Jesus said later, "the
Counselor [Paraclete] will not come to you" (Jn. 16:7). John, of
course, is fully aware of the activity of the Spirit in the lives of
Jesus' disciples even during the time of Christ's incarnation,[34] but
as S. H. Hooke concludes, "Never until the Son of Man had
ascended up where he was before and the last Adam had become
a life-giving spirit, had it been possible for the Spirit to enter into
and become the life of the believer, producing in him the life of
Jesus...."[35] Calvary is the prelude to Pentecost.

Having sketched the historical setting and observed John's
explanation of Jesus' offer of living water, let us now look at the
Savior's promise of the effect that a satisfying draught from the
stream of the Spirit is to have on the believer.

3. The Savior's Promise (Jn. 7:38)

"He who believes in me, as the scripture has said, 'Out of his
heart shall flow rivers of living water.'" There was no punctua-

tion in the early manuscripts, so we do not know exactly how to punctuate these words of Jesus. "As the scripture has said" could go with the verb "believe" or with "out of his heart shall flow rivers of living water." The NEB renders it: "As Scripture says, 'Streams of living water shall flow out from within him.'" Here "him" refers to Christ, the rock from which the water flows (1 Cor. 10:4), rather than the believer. Some have even suggested that Jesus meant the water which flowed from the side of his body when the soldier stuck his spear into Jesus' side. John does bring Spirit and water and blood together in the three witnesses mentioned in 1 John 5:7. The Western fathers of the early church by and large understood Jesus' promise to mean that he was the source of the rivers of water.

The majority of modern commentators, however, following in the tradition of the Eastern fathers, take Jesus' words to mean that rivers of fresh water shall flow from the believer's inner being once the Spirit is poured out.[36] That Jesus is ultimately the source of the fresh streams of the Spirit is thereby not denied, but the gift of the Spirit to his followers makes them, in turn, sources of living water. As Behm puts it: "The believer whose thirst is quenched by Jesus is promised that his refreshed inward being will become a source of wider refreshing, and that he is to share with others in overflowing abundance that which he himself has received from Jesus."[37]

It has been argued that this interpretation cannot be sustained because there are no Old Testament passages that say living waters shall flow from the believer. But as Leon Morris points out, there is no Old Testament passage that says Christ is the source of living water either.[38] There are, however, several passages in the Old Testament which may well have served Jesus as a background for his promise that living waters were to flow from those who would be baptized with the Spirit. The writer of the Proverbs says: "The words of a man's mouth are deep waters; the fountain of wisdom is a gushing stream" (18:4). But even more apropos is Isaiah 58:11: "And the Lord will guide you continually, and satisfy your desire with good things, and make your bones strong; and you shall be like a watered garden, like a spring of water, whose waters fail not." One might even find a parallel in the Qumran texts: "You, O my God, have put into my mouth, as it were, rain for all (who thirst) and a fount of living waters which shall not fail."[39] Jesus may well have had in mind some Old Testament passage which speaks of the righteous man as a channel of fresh waters when he claimed scriptural support for his promise.

In the older English versions, we read that living waters shall flow from the "belly" of the one who believes. Since that word has a pejorative ring in modern English, most versions today translate it as "heart," "inner being," or simply as "from within him." Jesus spoke Aramaic and may have used the word "body," which at times means "person," but then we might have expected the Greek to have "body" also.[40] The Greek word *koilia* basically means "hollow," and is used for the womb, the stomach, and the "inward parts."[41]

It has been suggested that the language of Zechariah influenced the choice of words here. The prophet foresees the day when living waters shall flow from Jerusalem (14:8), and since Jerusalem was the navel of the earth in rabbinic tradition (Jubilees 8:19), it is quite possible that "belly" was chosen in the light of this background.[42] The prophecy, then, was transferred by Jesus from the city to the individual believer.

But what does Jesus' promise of the Spirit which will make the believer a source of living waters for others mean practically? How are we to describe the "abundant life"? Does it mean a life of ecstasy? Does it mean that we radiate health, energy, and vitality, with never a sign of weakness or failure in our Christian lives? If so, then obviously the abundant life is promised only to a select few. Certainly Paul did not understand the life in the Spirit in that way. This Spirit-filled apostle still boasts in his weakness (2 Cor. 12:9). He could have boasted about his ecstatic experience when he was caught up in the third heaven (2 Cor. 12:2ff.). What a popular paperback story that would have made! Instead he prefers not to talk about it. In the same paragraph he will talk about his humiliating experience of slithering down the wall of

Damascus in a basket to escape from his enemies. His experiences in Asia had been so harrowing that he nearly despaired of life (2 Cor. 1:8). Abundant life? Yes! Power through weakness. Not very bubbly, I grant; but deep and strong.

Jesus promises those who thirst for the living waters a draught that will slake their thirst. He promises to meet the deepest needs of their hearts. He assures them of the forgiveness of sin and acceptance by God. But there is more! If that were all, then the Christian life might be compared to a pond with plenty of water but with no outlet. Such a pond would turn into a Dead Sea, which receives the waters of Jordan but does not channel them anywhere.

The abundant life which Jesus promises includes deliverance from the imprisonment to our ego. It is an outgoing life. It means that we pray not only for ourselves but for others also; that we spend time not only for ourselves but for others; that we feed and clothe not only ourselves but others; that we nurture not only our own souls but share the water of life with others; that we spend money not only on ourselves but on others.

The abundant life is lived in very mundane circumstances. It is beset with weakness, disappointment, and failure. Those who live the abundant life have their ups and downs, are emptied and filled again, are raised up and brought low (Phil. 4:12). They suffer blows to their egos, have wounded feelings, hurts, and traumas. But they are built up again. The abundant life has little in common with "the feel good movement."[43] Bookstores are filled with pop volumes promising to iron out all our kinks and to relieve us of all feelings of failure and guilt, to give us poise and self-fulfillment. But the abundant life which Jesus offers is one in which we invest our lives in others and in the process discover that his power is made perfect in our weakness. And what are the conditions for this life? Only one is mentioned: "He who believes in me . . . out of his heart shall flow rivers of living water."

From the promise of a new birth by the Spirit (Jn. 3:5), and an abundant life in the Spirit (Jn. 7:37-39), we turn now to the promise of the Paraclete.

D. The Coming of the Paraclete

It seems as though all the references to the Spirit in John's Gospel point to the period after the death and resurrection of Jesus. The only exception is the presence of the Spirit in the life and ministry of Jesus (1:32; 3:34).[44] This orientation to the future is most explicit in Jesus' promises of the coming Paraclete.

The word Paraclete is peculiarly Johannine. It appears in the fourth Gospel four times; it is found elsewhere in the New Testament only in 1 John 2:1, where Jesus is said to be the Paraclete, serving as a heavenly intercessor or advocate with the Father, entering his plea for his own people who often fail.[45] Our interest at the moment, however, lies in John's Gospel, where Jesus promises to send "the other Paraclete," namely the Holy Spirit.

1. The Meaning of Paraclete

The word *parakletos* in common Greek functioned both as a verbal adjective and as a noun, in the sense of a "person called in to help, summoned to give assistance," particularly as a legal adviser or helper or advocate in court.[46] Since the Synoptics promise Christ's followers the help of the Holy Spirit when they stand before human courts (e.g., Mt. 10:20), it would not be wide of the mark to see in the word *parakletos* a forensic meaning; in fact Old Latin versions render it as *advocatus*. However, the legal meaning of the term is not strictly adhered to in John's Gospel. With the exception of John 16:8-11, *parakletos* seems to have "the broad and general sense of 'helper.' "[47]

Older versions (Wycliffe, Luther, KJV) rendered *parakletos* as "comforter," but in none of the New Testament passages is this meaning appropriate. If, however, the English word "comfort" (or the German *Trost)* is taken in its original sense of "making strong" (Latin: *con*—"with," and *fortis*—"strong"), one comes closer to the meaning of "helper."[48]

There is a bewildering variety of translations in English versions.[49] The RSV and NIV translate *parakletos* as "Counselor"; J. B. Phillips gives it as "someone to stand by you"; Ronald Knox has "he who is to befriend you"; Moffatt, GNB, and the

Twentieth Century New Testament translate it as "helper"; NEB
and JB give it as "Advocate." Clearly there is no one English word
that can render *parakletos* adequately, especially since the
nuances of the word change with the contexts in which it is found.
Perhaps we do best to stay with a transliteration: Paraclete.

References to the Paraclete are found in John's Gospel only
in Jesus' farewell discourse, given very likely at the last supper.
What strikes us is the close relationship between Jesus and the
coming Paraclete. He will come only after Jesus departs (Jn. 16:7).
The Father will send him at Jesus' request (14:16) and in Jesus'
name (14:26). He will take what belongs to Jesus and declare it to
the disciples (16:14). He will glorify Jesus (16:14) and remind the
disciples of what Jesus said (14:26) and bear witness on behalf of
Jesus (15:26, 27).

A question that naturally arises is whether there is anything
in the Old Testament or in Jewish literature that could illuminate
such a tandem relationship. One is reminded of Joshua who succeeded Moses, or Elisha who followed Elijah. In both instances
the successor received the same spirit through the laying on of
hands (Deut. 34:9; 2 Kings 2:9, 15). In similar fashion one might
say that the Holy Spirit, who rested upon Jesus during his
ministry, was passed on to his followers after his departure.

Raymond Brown sums up his survey of biblical and Jewish
backgrounds to the concept of *parakletos* in this way:

> We find scattered in Jewish thought the basic elements that appear in the
> Johannine picture of the Paraclete: a tandem relationship whereby a second
> figure patterned on the first, continues the work of the first; the passing on
> of his spirit by the main salvific figure; God's granting a spirit that would
> enable the recipient to understand and interpret divine deed and word au-
> thoritatively; a personal (angelic) spirit who would lead the chosen ones
> against the forces of evil; personal (angelic) spirits who teach men and
> guide them to truth. Wisdom that comes to men from God, dwells within
> them, and teaches them, but is rejected by other men. And in the passages
> describing these various relationships and spirits there is much of the vocab-
> ulary of witnessing, teaching, guiding, and accusing that appears in the
> Johannine Paraclete passages, including the title "Spirit of Truth."[50]

With this background let us now turn to the Johannine texts

to examine more closely the functions of the Paraclete that Jesus promises to send.

2. The Functions of the Paraclete

(a) *An Abiding Presence.* "And I pray the Father, and he will give you another Counselor, to be with you for ever, even the Spirit of truth, whom the world cannot receive, because it neither sees him nor knows him; you know him, for he dwells with you, and will be in you" (Jn. 14:16, 17).

Here the Paraclete is given by the Father at the Son's request; at verse 26 the Father sends him in Christ's name; at 16:7 Christ sends him; at 15:26 he proceeds from the Father. There is, however, no significant difference between these expressions.[51]

Our passage is unique in that the Holy Spirit is called "another Paraclete," implying that Christ is also a Paraclete. Jesus is nowhere called a Paraclete (see 1 Jn. 2:1), but, as Brown observes, "virtually everything that has been said about the Paraclete has been said elsewhere in the Gospel about Jesus."[52] Similarly John Marsh: "He has himself been their counsellor while he has been with them; now that he is going away their plainest need is for counsellor of comparable stature."[53]

This "other" Paraclete is described as the "Spirit of truth" (an expression found three times: 14:17; 15:26; 16:13). Already in this chapter (14:6) Jesus has declared himself to be the truth; the "Spirit of truth" should then be taken as an objective genitive, meaning "the Spirit who communicates truth."[54]

The coming of this Spirit of truth marks off the disciples from the world which does not discern the presence of the Spirit. Because of a wrong attitude toward's God's salvific work in the world, the world (i.e., humanity alienated from God) is unaware of the Spirit's working. With Jesus' followers the matter is quite different; they know the Paraclete, who not only remains "with" them but will be "in" them. For this reason the disciples need not fear Jesus' departure, for he will not leave them desolate; he will come to them; not as in the days of his flesh, but by his *alter ego*, his representative, the Paraclete.

In contrast to Old Testament times when the Spirit of God often appears as naked power, the coming Paraclete is to be clothed with the personality and character of Jesus. In fact he is later called "the Spirit of Jesus" (Acts 16:7). By dwelling "with" and "in" the believers, the Paraclete will universalize the presence of the risen Lord, making it possible for Jesus' followers all over the world to have an even more intimate relationship with Christ than was possible in the days of his incarnation.

(b) *An Authoritative Teacher.* "But the Counselor, the Holy Spirit, whom the Father will send in my name, he will teach you all things, and bring to your remembrance all that I have said to you" (Jn. 14:26).

The Paraclete, who is called the Spirit of truth in verse 17, is now spoken of as the Holy Spirit (the only place in the Gospel of John where the expression is found). The Holy Spirit, says Jesus, will be sent by the Father in Jesus' name; this means, among other things, that the Paraclete will continue the work that Jesus began.

The particular function of the Paraclete according to John 14:26 is that of teacher: "He will teach you all things." "All things" does not suggest that he will teach Christ's followers more than Jesus himself taught. Perhaps it means, as Morris suggests, "all that you need to know."[55] In fact the teaching of the Paraclete is explained as a bringing to remembrance all things that Jesus had said. There were many things that Jesus taught which the disciples did not comprehend because of the historical situation they were in. In the post-resurrection situation many of Jesus' sayings would take on a new significance. The Paraclete will not dispense with the teachings of Jesus, nor teach things contrary to what Jesus said, but he will bring them to remembrance and illuminate them. "There is no independent revelation through the Paraclete, but only an application of the revelation of Jesus."[56]

Essentially the same thing is said of the Spirit of truth in John 16:13, 14: "When the Spirit of truth comes, he will guide you into all the truth; for he will not speak on his own authority, but whatever he hears he will speak, and he will declare to you the things that are to come. He will glorify me, for he will take what is mine and declare it to you."

There are vistas of truth which the disciples could not grasp prior to the cross and the exaltation, but the Spirit of truth would guide them into "all the truth." (The Greek has an article before truth; Jesus did not mean that the Spirit would necessarily guide his followers into any and every kind of truth but the truth as it is in Jesus' person, his work and his words.) The Spirit has bound himself to the teachings of Jesus. And when Jesus says the Spirit will "declare . . . the things that are to come," he does not mean that the Spirit will give Christ's followers a blueprint of future events. The meaning is rather that the Spirit will lead Christ's followers into the deeper significance of the cross and the resurrection, which from Jesus' standpoint were still future events. Without the Spirit's illumination Christ's death would have been utter tragedy; under the Spirit's guidance, however, Jesus' followers saw in it the victory of God.

> What the free Spirit of God has to reveal to the Church is therefore not new revelations, new doctrines, new promises, which go beyond things that Jesus himself said or even complement and add to them. It is not said of the Spirit that he will lead the Church into new truth, but into all truth. . . . Jesus is followed by no new revealer; in him, once for all, the revelation of God is given to the world. This revelation is inexhaustible. But the new insights bestowed on the Church by the Spirit do not add to or surpass what Christ himself revealed. . . . The Spirit cannot say more than Jesus. . . . The Spirit cannot give a new revelation, but through the preaching of his witnesses he will cause everything that Jesus said and did to be revealed in a new light.[57]

The Spirit's work will be totally Christocentric. He will glorify Christ by taking the things of Christ and declaring them to his disciples. Just as Jesus glorified the Father by revealing him to people, the Paraclete glorifies Jesus by revealing him to people.

When undue emphasis is put on the Holy Spirit in comparison to the work of Christ, it is worth remembering that this is just as wrong as a neglect of the doctrine of the Holy Spirit. Also, it is important that when people claim to have received "messages" from the Holy Spirit, these messages must always be tested by what Jesus taught.

(c.) *An Effective Witness.* The Paraclete's role is not only to assure Christ's followers of Jesus' presence with them and to be their authoritative teacher, but he is also to function as an effective witness. "But when the Counselor comes, whom I shall send to you from the Father, even the Spirit of truth, who proceeds from the Father, he will bear witness to me" (Jn. 15:26).

Once again (as in 14:17) the Paraclete is called the "Spirit of truth" who "proceeds from the Father." This phrase made its way into the fourth-century creeds to describe the eternal procession of the Spirit from the Father. But it should be noticed that the present tense stands parallel to the future "I will send," and should, therefore, not be used to speculate about the interior life of God.[58]

What is unique about this passage is that the Paraclete, the Spirit of truth, shall witness to Jesus. Immediately following this promise (v. 26), Jesus explains that his disciples shall also be witnesses (v. 27). The Spirit does not do his work of witnessing to Jesus apart from the disciples, who had been with Jesus from the beginning (15:27). The witness of the Spirit and the witness of the Father stand in relation to each other, much in the same way as the witness of the Father is related to that of the Son. Jesus' words anticipate Acts 1:8, where the disciples are promised power "when the Holy Spirit has come upon you; and you shall be my witnesses."

Since the context of John 15:26 is that of hatred of Jesus' disciples by the world and persecution, it may be that the word "witness" here has something of a forensic meaning as well. "The Spirit, so to speak, conducts Christ's case for Him before the world."[59] This would be in line with Jesus' promise that the Spirit would tell them what to say when dragged before human courts (Mk. 13:11).

(d.) *A Prosecuting Attorney.* "Nevertheless I tell you the truth: it is to your advantage that I go away, for if I do not go away, the Counselor will not come to you; but if I go, I will send him to you.

And when he comes, he will convince the world concerning sin and righteousness and judgment: concerning sin, because they do not believe in me; concerning righteousness, because I go to the Father, and you will see me no more; concerning judgment, because the ruler of this world is judged" (Jn. 16:7-11).

In this final passage in which the Holy Spirit is called the Paraclete, his function is clearly forensic. To translate *parakletos* as "comforter" or even as "helper" would seem inappropriate in this context. Moreover, the Spirit is not so much a counsel for the defense in this passage, but rather he is counsel for the prosecution. The world is standing in the dock, as it were.[60]

Jesus' words about his imminent departure must have seemed disastrous to the disciples. Actually, as Jesus explains, his departure would be for their profit. Not only would the disciples no longer be dependent on the visible, bodily presence of Jesus, but Jesus' departure, his exaltation to the right hand of God, would open the way for the Spirit to come upon the disciples in all its fullness. There would then be no more barriers of space and time to prevent the disciples from being in intimate contact with Jesus.

John 16:7-11 is unique, however, not in what it says about the Paraclete's activity in the lives of the disciples, but in its prediction of what he will do in the world. The Paraclete, Jesus explains, will act as the world's prosecutor. He will function in an elenctic capacity. The Greek verb *elegcho* has a number of meanings,[61] but in this text it has to do with cross-examination for the purpose of proving the opponent wrong and convicting him. The Paraclete will "expose," "bring to light," "convict" the world. How he does this John does not say, but certainly one way is through the witness of the church. By the proclaimed Word the Spirit works in people's consciences. If those who proclaim the gospel did not have the conviction that the Spirit worked in the hearts of their hearers, they would have every reason to despair.

The prosecuting and convicting activity of the Paraclete is to take place in three areas: sin, righteousness, and judgment. Jesus then goes on to explain why the world is wrong in these areas. The explanation is admittedly somewhat enigmatic, but it opens up for us new dimensions in the Spirit's activity.

First, the Spirit will convince the world concerning sin "because they do not believe in me." The basic sin of fallen humanity is unbelief. The rejection of Jesus is the type and crown of all sin, even though it is not the only sin that the world is guilty of.[62] Other sins, however, are related to this basic sin of unbelief. The Paraclete will focus on the sin of unbelief which led wicked humanity to crucify God's Son. However, those who killed the historical Jesus are but the forebears of people in every generation who are hostile to Jesus and reject him. When Peter preached his Pentecost sermon, the Spirit convinced his hearers that they were guilty before God for having rejected his envoy, Jesus Christ; by the Spirit the Word cut to the heart (Acts 2:37) and they turned to Christ in repentance and salvation. Gentiles, however, were no less guilty of unbelief than were Jews—as the sermons in Acts clearly show.

Second, the Spirit will convince the world of righteousness "because I go to the Father." By going to the Father, Jesus was proved to be in the right; he was vindicated. When the Paraclete comes, Jesus says in effect, he will convince the world that the judgment of the Sanhedrin and of Pilate was a travesty of justice. He was not a criminal. God reversed the judgment of man by raising his Son from the grave and exalting him to his right hand. The Jews had regarded Jesus' claims to divine sonship as blasphemous, accused him of being a deceiver, and put him to death for his sins. But the Paraclete would show that all of Jesus' claims were legitimate; the Father certified him by taking him to glory. Perhaps a line from a Pauline hymn underscores this truth: "He was manifested in the flesh, vindicated in the Spirit" (1 Tim. 3:16). For the disciples the coming of the Spirit will be proof that Jesus is with the Father.[63]

Third, the Spirit will convince the world of judgment, "because the ruler of this world has been judged." It is a dominant theme of the New Testament that in the very act of Jesus' death, the dominion of Satan came to an end. The hour of Jesus' passion represented a confrontation with the prince of this world. In being victorious over death, Jesus was victorious over the archenemy of humanity. While God's final judgment still lies in the future when Satan will be forever vanquished, the tide of the battle turned against Satan at the cross and the victory over all evil powers is already evident. Satan is essentially a defeated foe. The Paraclete will convince the world of this. We should not overlook the fact, however, that the Spirit also convicts unbelieving man of judgment to come. Moreover, in this passage final judgment is seen as taking place proleptically in the judgment of the ruler of this world at the cross and the resurrection of Jesus. The Spirit will convince people through the gospel that the world is wrong in thinking that Jesus was judged for wrongdoing; not he, but the prince of this world, was judged at the cross. That corrective insight can come to persons, blinded as they are by sin, only by the work of the Spirit.[64]

3. The Significance of the Paraclete for John's Readers

Whereas it is impossible to assign a date for John's Gospel with any degree of accuracy, it has generally been placed last among the Gospels (or even among New Testament books in general). Be that as it may, it must have been unsettling, to say the least, when the last of the apostles passed off the scene. There was a rumor that John would not die, but Jesus dispels that rumor (Jn. 21:23). We can only imagine how important the Paraclete passages of John must have been for the early readers, when those who had been in the confidence of Jesus had died.

The apostles would pass off the scene, to be sure, but the Holy Spirit, as Jesus had promised, would continue to guide and to teach his people. The Paraclete would take Jesus' place; he would make the absent Lord's presence real to his followers in a way he could never have done by his bodily presence or by his personal representatives, the apostles. In fact, the witness of the apostles after Pentecost had also been the witness of the Holy Spirit speaking through them, and the Spirit's witness would not cease with the death of the eyewitnesses.

Another problem that the early church faced was that of the delay of the parousia. That there were serious questions about the delay of Christ's coming can be seen, for example, by the explanations given in 2 Peter 3:3-8. The outpouring of the Spirit, as Peter had explained (Acts 2:17, quoting Joel 2:28f.), was a sign that the last days had begun, but he also knew that the final chapter had not yet been written. The promise of Jesus to send the Paraclete, which only John records, must have been very meaningful for those who felt Christ's absence so keenly. During this time of waiting Jesus was not entirely absent; he was present by his Spirit; he had not left them orphans, he had come to them, just as he had promised.

Michael Green writes:

> Jesus had not left them orphans: he had come to them in the person of the Spirit, who was not only the special gift of the messiah to the messianic people in order to enable them to know his continued presence with them, but was the first installment of the Age to Come, the pledge that the last days which had dawned with Jesus of Nazareth would, one day, come to God's perfect conclusion.[65]

E. The Breath of the Spirit

Aside from the trinitarian baptismal formula found in Matthew's Gospel (28:19), John is the only evangelist who makes specific reference to the Holy Spirit after the resurrection of Jesus from the dead. According to Luke, Jesus did assure his disciples that he would send "the promise of the Father," and he commanded them to stay in Jerusalem until they be "clothed with power from on high" (Lk. 24:49). And while Jesus had the Pentecost experience in mind, no doubt, the Spirit is not mentioned here explicitly.

John stands alone in reporting that on the first Easter evening, when the disciples met together behind locked doors for fear of what the Jews might do to them now that Passover was over, Jesus came into their midst and greeted them. Upon greeting them with the conventional Jewish greeting ("Peace to you," a greeting which in this case obviously was more than conventional), he showed them his hands and his side, presumably with the wound prints.

This elicited a joyous response on the part of the disciples. In his last discourse, when Jesus promised the coming of the Paraclete, he gave his peace to his disciples as his farewell (Jn. 14:27, 28); now as risen Lord, he gives them his peace as greeting, for he is about to bestow his Spirit upon them. He had told them earlier that they would be sad when he left them, but that he would come back to them and their sorrow would be turned into joy (Jn. 16:20). In Jewish thought peace and joy were marks of the age to come. And when it is remembered that the age to come was to be inaugurated with the outpouring of the Spirit, we can see why John would want to bring "peace" and "joy" and "the coming of the Spirit" together. After greeting them a second time, Jesus gave his disciples the Great Commission; and having breathed on them, said: "Receive the Holy Spirit!" (Jn. 20:19-23).

How shall we relate the coming of the Spirit on this first Christian Easter to the coming of the Spirit at Pentecost?

1. Two Bestowals of the Spirit?

For some scholars it appears a waste of time to attempt to harmonize John 20 with Acts 2. They say either John or Luke is in error chronologically, for there was but one occasion when the Spirit was bestowed. Barrett seems to take this position when he writes: "It is probable that to the first Christians the resurrection of Jesus and his appearances to them, his exaltation . . . and the gift of the Spirit, appeared as one experience, which only later came to be described in separate elements and incidents."[66]

Theodore of Mopsuestia also held that there was but one Pentecostal outpouring of the Spirit and that what Jesus did on the resurrection day was but symbolic of what would happen at Pentecost. Jesus did not really give his disciples his Spirit at Easter but acted figuratively by way of promise. This view was condemned by the Second Council of Constantinople (AD 553).[67] Dunn suggests another way of expressing Theodore's view (although Dunn rejects that approach):

To avoid the historical contrast between the "Lukan Pentecost" and the "Johannine Pentecost" it has been periodically argued that 20:22 does not depict an actual giving of the Spirit, but only points forward to Pentecost proleptically, as though Jesus was saying, "When you hear the sound of the wind (=*pneuma*= breath) then you will receive the Spirit." This is an unsupported speculation which does too little justice to the text.[68]

Another approach is to take the two accounts as factual descriptions of two quite independent "givings" of the Spirit. John, in that event, reports the preliminary bestowal of the Spirit and Luke the Pentecostal outpouring.[69] We cannot deny that the circumstances surrounding the bestowal of the Spirit in John are very different from those in Acts. Also, as Morris points out, the Pentecostal outpouring led to the proclamation of the gospel, something that did not follow upon the bestowal of the Spirit in John (at least it is not recorded).

Those who hold to two separate "bestowals" of the Spirit point out that the gift of the Spirit at Easter is related to the forgiveness of sin, whereas the gift at Pentecost is related to being able to do mighty works; or the gift at Easter was an individual gift, whereas the Pentecost outpouring was ecclesiastical. Others have suggested that the gift at Easter was transitional and anticipatory, whereas the gift on Pentecost is complete and definitive, one being potential, the other actual. F. F. Bruce suggests that the gift of the Spirit at Easter "may be regarded as an inward anticipation of the outward manifestation of Pentecost."[70] Still others take the gift of the Spirit at Easter to be Christ's way of helping his disciples to recognize him as risen Lord, since he had promised to send the Holy Spirit when he would return to them after his temporary departure.[71]

If we do hold to two separate bestowals of the Spirit, we must not follow those who then infer from this double experience that this is the pattern for all believers: a gift of the Spirit bestowed at conversion (the Easter gift) and a baptism of the Spirit later (the Pentecostal experience).[72]

Whenever Christians seek to imitate in their own experience the sequence of the great events of salvation history, they are bound to get themselves into trouble. By faith these past events—the cross, the resurrection, Pentecost—become a present reality for us, but we can never go back in time and relive the experiences of the founders of the church.

Another approach to the problem of the two accounts of the Spirit's coming is to hold to one single event when the Spirit was given, but to see in the Johannine and Lucan accounts two different theologies—not contradictory but complementary. Michael Green writes:

> The important point is not to try to harmonise this account with that of Luke in the Acts—after all, John in all probability never read Luke's work, and presents the material in a very different manner and with different aims. I do not think we get much further by supposing that Jesus gave two insufflations of his Holy Spirit, one in John's upper room, and one at Luke's Pentecost. No, the point they both make is that Jesus was equipped for his messianic mission by the Spirit promised for the last days; that this Spirit was not available to others in the days of his flesh; and that after his death and resurrection the last days were extended, so to speak, by the followers of Jesus inheriting his mission, his authority and his Spirit. On this point the evangelists are agreed.[73]

Dunn writes in similar vein:

> It will simply not do to cite John 20:19-23 against Luke's dating of the outpouring of the Spirit. John's presentation of the gift of the Spirit is almost wholly inspired by theological considerations—in particular his desire to bring out the theological unity of the climactic salvation events of Jesus' ministry.[74]

John Marsh muses,

> If John were asked why he put the great commission, the new creation and the gift of the Spirit together with the pardoning authority of the Church all on the evening of Easter Day, he would in all probability say that each was inextricably bound up with the moment of the glorification of the Lord that no other place would possibly display their meaning half so well.[75]

The objection that the two accounts could not refer to the same event, since the Spirit could be given only after Jesus' ascension, is countered by inferring from John 20:17 that Jesus did ascend on the day of the resurrection. His post-Easter appearances, then, were actually appearances of the ascended Lord, appearances which ceased with the ascension described in Acts 1. Brown comments:

> What is interesting is that both authors place the giving of the Spirit after Jesus has ascended to his Father, even if they have different views of the ascension. For both of them the Spirit's task is to take the place of Jesus, to carry on his work, and to constitute his presence in the world.[76]

However we explain the unity or diversity of John 20:22 and Acts 2, we cannot deny the fact that the Gospels are more than historical records; they are "good news," and each evangelist puts his own theological stamp on his presentation of the materials. Nevertheless, it appears to be too simple a solution to say that John 20 is but a Johannine variant of the Lucan Pentecost account. The historical contexts of the two accounts are so different that it is perhaps best to view them as describing two different events.

2. The Gift of the Spirit

The bestowal of the Spirit, as recorded by John, follows upon the commissioning of the disciples (Jn. 20:21, 22). By showing them his hands and his side, Jesus was saying that he had completed the work of redemption for which the Father had sent him. Now the message of salvation must be carried into the world. John had explained earlier that the Spirit was not given previously because Jesus had not yet been glorified (Jn. 7:39); but now Jesus has been glorified (in John the cross is part of that glorification), so the Spirit is now available. That Jesus had anticipated the mission of the disciples can be inferred from numerous texts; we need only to refer to Jesus' prayer in John 17:18: "As thou didst send me into the world, so I have sent them into the world." The witness of the Paraclete, Jesus had explained, would go hand in hand with the witness of the disciples (Jn. 15:26, 27), and so the witness of the disciples and the gift of the Spirit are brought together in this text.

As the Father sent Jesus, so Jesus sends his disciples. Their mission proceeds from his mission; it is a continuation of it; indeed, it must be patterned after it. Moreover, just as Jesus was endowed with the Spirit to accomplish his task, so the disciples must be equipped with the Spirit to carry out their commission. Consequently our Lord "breathed" on them. This is the only occurrence of this verb *(emphusao)* in the New Testament. It is found, however, in the creation account, where God breathes the breath of life into man's nostrils (LXX, Gen. 2:7), as well as in Ezekiel 37:7-10, where God's breath blows upon the valley of the dead. It is not unlikely, therefore, that these passages were in John's mind when he recorded Christ's breathing on his disciples. As God breathed upon the first man, so Jesus, fresh from the tomb—as a "life-giving Spirit," as Paul calls him—shares his living breath with his disciples, and initiates the church by his warm, personal, and self-giving breath. The church is a new creation constituted by the Spirit of the risen Lord.[77]

According to Luke 24:46-49, the disciples are told to proclaim the forgiveness of sins once the "promise of the Father" has been sent. Somewhat similarly here in John, the Great Commission, which can be carried out only in the power of the Spirit, involves the offer of the forgiveness of sins. "If you forgive the sins of any, they are forgiven; if you retain the sins of any, they are retained" (Jn. 20:23). John does not mention "preaching" as does Luke, but that may be inferred from the commission to forgive sins—a commission that follows upon the insufflation with the Spirit.

The authority to forgive sins in no way contradicts the fundamental teaching of the Scriptures that only God can forgive sins. The disciples are here authorized to serve as God's agents. But this authority should not be restricted to the apostles, and certainly Jesus was not speaking of the gift of absolution which the apostles could pass on to other church leaders. We should rather think of the disciples on that first Easter evening as representatives of the entire church. Even if that is not the case, we must still ask what it means when the church offers (or denies) forgiveness.

In a general sense, whenever the church proclaims the gospel
it offers God's forgiveness of sins. With that offer of forgiveness
goes the warning that if the sinner does not repent, his sins are
retained and there is no hope of salvation. In the words of Barclay:
"This sentence lays down the duty of the Church to convey forgiveness to the penitent in heart, and to warn the impenitent that
they are forfeiting the mercy of God."[78] It should be recalled that
one of the functions of the Paraclete was to convict the world of
sin (Jn. 16:8ff.). Here Jesus bestows the Holy Spirit on his disciples; as they proclaim the gospel, the Spirit convinces and convicts people of their sins so that they can repent and be forgiven.
Those who refuse suffer the consequences of unforgiven sin.

However, the saying about the forgiveness of sin may also be
related to Matthew 18:18, where Jesus gives the disciples the
power to bind and to loose in the context of church discipline.
When an offender repents, the church forgives his sin; when he
refuses, he is excommunicated, and so his sin is retained. What is
problematic with this line of interpretation is that in John's Gospel
the authority to forgive sins is given in the context of the mission
of the disciples and not of church discipline. We must remember,
of course, that the Great Commission (Mt. 28:19, 20) includes not
only the call to preach and to baptize but also to discipline.

Since the Great Commission in its Matthean form is related
to baptism, some have interpreted Jesus' words about forgiving
and retaining sins to apply to the church's admission (or rejection)
of baptismal candidates. That there is a close connection between
baptism and the forgiveness of sins is plain from Peter's sermon on
the day of Pentecost (Acts 2:38), but the view that the forgiveness
and retaining of sins, of which Jesus speaks in our passage, has to
do with the admitting or rejecting of baptismal candidates seems
somewhat farfetched.

Perhaps it is impossible to be precise in our interpretation of
what it means for the church to forgive sins. That the authority to
forgive sins is related to the Great Commission cannot be denied.
The "sending" of the disciples is modeled on the "sending" of
Jesus by the Father. Jesus' mission divided humanity. Some

believed and were forgiven; others persisted in unbelief and their sin remained. So the mission of the disciples will call forth the hatred of the world but cause others to believe (Jn. 17:14, 20). "The disciples both by deed and word cause men to judge themselves: some come to the light and receive forgiveness; some turn away and are hardened in their sins."[79]

The Great Commission, however, which brings with it both forgiveness and judgment, cannot be carried out without the gift of the Holy Spirit. That explains why the right to forgive sins follows upon the bestowal of the Spirit. And if we be permitted to extend the application of Jesus' promise to embrace other aspects of the life of the church, it can also be said that where the Spirit indwells a Christian community, it can offer forgiveness in the name of Jesus to all who repent. It can also assure baptismal candidates that God in his grace has forgiven their past, and it can forgive members of the Christian community who fail and need to be restored. By the same token, where sinners remain obdurate, their sins are retained and call forth the wrath of God.

In this first part of our study we have focused on the pre-Pentecost period. From the prophetic hopes of the Old Testament prophets, we moved into the dawn of the new era. We listened to John the Baptist announcing the coming baptism with the Spirit by the greater one. We witnessed the activity of the Spirit in the birth and ministry of Jesus who, above all others, was the bearer of the Spirit. Finally we took note of the rich promises of Jesus regarding the coming of the Spirit as these are found in the fourth Gospel. In the second part of this study we shall devote our attention to the coming of the Spirit at Pentecost and its profound and diverse activity in the early church.

PART TWO
The Coming of the Spirit

CHAPTER 5

The Initial Outpouring of the
Spirit at Pentecost

What the prophets of old had hoped for, what John the Baptist had anticipated, and what Jesus had predicted was fulfilled on the day of Pentecost. Pentecost marked the final stage of salvation history; it put the capstone on Christ's work of redemption. From the start of his ministry, Jesus had looked forward to the coming baptism with the Spirit (Acts 1:5). The climax of Jesus' ministry was not only the cross and resurrection, but the ascension and Pentecost. "It was only at Pentecost by the gift of the Spirit that the benefits and blessings won by Jesus in his death, resurrection, and ascension were applied to the disciples."[1]

Jesus had on one occasion said: "I came to cast fire upon the earth; and would that it were already kindled! I have a baptism to be baptized with; and how I am constrained until it is accomplished!" (Lk. 12:49, 50). Whether the fire which Jesus came to cast upon the earth was the fire of judgment, in keeping with the Baptist's prediction that Messiah would baptize "with the Holy Spirit and fire" (Lk. 3:16), or whether the reference is to Pentecost, is not altogether certain. It may be that both meanings were present, for the coming of the Spirit at Pentecost would not only

101

kindle a flame, but also cause a division of humankind into believers and unbelievers (a division which Jesus mentions immediately following the reference to his baptism, Lk. 12:51).

It is significant, however, that the prediction of the fire that Jesus had come to cast on earth is coupled with his words about his death, which he calls a baptism. This baptism, then, is no accident, but it is the goal toward which our Lord moves, for without that baptism the fire cannot fall. On the first Whitsunday, the fire was lit. The work of the suffering servant, into which Jesus had entered when he was baptized in the Jordan, was continued in the baptism of his death, and completed in the baptism with the Spirit on Pentecost (Acts 1:5).

Following his resurrection from the dead our Lord appeared to his disciples repeatedly during the forty days prior to his ascension. Since the number forty is so common in the Bible, it may well be that Luke was alluding to the forty days of divine revelation to Moses on Mt. Sinai. There the leader of the people of God was given his program for action; here the new Moses, Jesus Christ, instructs the leaders of the new people of God.

Several of these post-resurrection appearances took place in Galilee where the risen Lord went to meet his disciples (Mk. 16:7). At the end of the forty days, however, they were back in Jerusalem. The reason for the return to Jerusalem was presumably the eschatological significance of Jerusalem. The immediate occasion for returning to Jerusalem at this time was the celebration of the great pilgrim festival, Pentecost.[2]

Once in Jerusalem, Jesus charged them not to depart from the city but to wait for the promise of the Father (Acts 1:4), the baptism with the Spirit (Acts 1:5), the endowment with power for their calling to be witnesses (Acts 1:8)—a commission given to them "by the Holy Spirit" (Acts 1:2).

Let us see how this promise of Jesus was fulfilled, first on the day of Pentecost, and then in the ongoing work of the church.

A. The Day of Pentecost in Jewish Thought

The Jewish festival of Pentecost, as the word suggests, was

celebrated fifty days after Passover. It was one of the three pilgrim festivals of Israel. Pentecost marked the end of the grain harvest. The two loaves waved before the Lord at Pentecost completed the sheaf-offering made at Passover. And just as the Jewish Pentecost completed the Passover, so the coming of the Spirit at Pentecost completed the first Christian Easter, when Christ, our passover, died for our sins and rose victoriously from the grave.[3]

The two loaves offered at Israel's Feast of Weeks, known in Greek as Pentecost, were called the firstfruits (Lev. 23:17; Num. 28:26). Whereas the sheaves of grain offered at Passover were also called the firstfruits, the real feast of firstfruits was Pentecost.[4] Luke nowhere uses the word firstfruits in his account of Pentecost but, as de Vaux suggests, the very word "Pentecost" had become synonymous with "firstfruits."[5] Luke may well be suggesting that the 3000 believers who formed the nucleus of the new people of God were the firstfruits of the full harvest that would follow once the gospel would go to the ends of the earth. Since Paul calls the Holy Spirit the firstfruits of the harvest that still awaits us (Rom. 8:23), the first Christian Pentecost should perhaps be thought of as a festival of firstfruits.

Pentecost, or *shabuoth* as it was known in Judaism, was always a day of rejoicing. Indeed it was God's command that Israel should rejoice at the Feast of Weeks (Deut. 16:10f.). Gifts were to be given to sons, daughters, servants, Levites, sojourners, the fatherless, and widows. There was no more appropriate day in the Jewish calendar on which the Spirit, which is supremely a Spirit of joy (Gal. 5:22; Rom. 14:17), should have been given. The first Christian Pentecost opened up wells of joy for the new people of God. The fact that the Spirit was given to all classes of people present may be reminiscent of the distribution of gifts to the various groups at Israel's Festival of Weeks. So closely is the Spirit and joy related in the New Testament that Lampe feels justified in assuming that when the Ethiopian eunuch went on his way "rejoicing" (Acts 8:39), or when the Philippian jailer "rejoiced" with all his household (Acts 16:34), he was using the word as a synonym for receiving the Holy Spirit.[6]

Originally Pentecost was an agricultural festival but in New Testament times, apparently, it was celebrated as the anniversary of the giving of the law at Sinai (Jubil. 1:1; 6:7). Several of the circumstances that attended the coming of the Spirit find their parallels in the great event at Sinai when Israel was constituted a people of God.[7] Among other things it was a Jewish tradition that all nations had been present at Sinai and that all had been given the law in their own language,[8] but that only Israel had accepted the covenant. This tradition has no Old Testament support, but it is interesting to find in Luke's account of the first Christian Pentecost a catalog of nations representing all humanity (Acts 2:5-13). Moreover, the noise and the fire in Luke's account are reminiscent of the noise and fire that attended God's coming to Sinai to give Israel his law and to form a band of slaves, whom he had redeemed out of bondage, into his own people.

In Qumran, Pentecost was a day for the renewal of the covenant with Yahweh.[9] Since the promise of the Spirit lies at the heart of the promise of a new covenant (e.g., Ezek. 36:24-26; 2 Cor. 3), Pentecost may be viewed as the fulfillment of that promise. By putting his Spirit into the hearts of his people as the prophets had promised, God established his new covenant with a new people.[10]

Some familiarity with the Pentecost festival as it was celebrated in ancient Israel and in Judaism enriches our understanding of Luke's account of the first Christian Pentecost. We turn now to some of the circumstances associated with the coming of the Spirit.

B. Circumstances Associated with the Coming of the Spirit
1. The Noise from Heaven

When the day of Pentecost arrived, the hundred and twenty were together in one place. "And suddenly a sound came from heaven like the rush of a mighty wind, and it filled all the house where they were sitting" (Acts 2:2). In the Old Testament, God's presence is often recognized by what is heard (Gen. 3:8; 1 Sam. 3:4ff.; Ex. 33:20ff.). Philo reports that when God gave the law, he caused a noise (*echos*, as here) which changed to fire and was perceived as tongues (*dialektos*, as here).[11]

A wind or whirlwind also represent the divine presence or the mysterious working of God in the Old Testament (1 Kings 19:11; Job 38:1). In Ezekiel 37:9-14 the wind (*ruach*, spirit/wind) blows upon the corpses, filling them with new life. Jesus said the Spirit was like the wind that blows where it wills (Jn. 3:8).

Pentecost began with a "blast," a rushing mighty wind, not a light, gentle breeze. Noise and violence—emotional, vocal, or physical—have no value in themselves, but here God was at work and there was no mistake about it. As the "wind of God" blew at the beginning of the first creation, so God's wind blew at Pentecost, creating the church.

That this wind came "suddenly" is another way of saying that when God's time comes, he acts and nothing can stop him. We are reminded of Malachi's prediction that the Lord will "suddenly" come to the temple (3:1),[12] and of the announcement of Christ's birth when "suddenly" there was with the angel a multitude of the heavenly host praising God (Lk. 2:13f.).

2. The Tongues of Fire

"And there appeared to them tongues as of fire, distributed and resting on each one of them" (Acts 2:3). Fire, like wind, is a sign of the presence of God (Ex. 3:2f.; 19:18); indeed, fire and wind are sometimes linked together (Is. 29:6; 30:7f.).

John the Baptist had predicted that Jesus would baptize with the Holy Spirit and "fire." Joel had also mentioned fire as an accompaniment to the outpouring of the Spirit in the latter days (Joel 2:30). In these passages, however, the reference seems to be to judgment, whereas Pentecost was a gracious visitation of God. It is possible, nevertheless, that Luke thought of the coming of the Spirit as inaugurating the eschatological judgment through the preaching of the gospel, by which humanity is divided into believers and those who reject the gospel.[13]

The tongues of fire distributed themselves and rested (sat) on each one of them. The expression is reminiscent of the Spirit descending upon Jesus and remaining on him (although a different verb is used for "remain" in John 1:32). It may be a symbolic way of saying that God's favor rested on them.

That neither wind nor fire should be understood prosaically can be seen from the fact that Luke is careful to say "like" wind and "as of fire." He does, however, want to impress us with the fact that these unusual phenomena were actually witnessed by the early believers in the upper room and that the author is not simply describing a subjective experience of visionaries.

> What came to them came not from the depths of their subconscious, individual or collective, but from beyond themselves, outside themselves. It was the experience of divine power unexpected in its givenness and in its accompanying features which probably determined the elements of the vision. [14]

As the Spirit came upon the hundred and twenty, "they were all filled with the Holy Spirit and began to speak in other tongues, as the Spirit gave them utterance" (Acts 2:4).

3. Speaking in Tongues

In the predictions of the coming of the Spirit, a variety of verbs are used: "clothed with power" (Lk. 24:49), "receive" (Jn. 7:39), "baptized" (Acts 1:5), "come upon" (Acts 1:8). When the Spirit came Luke says simply that the recipients were "filled with the Holy Spirit" (2:4). Clearly in this passage "to be filled" is used as the equivalent of "to be baptized" with the Spirit. Or, taking a word from Joel 2:28, Luke describes the coming of the Spirit at Pentecost as "poured out" (Acts 2:33). Marshall writes:

> Our conclusion is that Luke refers to the Pentecost experience of the disciples as a filling with the Spirit, and that this means the same as the baptism of the Spirit, the gift of the Spirit, and so on. The choice of the particular term "filling" in this context rather than any of its synonyms is with a view to the prophetic inspiration which accompanied the gift on this particular occasion. [15]

When the Spirit came at Pentecost those sitting in the upper room were filled with the Spirit (stressing the rich profusion of

God's gift) and began to speak in other tongues. Strangely, in the promises of the coming of the Spirit there are no suggestions anywhere that the recipients of the Spirit would speak in other tongues, although there is a rabbinic tradition that every nation heard the law given at Sinai in its own tongue.[16] Moreover, there is no indication that those who waited for the Spirit in the upper room sought this gift, or that some received the gift of tongues and others did not. The gift of tongues at Pentecost enabled the recipients to proclaim the good news of God's salvation to the multitudes in their native tongues (Acts 2:8).

There are only three references to speaking in tongues in the book of Acts: in Jerusalem on the day of Pentecost (2:6), in the house of Cornelius at Caesarea (10:46), and when Paul dealt with the disciples of John the Baptist at Ephesus (19:6). It is not certain that the gift of tongues bestowed subsequent to Pentecost was employed in the proclamation of the gospel. That there were other kinds of tongues seems obvious from Paul's letter to the Corinthians (1 Cor. 12—14). According to 1 Corinthians the gift of tongues was not given to all believers. Moreover, the tongues in Corinth were unintelligible, for they called for an interpreter. In contrast to Pentecost, where the gift of tongues enabled the recipients to proclaim the gospel so that others could hear it in their own language, tongues elsewhere in the early church belong to the language of devotion, prayer, and song. The speaking in tongues at Pentecost, then, appears to have been a unique phenomenon.

That there should be such unusual phenomena when the Spirit came at Pentecost should not surprise us. In every deep spiritual movement there are unusual manifestations. Since there is speaking in tongues even in non-Christian religions, some interpreters have tried to give naturalistic explanations for tongues at Pentecost.

It has been suggested, for example, that to speak in tongues is simply a Hebrew idiom, meaning to speak with excitement, enthusiastically, vigorously, and with feeling. Such a view, however, has no foundation in Luke's account. An even more incredible explanation is that people from all over the Roman world simply understood what the apostles were saying in spite of their Galilean dialect. That the visitors in Jerusalem could have understood the apostles if they had spoken to them in Greek, the language of the Greco-Roman world, must be accepted. However, God broke through all language barriers at Pentecost so that the visitors understood the message in their local dialects, in order to convince them that the Spirit had in fact come.

Moreover, a comparison of the language of Acts 2 with that of the account of the confusion of tongues in Genesis 11 will show a number of parallels. It has even been suggested that Genesis 11 was one of the pericopes read during the Jewish Festival of Weeks. Whereas Genesis 11 describes how God's judgment confused human languages, at Pentecost he breaks through these barriers and unites hearers from many lands under the Word given by the power of the Spirit.

Luke is known as a rather reliable historian. It is not worthy of him, therefore, to say that the report of speaking in tongues at Pentecost is a literary construction based upon the reports of glossolalia in Christian churches and the rabbinic legends of the giving of the law at Sinai.

Some interpreters maintain that the Pentecostal speaking in tongues represents the same phenomenon as found in the later Corinthian church; they suggest that what the visitors heard was not coherent or even intelligible speech. Some hearers, so the explanation goes, seemed to identify the sounds uttered by the disciples with the languages of their homeland; others thought it was gibberish and in fact suggested that the apostles were drunk (Acts 2:13). Luke, however, reports that they did, in fact, hear them telling about the great works of God in their own tongues (Acts 2:11).

By breaking through the language barriers, the Holy Spirit was pointing the church to its mission: to be a proclaiming church. The gift of tongues was not given to lighten the labor of the missionary in learning foreign languages; it was designed rather to remind the church that the gospel must be proclaimed to every tribe and tongue. As far as we know, this Pentecostal experience was never repeated; it was unique.

As was often true in the Old Testament and in the Lucan infancy narratives, when the Spirit was given to individuals, they were inspired to proclaim God's Word—to prophesy. In his Pentecost sermon Peter quoted Joel 2:28 in which the prophet predicted that when the Spirit would be poured out, prophecy would be reborn. As it happened, the disciples of Jesus, who had fled when Jesus was captured and had hid behind closed doors for fear of the Jews, became courageous preachers of the the gospel by the Spirit's power. This is not the place to analyze Peter's sermon, except to call attention to the fact that when those who were convicted by his message asked what they should do, Peter explained: "Repent, and be baptized every one of you in the name of Jesus Christ for the forgiveness of your sins; and you shall receive the gift of the Holy Spirit" (Acts 2:38).

C. The Offer of the Gift of the Spirit in the Gospel
1. Repentance, Baptism, and the Gift of the Spirit

Whereas elsewhere in Acts only one or two conditions for experiencing God's salvation are given, here Peter's call represents a combination and coordination of a number of conditions. One condition that has to be met before the Spirit can be received is repentance. The call to repentance characterizes the speeches of Acts, even though the word itself is not always mentioned. In the earlier speeches addressed to Jews, the hearers are called upon to repent from the awful sin of having participated in killing God's Messiah (Acts 2:23; 3:1f.). Gentiles are called to repent of idolatry (Acts 14:15; 17:22ff.). However, the sermons in Acts cannot be stereotyped.

Although it is not reported that Peter urged his listeners to believe in Jesus, those who responded to his message are called the believing ones (Acts 2:44). Also Luke reports that "those who received his word were baptized" (Acts 2:41). This diversity cautions us against looking for the same words whenever Luke describes the conversion of those who accepted the gospel. If then

Peter here called his audience to "repent" and later Paul told the jailor and his house to "believe in the Lord Jesus, and you will be saved" (Acts 16:31), there is no essential difference in meaning. We may recall Jesus' message, in which these two terms are combined: "Repent, and believe in the gospel" (Mk. 1:15). If one were to make a distinction between "repentance" and "faith," then repentance represents the negative aspect of conversion— the turning away from sin (behind conversion and repentance in Greek lies the Hebrew word *shub* meaning to turn or return); faith, on the other hand, represents the positive aspect—the turning in trust and commitment to Christ.

That repentance and faith are necessary preconditions for the conferral of the Spirit stands to reason. What some readers find troublesome, however, is the close link that Luke establishes between repentance, forgiveness, and baptism as necessary requirements for the reception of the Spirit. The uneasiness about this close connection probably stems from a reaction against baptismal regeneration—an erroneous doctrine which has been found in some church traditions through much of the Christian era. If we recognize that Peter is not teaching anything of the sort, we should have less difficulty with the close relationship of repentance, baptism, and the forgiveness of sin. In the early church these were all part of one experience.

Perhaps it should be observed that forgiveness of sin is as closely related to repentance and the gift of the Spirit as it is to baptism. And since these were all part of the one experience by which people were initiated into the church, there was no need for exact chronological sequence when describing the experience. F. F. Bruce writes:

> If it be realized that repentance and faith, with baptism in water and reception of the Spirit, followed by first communion, formed one complex experience of Christian initiation, then what is true of the experience as a whole may be predicated of any element in it. We may make logical distinctions between this and that element, but such distinctions need not have been present in the minds of Paul's converts who knew that they had been "washed . . . sanctified . . . justified in the name of the Lord Jesus Christ and the Spirit of our God."[17]

It is possible, of course, to interpret the formula "for the forgiveness of sins" *(eis ephesin ton harmartion)* as "on the basis of forgiveness of sins"; this would mean that baptism follows only upon repentance and forgiveness (for this meaning of *eis*, see Matthew 10:41; 12:41). In fact one might even take the phrase to express result rather than purpose: baptism follows forgiveness of sins as consequence, it does not effect the forgiveness of sins. But all such explanations are unnecessary when one remembers that the New Testament writers vary their vocabulary considerably when speaking of conversion. They never seem to be overly concerned about observing the proper sequence in wording when they describe an experience which has a number of facets.

It should not be insisted upon, however, that the gift of the Spirit was withheld until the precise moment when these new converts were baptized with water. The experience of those who heard Peter in the house of Cornelius would bear this out, for they received the Spirit before they were baptized (Acts 10:44-48).

Hull is probably correct in observing that the preconditions for the gift of the Spirit which Peter enunciated in his Pentecost sermon were repentance, faith in Jesus, and the willingness to be baptized.[18] He goes on to say that "the distinction between the willingness to be baptized and baptism itself means that Luke sees no inconsistency and indeed, that there is no inconsistency in the reception of the Spirit sometimes before and sometimes after baptism."[19]

The command to be baptized with water occasioned no surprise in the hearers, since baptism was well-known to them. Not only were Gentiles baptized when they became members of the Jewish synagogue, but John the Baptist had baptized fellow Jews who repented of their sins and declared their intention to begin a new way of life in anticipation of the coming Messiah. The church continued the practice of initiating its converts into the Christian community through water baptism.

In contrast to John's baptism, the Christian church baptized in the name of Jesus. The Trinitarian baptismal formula (Father, Son, and Holy Spirit, Mt. 28:19) does not appear to have been used in the early stages of the church's life. Perhaps Jesus' command to baptize converts in the name of the Father, Son, and Holy Spirit had not been understood as a formula to be quoted at baptism; it may also be that when the early church baptized in the name of Jesus, his name by synecdoche (a figure of speech in which a part is used to represent the whole) stood for the Trinity. Jesus had not said: "When you baptize, then say these words." And even in the Trinitarian formula, "name" is singular, not plural. As Bietenhard puts it: "Baptism into the name means that the subject of baptism, through fellowship with the Son who is one with God, receives the forgiveness of sins and comes under the operation of the Holy Spirit."[20] That the Trinitarian formula may have been used quite early in the history of the apostolic church seems to be reflected in Paul's observation regarding the Corinthian converts who are said to have got themselves washed "in the name of the Lord Jesus Christ and in the Spirit of our God" (1 Cor. 6:11). (Notice here all the members of the Trinity.)

A much more important distinction between John's baptism and Christian baptism is the fact that John's was with water only, whereas in Christian baptism water and Spirit go together. With John there is a contrast between water and Spirit, for only after Pentecost could the two be combined. Jesus anticipated this combination when he explained to Nicodemus that he needed to be born of "water and the Spirit" (Jn. 3:5). "The outward form of baptism in water remained unchanged, but its significance was now immeasurably enhanced."[21] At Pentecost the greater one, whose coming John the Baptist had predicted, baptized all those who repented with his Spirit, and they expressed this by being baptized with water.

Peter's promise of the gift of the Holy Spirit needs to be singled out for special observation.

2. The Gift of the Spirit Following Pentecost

Jesus had promised his disciples that in a few days they would be baptized with the Spirit (Acts 1:5); they would be endowed with power when the Spirit would come upon them

(Acts 1:8). This was fulfilled on the day of Pentecost when the 120 were filled with the Holy Spirit (Acts 2:4) and the 3000 responded in repentance and faith, were baptized, and received the gift of the Spirit.

Peter, however, went beyond the present moment and held out the gift of the Spirit both to Jews and Gentiles who would hear the gospel and turn to Christ in faith. No matter how Peter may have understood Joel's prophecy that in the last days God would pour out his Spirit upon "all flesh," he was convinced that the gift of the Spirit was not restricted to the 120 or even to the 3000 Pentecostal converts. Peter went on to say: "For the promise is to you and to your children and to all that are far off, every one whom the Lord our God calls to him" (Acts 2:39).

The "gift" of the Spirit must not be confused with the "gifts" of the Spirit. There were gifts as well, to be sure, but that is not what Peter meant when he offered the gift of the Spirit to all those who would believe. And this gift was made available not only to those who waited in the upper room, nor only to the Pentecostal visitors, but "to your children," says Peter. The "children" are the descendants, the future generations. One must not read the later practice of infant baptism into this text. The "children" would have to repent just like those who received the word at that first Pentecost if they were to receive the gift of the Holy Spirit.

The promise of the Spirit to the "children" paralleled the promise of the Spirit to "all that are far off." Those "far off" in the language of the Old Testament (Is. 57:19) and of Jewry were the Gentiles. Although Peter might have had diaspora Jews in mind when he spoke of those "far off," in contrast to Palestinian Jews who were "near," then Paul makes it very clear that those "far off" were the Gentiles ("And he came and preached peace to you who were far off," Eph. 2:17).

It is worth noting that Peter in fact threw the door open wide when he added: "and to every one whom the Lord calls." The gift of the Spirit is bestowed upon all who hear God's call in the gospel and respond to that call. The language used here stresses the fact that God takes the initiative in our salvation. Peter very likely derived his terminology at this point from Joel 2:32. Following the promise of the eschatological outpouring of the Spirit (Joel 2:28-31), Joel adds that the survivors of the day of the Lord "shall be those whom the Lord calls" (v. 32). Since God is the God of both the Jew and the Gentile, his grace is conferred on both, and so the gift of the Spirit is now available to all whom he calls. Whether or not Peter fully realized the implications of what he said when he held out the gift of the Spirit to all whom the Lord would call, is hard to say. When the Spirit directed him to the Gentiles (Acts 11:12), he obeyed. Subsequently he defended his action before the Jerusalem congregation, and later explained to the Jerusalem Council that God had given the Gentiles "the Holy Spirit just as he did to us" (Acts 15:8).

The miracle of Pentecost is a historical event which cannot be repeated. It is the birthday of the church. The gift of the Spirit, however, is available to all future generations as long as this age of grace lasts. For that reason it is hermeneutically improper to insist, as some do, that all believers must experience what the 120 experienced: wait in some upper room (sometimes called the doctrine of "tarrying") until the Spirit comes upon them. What we can say with certainty, however, is that all who repent, receive the forgiveness of sins, and are baptized with water in the name of Jesus will receive the gift of the Holy Spirit. Dunn writes,

> In one sense, therefore, Pentecost can never be repeated—for the new age is here and cannot be ushered in again. But in another sense Pentecost, or rather the experience of Pentecost, can and must be repeated in the experience of all who would become Christians. As the day of Pentecost was once the doorway into the new age, so entry into the new age can only be made through that doorway.[22]

A new people of God was born on the day of Pentecost. Like the sacred remnant of which the prophets speak, they too represented the genuine people of God in the midst of an apostate Jewish nation. In fact Peter called upon his hearers to save themselves "from this crooked generation" (Acts 2:40). "Peter's words reflect the conviction of the early Christians that they formed the faithful remnant of Israel."[23] Here we have a clear indication that the church, the new people of God, is no longer to be identified with Israel as a nation, even though the first converts were mostly Jews.

By the baptism with the Spirit the church was brought into being and the members of this new people of God "devoted themselves to the apostles' teaching and fellowship, to the breaking of bread and the prayers" (Acts 2:42). Their life was characterized by a new power to witness; they were filled with infectious joy; they willingly shared their material goods; they were highly respected in the community. The result was that the Lord added to their number day by day (Acts 2:47).

As Peter had explained, the outpouring of the Spirit at Pentecost was not to be limited to the Jerusalem community. The fresh waters of the Spirit, as the prophets had described the coming of the Spirit, burst their banks and spread over a vast terrain, bringing new life and fruitfulness to parched souls. One of these "overflows" occurred in Samaria.

CHAPTER 6

The Continuing Overflow of the Spirit to Other Believers

The church in Jerusalem had grown to a large body of believers. At first they were held in high repute by their Jewish contemporaries. Eventually, however, the separation of the church from the Jewish community, particularly as this was advocated by the Hellenist Stephen led to a persecution which hit believers of Hellenistic background particularly hard. One of these Jerusalem saints who was forced to leave the city was Philip. This man of God, whom Luke first brings upon the scene as one of the seven "deacons" (Acts 6:5), took a very daring step and preached the gospel to the Samaritans (Acts 8:1-13).

A. The Receipt of the Spirit by the Samaritans
1. The Conversion of the Samaritans

The deep hatred between Jerusalem and Samaria resulted from the breakup of David's kingdom after Solomon's death. Samaria became the capital of the Northern Kingdom under Omri. When Samaria fell, the Assyrians brought in Eastern peoples to live in the conquered kingdom of Israel. Judah also went into captivity. Later, when the exiles returned from Babylon and rebuilt

Jerusalem, the Samaritans, who were viewed by the Jews as a mixed race, offered their help, but were rebuffed. This led to an even deeper cleavage between the two communities. About a century before Christ, John Hyrcanus I conquered the Samaritans and destroyed their schismatic temple. When the early church was established, Samaria and Judea had been united politically under the Romans, but the hatred between the Jews and the Samaritans was still very intense. On numerous occasions the Roman governor, who resided at Caesarea, had to intervene in conflicts between the two factions.

Philip, however, had already grasped the fundamental truth that the church was not to be comprised of Jewish believers only but of converts from all nations. Having come into Samaritan territory, Philip "proclaimed to them the Christ" (Acts 8:5). The crowds heard the message and responded in faith to the gospel. To "give heed" to what was said by Philip (8:6) is the equivalent of "believed" (8:12). Philip's ministry was attended by manifestations of God's power in exorcism and healing. A sign that the new age was dawning also for the Samaritans was the great joy which the Samaritans experienced when they believed the gospel (8:8). Having put their faith in Christ, they were baptized with water, as were the new converts on the day of Pentecost (8:12). Philip had reaped where his Master had sown earlier, when the Samaritans were introduced to the Savior of the world through the witness of the Samaritan woman (Jn. 4).

2. The Delay of the Gift of the Spirit

When the apostles, who had not been driven from Jerusalem because they were still looked upon as orthodox Jews, heard that the Samaritans had received the word of God (8:14)—just as Jews and proselytes had received it on the day of Pentecost (Acts 2:41)—they decided to send the leading apostles, Peter and John, to Samaria. There is no suggestion that they had doubts about the reports of the conversion of the Samaritans; nor is there a hint that they wanted to assure themselves that Philip was doing the right thing or preaching the right gospel.

Rather, they seem to have regarded it as their responsibility to guide the ongoing work of the church. Perhaps the Jerusalem community had to be convinced by the apostles that the Samaritans had in fact accepted Christ. On the other hand, the Samaritan believers would certainly need to be assured by representatives from Jerusalem that they were welcome in the community of the saints.

However, when Peter and John arrived, presumably to extend the right hand of fellowship to these recent converts from the Samaritans, they discovered that they had not yet received the Holy Spirit. Contrary to what Peter had proclaimed at Pentecost, namely, that the gift of the Spirit would be given to all who repented, the Samaritans, who had believed and had been baptized, had not yet received the Holy Spirit. The apostles then laid hands on them and prayed that they might receive the Spirit (Acts 8:14-16).

The experience of the Samaritans was not typical of other conversions and, as Michael Green puts it, "Luke records it *because it is not typical.*"[1] Various attempts have been made to explain this unusual experience. There are those who argue from silence that the Samaritans had received the gift of the Spirit when they believed, but the "gifts" of the Spirit had not yet been bestowed. The apostles (so the argument goes) laid hands on them for the purpose of receiving charismatic gifts. But the text says explicitly that they had not yet received the Holy Spirit (Acts 8:16). Moreover, the text has it that they did receive the Holy Spirit in answer to prayer when Peter and John laid hands upon them (8:17). There may well have been gifts also, but that's not what the text says. It is wrong, therefore, to use this passage to teach that believers must at some point after conversion receive the baptism of the Spirit in order to be endowed with spiritual gifts.

Then there are those who deny that the Samaritans were genuinely converted in the first place. They read this story in the light of the Pauline teaching that those who do not have the Spirit of Christ are not genuine believers (Rom. 8:9). The language of the text, however ("gave heed," "believed," "received the word of God"), makes it unequivocally clear that the Samaritans were true believers. It would be wrong to say that their conversion took place when Peter and John laid hands on them and they received the Spirit. To say, as does Dunn, that the Samaritans had fixed their attention on Philip, not on Christ, misreads the text. The argument that their faith was not genuine, on the grounds that Simon Magus, whose faith turned out to be spurious, had also believed and was baptized as the rest of the Samaritan believers, cannot stand.[2] It is an attempt to paint Luke's account with a Pauline brush.

Some who refuse to accept the faith of the Samaritans as genuine argue that they believed with the "mind" and not with the "heart." Later, when Peter and John laid hands on them and they received the Holy Spirit, their faith became real, it is said. But Peter and John did not question the faith of the Samaritans, nor did they give them instructions on how to make their faith real. In fact they did not ask the Samaritans to do anything—such as confess their sins, pray, fast, or the like.

Evidently Philip had preached the full gospel but the experience of the Samaritans was not yet complete. There is no insinuation either that Philip lacked ecclesiastical clout and that the leading apostles had to be called to confirm the genuineness of the faith of the Samaritans.[3] When Philip later baptized the Ethiopian official, the latter went on his way rejoicing, and certainly the "layman" Ananias, who laid hands on Paul, had no more ecclesiastical authority than Philip. Even more fanciful is the suggestion that the Samaritans had been baptized but needed to be confirmed by the apostles from Jerusalem. One must not read later church practices back into this early period of the church. Neil says quite correctly, "Luke is thus not concerned with anchoring later ecclesiastical practice in the fluid and 'irregular' form and order of the primitive church. . . ."[4]

The explanation for the delay of the Spirit in the experience of the Samaritans lies rather, we think, in another direction. F. F. Bruce points out that "in the present instance, some special evidence may have been necessary to assure the Samaritans, accustomed to being despised as outsiders by the people of Jerusalem, that they were fully incorporated into the new community of the people of God."[5] Professor Lampe argues similarly that the Samaritans, so long the objects of disdain, needed a special gesture from the leaders of the Jerusalem church to incorporate them into the Spirit-possessed fellowship of the new people of God.[6] The imposition of hands, then, was primarily a token of fellowship and solidarity.

F. D. Bruner suggests that the gift of the Spirit was withheld till the Jerusalem apostles could come and see the Samaritans receive it—see it with their own eyes. He goes on to say:

> The Samaritans were not left to become an isolated sect with no bonds of union with the apostolic church in Jerusalem. If a Samaritan church and a Jewish church had arisen independently, side by side, without the dramatic removal of the ancient and bitter barriers of prejudice between the two, particularly at the level of ultimate authority, the young church of God would have been in schism from the inception of its mission.[7]

Michael Green is of the same persuasion:

> If the Holy Spirit had been given immediately upon profession of faith and baptism by the Samaritans this schism might have continued, and there would have been two churches, out of fellowship with each other.... It was not so much an authorisation from Jerusalem or an extension of the Jerusalem church, as a divine veto on schism in the infant Church, a schism which could have slipped almost unnoticed into the Christian fellowship, as converts from the two sides of the "Samaritan curtain" found Christ without finding each other.... It was for this reason, I believe, that God made delay on this occasion.[8]

All the conditions for the receipt of the Spirit evidently had been met, but the gift was delayed until the leaders of the Jerusalem church were on the scene to dismantle the old walls of enmity and to welcome these new converts into the community of the saints.

This was a pioneer situation and the story is not told to give us a pattern of Christian experience; for just as we cannot relive the Jerusalem Pentecost event, so we cannot imitate the

Samaritan Pentecost experience. If we could, what would we do with the experiences of Paul, Cornelius, and others, where the pattern is quite different? Luke is really not interested in giving us tidy theological schemes. The book of Acts is not a handbook on Christian initiation.[9] The book illustrates, rather, the freedom with which the Spirit works.

John R. W. Stott says that "a doctrine of the Holy Spirit must not be construed from purely descriptive passages in the Acts. It would be impossible to build a consistent doctrine from them because there is no constancy about them."[10] On the conversion of the Samaritans, Stott goes on to say:

> The reason why the Spirit was not given seems to lie in the historical situation. And since this historical situation was unique and cannot be repeated (the Jewish-Samaritan schism having long since been swallowed up by the universal-Christian mission), I cannot myself see how the abnormality in the Samaritan reception of the Spirit could be taken as a precedent for today.[11]

The experience of the Samaritans was so clearly abnormal, it is difficult to see how their experience could be held up as a norm for spiritual experience today. That the Samaritan experience cannot be viewed as normative for believers is underscored by another church-founding event in which the sequence of Christian experience is quite different—the conversion of Cornelius and his household (Acts 10).

B. The Falling of the Spirit on the Gentiles

It took a special revelation from heaven to convince Peter that the Gentiles, too, had been embraced in Christ's plan of redemption. Together with several Jewish brethren, he risked "contamination" by entering the house of a Gentile God-fearer, Cornelius. As Peter shared God's saving message with the household and friends of Cornelius, the Holy Spirit fell on those who heard the Word (Acts 10:44). One gets the impression that the sermon was interrupted by the response of the hearers and the bestowal of the Spirit.

The Jewish believers with Peter were dumbfounded when they saw that the Holy Spirit had been poured out on the Gentiles (10:45). Of Paul it was said that when he was converted, he was "filled" with the Spirit; here the verbs "fall" (10:44), "pour" (10:45), and "receive" (10:47) are used to describe the coming of the Spirit on the hearers. These are just a few of the many terms for the coming of the Spirit; when they are used to describe Christian initiation, they mean essentially the same thing.

If we should ask how the Jewish brethren recognized the fact that the Spirit had been poured out on the hearers, one might answer that these new converts spoke in tongues (Acts 10:46). But it should be noted that this was a gift which they received when they turned to Christ; it was not something they sought for after conversion. Also, in the three instances where tongues are mentioned in Acts (Acts 2, 10, and 19), they come to an entire group at once. Just what form the speaking in tongues took in Cornelius' household, we do not know, except that the converts praised God. The phenomenon seems quite different from the Jerusalem Pentecost, when the gospel was proclaimed in other tongues.

Perhaps it would not be wrong to speak of a Jewish Pentecost (Acts 2), a Samaritan Pentecost (Acts 8), and a Gentile Pentecost (Acts 10). If, as Jesus explained (Acts 1:5), the baptism of the Spirit took place at the Jewish Pentecost, then it could legitimately be said that the Samaritan and Gentile experience was also a baptism of the Spirit, as new churches were founded and members were initiated into the body of Christ. We have good reason to say that, because Peter, when he reported on the conversion of Cornelius and his household, told the Jerusalem church that when he had seen the Holy Spirit fall on the Gentiles, he was reminded of Jesus' words: "John baptized with water, but you shall be baptized with the Holy Spirit" (Acts 11:16).

Once the Spirit had come upon his hearers, Peter asked: "Can any one forbid water for baptizing these people who have received the Holy Spirit just as we have?" (Acts 10:47). Someone might argue that the conditions laid down by Peter in his Pentecost sermon for the receipt of the Spirit had not yet been met.

Nothing is said about repentance or faith. This illustrates Luke's freedom in reporting conversion stories. Later, when Peter defended his preaching in Cornelius' house, he mentioned that "God gave the same gift to them as he gave to us" when he *believed* in the Lord Jesus Christ (Acts 11:17). Moreover, the Jerusalem congregation recognized, after Peter reported on the conversion of these Gentiles, that God had in fact given *repentance* to the Gentiles (11:18). Later, at the Jerusalem Council, Peter argued for the inclusion of the Gentiles by reminding his brothers that God chose him even before Paul to preach the gospel so that the Gentiles should hear the Word of God and *believe* (Acts 15:7, 8). He added that God had cleansed their hearts by faith (15:9).

Since all the conditions for water baptism had been met, Peter "commanded them to be baptized in the name of Jesus Christ" (Acts 10:48). The greater act had been bestowed; the lesser could not be withheld. In his report to Jerusalem, Peter said that he would have resisted God if he had denied baptism to these Gentiles (11:17). Bruner observes:

> The intimate connection between baptism and the Spirit established at Pentecost (2:38, 39), dramatically confirmed at Samaria (8:14-17), finds expression again here in Caesarea. Since it was evidently impossible for the apostles to associate the gift of the Holy Spirit with anything but baptism, the new converts were immediately baptized (10:48).[12]

It is interesting that the order of events in chapter 10 are different from those in chapter 8. In the case of the Samaritans there was faith, baptism, then the gift of the Spirit; in the story of the conversion of Cornelius' household, the order is faith, the gift of the Spirit, then baptism. Both accounts are descriptive rather than prescriptive. Bruce observes that "if we think of the separate elements in Christian initiation—repentance and faith, baptism, laying on of hands, reception of the Spirit—Luke does not seem to regard any one sequence as normative."[13] If, however, we take into account what Paul taught about the relation of faith, the gift of the Spirit, and baptism, then the order as found in Acts 10 seems to have been the more normal order.

In chapter 19 there is another rather unique account. What makes it so unique is that it is the only instance in which people were rebaptized. I am referring to the disciples of John the Baptist in Ephesus.

C. The Coming of the Spirit on the Ephesian Disciples

When Paul arrived at Ephesus on his third missionary journey, he encountered about twelve Jews whose knowledge of the Christian faith was incomplete. They may have received their instruction about the Christian life from a source similar to Apollos' source. And just as he needed further enlightenment by Priscilla and Aquila (Acts 18:26), so Paul led these Ephesian disciples into a fuller understanding of the gospel.

The question has often been debated as to whether this Ephesian dozen was really Christian or not. The word "disciples" is the normal description for Christians in the book of Acts (Acts 16:1; 18:27; etc.). When Paul met them in Ephesus, he took them for true disciples of Jesus. However, he must have detected a deficiency in their life, so he asked them: "Did you receive the Holy Spirit when you believed?" (Acts 19:2). Their answer made it clear that their Christian experience was, at best, a truncated one. Stott asks whether it can be seriously maintained

> that people who have never heard of the Holy Spirit, nor have been baptized in the name of Jesus, nor even apparently believed in Jesus, were true Christian disciples? Surely not. If they were anybody's disciples, they were disciples of Apollos and of John the Baptist. They were not clearly converted Christians. They certainly cannot be regarded as typical Christian believers today.[14]

Upon further probing Paul discovered that they were disciples of John the Baptist. It is hard to determine whether they had been followers of the Baptist in Judea who later settled in Ephesus, or whether they had been introduced to John's teachings and baptized "into John's baptism" (Acts 19:3) in Ephesus by a disciple of the Baptist. That they must have known about the Holy Spirit is almost certain, for even the Old Testament has much to say about God's Spirit (the term "Holy Spirit" is, of course, rare). Moreover, if they had paid any attention to the Baptist's teaching, they must have known about the promise of the coming one who would baptize with the Holy Spirit. What they did not know, however, was that the Spirit had in fact been given. If they were Palestinian disciples of John, they may have left the country before the Pentecostal outpouring of the Spirit. In any case, what normally happens when people believe in Jesus had not happened in their case; they did not have the Holy Spirit.

Paul gave them fuller instruction about Christ and they were baptized with water in the name of the Lord Jesus. It is nowhere suggested that the disciples of Jesus who had been baptized with John's baptism were rebaptized when the Holy Spirit came upon them at Pentecost. Evidently the receipt of the Spirit at Pentecost transmuted John's baptism into Christian baptism in their case. But the Ephesian disciples of John were not Christians in the full sense of that word; they were living on this side of Pentecost. It may even be that they had been baptized with John's baptism *after* Pentecost and for that reason their baptism was not simply transmuted into Christian by the receipt of the Spirit. When they were fully instructed in the Christian faith, they received the Holy Spirit and were then baptized in the name of Jesus.

Here then we have a very unique situation. And to recognize that goes a long way in solving this problem text. Those who want to use this passage to teach that salvation is experienced in two stages fail to recognize that there are no analogies to this singular event in our day. Here were people who were baptized with John's baptism and were subsequently taught the Christian faith and then rebaptized with water. To argue that they were genuine Christians who had already received the gift of the Spirit, but had not been "baptized" with the Spirit (the second work of grace), is to read something into the text that is not there.

It should be noticed that Paul assumed that faith was all that was required to receive the Holy Spirit. "Did you receive the Holy Spirit when you believed?" was his question (19:2). He did not ask: "Have you prayed for the Spirit-baptism?" "Have you emp-

tied yourself of self and sin?" "Have you yielded yourself completely to God?" "Have you had hands laid upon you?" All that
was needed to receive the Holy Spirit was faith in Jesus Christ.
Paul did not offer to lead them to "higher things," but he gave
them the fundamentals of the faith. When they grasped these
they were baptized in Jesus' name. Paul then laid hands on them
and the Holy Spirit came upon them (19:6). The laying on of
hands was mentioned at Samaria and Ephesus, not only as part of
the baptismal rite, but also in connection with the gift of the
Spirit. Hull is probably right when he comments that "reference is
made to it on these two occasions only because, in Luke's view,
these two cases were quite exceptional."[15]

As evidence that they had received the Holy Spirit, Luke
mentions that they spoke in tongues (Acts 19:6). Two quite opposite conclusions have been drawn from the fact that Luke mentions only three occasions when believers spoke in tongues. Some
insist that this shows that it was an unusual phenomenon; for that
reason Luke mentions it only on these occasions. Others infer that
it was so common that Luke did not bother to mention it in the
other conversion stories. In a sense both these views are arguments from silence; we can say only what the text says, not what it
does not say. Marshall writes: "The fact that the gift of tongues is
so rarely listed with the reception of the Spirit in the New Testament indicates that it was not regarded as a normative or
necessary accompaniment of spiritual experience."[16] In any case
the speaking in tongues by the Samaritans and Ephesian believers
is distinct from the tongues spoken at Pentecost. There is no mention of the proclamation of the gospel in other tongues in the case
of the Samaritans or the Ephesians.

From our survey of events in Acts in which the Spirit comes
upon various people when they believe in Christ, we noticed that
Luke varies his vocabulary considerably in describing these
experiences. The Samaritans "received the Holy Spirit" (8:17);
Paul was "filled with the Holy Spirit" at conversion—equipped
for his apostolic ministry (9:17); the Spirit "fell" on the hearers in
Cornelius' household, and Peter and his countrymen were

amazed that "the gift of the Holy Spirit had been poured out," and so he could not prevent them from being baptized since they had "received the Holy Spirit" (Acts 10:44-47); and the Holy Spirit "came upon" the Ephesian disciples of John (19:6).

In all of these conversion stories, repentance or faith is the only condition for the conferral of the Holy Spirit. Nowhere in the New Testament is a second work of grace described for us. We recognize, of course, that people experience God in different ways, and there are many who have had a transforming experience some time after their conversion. We do not question or minimize these experiences, but it is exegetically illegitimate to use the conversion stories of the Acts to justify such "second" experiences.

Having surveyed the events in which Luke reported group conversions, events at which people of various backgrounds were baptized by the Spirit into the body of Christ, we now want to point out that initiation into the Christian faith is not the end of Christian experience. Again and again we read in Acts of individuals or groups of individuals who were known to be full of the Spirit or who experienced an infilling of the Spirit after they were converted. We must take a closer look, therefore, at the passages in Acts that speak of the fullness of the Spirit.

CHAPTER 7

The Fullness of the Spirit in the Early Church

Baptism with the Spirit is the initial experience of Christians in response to repentance and faith. The fullness of the Holy Spirit, on the other hand, is intended to be the continual state of the Christian. John R. W. Stott writes:

> When we speak of the baptism of the Spirit we are referring to a once-for-all gift; when we speak of the fullness of the Spirit we are acknowledging that this gift needs to be *continuously and increasingly appropriated*.... The baptism was a unique initiatory experience; the fullness was intended to be the continuing, the permanent result, the norm. As an initiatory event the baptism is not repeatable and cannot be lost, but the filling can be repeated and in any case needs to be maintained.[1]

In similar vein writes Michael Green:

> While baptism in the Spirit is the initial experience of Christians, brought about by the Spirit in response to repentance, faith and baptism, the fulness of the Holy Spirit is intended to be the continual state of the Christian. It is not a plateau on to which you are ushered by some second stage in initiation, a plateau which separates you from other Christians who have not had the same experience. The New Testament gives no support to that view whatsoever. In plain language, we are meant to be progressively filled with the Spirit of our Saviour Jesus Christ.[2]

128

Interestingly, no one in the New Testament ever claims that he or she is full of the Holy Spirit; it is always a testimony that others give. The fullness of the Spirit evidently leads to a joyous self-forgetfulness, so that one does not make great claims about one's own spirituality. If then someone should ask me: "Have you been baptized with the Holy Spirit?" I would say without hesitation, "Why, yes! Otherwise I could not be a member of the body of Christ." But if someone should ask me: "Are you full of the Holy Spirit?" I would humbly acknowledge: "That is my constant prayer and concern; but I will leave that judgment to others."

In order to grasp what it means to be full of the Spirit, we intend to survey the "fullness" passages in the Acts. It should be stated at the outset that in some cultures persons are not thought of as being empty; therefore, to be filled with the Spirit strikes people as strangely humorous. "The implication is that our Western logical concept that something which is full cannot be filled any further is misleading if applied to the Spirit."[3] It must be recognized that "to be filled with something" is a figure of speech for being dominated by something or someone, or to be wholly taken up with something. If, for example, a person constantly talks politics, we might say he is full of politics; another might be full of sports; or a young man may be full of girls, as we say colloquially. Therefore, to say that someone is full of the Spirit means that the Spirit of Jesus, the risen Lord, dominates this person's life. To be full of Christ is no different from being full of the Spirit, for Jesus explained that when the Spirit would come he would glorify him.

There are at least seven passages in Acts in which Luke reports on people being full or being filled with the Spirit. We group these reports under four headings in an attempt to understand what it meant to be full of the Spirit in the early church.

A. The Fullness of the Spirit and Witness

The first "fullness" passage in Acts is found in 2:4. When the day of Pentecost arrived, the followers of Jesus "were all filled with the Holy Spirit."

Some find it problematic that Jesus should speak of Pentecost as the "baptism" with the Spirit which John had predicted (Acts 1:5), when Luke reports that the 120 were "filled" with the Spirit at Pentecost. At first blush it appears as if the two expressions are used interchangeably. Hull suggests that " 'to be filled' appears to be only a stylistic variant of the metaphor 'to be baptized,' which can also mean 'to be soaked, to be saturated.' "[4] If "filled" in Acts 2:4 should be considered the equivalent of "baptized" in Acts 1:5, then this would be the only instance where the two are used interchangeably. Perhaps it could be said that the outpouring of the Spirit at Pentecost, which led to the founding of the church, is the baptism of the Spirit (Acts 1:5 clearly says so), and the fullness which the 120 experienced was the result of that outpouring. John Stott writes: "Thus, the fullness of the Spirit was the consequence of the baptism of the Spirit. The baptism is what Jesus did (pouring out the Spirit from heaven), the fullness is what they received."[5]

Having been filled with the Spirit, the apostles immediately began to witness to the great saving acts of God in Christ. Indeed they spoke with other tongues and people heard them talk about the great things of God in their native dialects. Here were untutored Galileans, some of them fishermen, who were enabled by the Spirit to stand up before thousands and proclaim the good news. Just a few weeks before, all the disciples fled when Jesus was captured, and Peter had denied his Lord to save his own skin. Then, when Jesus died, they all hid behind closed doors for fear of the Jews. Now these same men stood in the public square and witnessed to their Lord.

If we had been there we might have asked Peter: "How can you do this?" Perhaps he would have answered: "I don't really know; the only explanation I can give is that the Spirit of Jesus helped me." Jesus had promised that when the Holy Spirit would come upon the disciples, they would receive power to be his witnesses (Acts 1:8). This promise was now being realized.

The next "fullness" passage again connects the fullness of the Spirit with witness. When Saul of Tarsus was stopped in his path of destruction on the way to Damascus, Ananias came to him and informed him that the Lord had sent him to tell Saul that he should receive his sight "and be filled with the Holy Spirit" (Acts 9:17). And why should Saul be filled with the Spirit? this newborn babe in Christ? Because he was a chosen vessel, and God was going to send him to the Gentiles to proclaim the unsearchable riches of Christ. Only a few days after his conversion, he argued mightily with the Jews in the synagogues of Damascus that Jesus was the Son of God (Acts 9:20-22). Then, after the Arabia interlude, he witnessed in Jerusalem; from there he went to Syria and Cilicia, where he carried on his witness for 14 years (unless the 14 years includes the Arabia interlude; Gal. 1:18; 2:1). From there he was called to Antioch, only to be thrust out by the Holy Spirit to take the gospel to the entire Mediterranean world.

In the prophecy of Joel which Peter quoted in his Pentecost speech, it was predicted that when the Spirit is poured out in the latter days, prophecy shall be reborn (Acts 2:18f.). Both sons and daughters are to be involved in this activity. It strikes us that, in the book of Acts, Christian women are a force to be reckoned with. Saul recognized this, as he dragged off both men and women to prison (Acts 9:2). Whereas in Judaism the testimony of a woman amounted to nothing, the first witnesses to the resurrection of Jesus were women, signaling a new day for womanhood. The Spirit equipped both men and women to witness to their faith.

"Witness" does not necessarily mean "preaching" in the formal sense, as that word is used today. But where God's people are filled with Christ's Spirit, they are concerned that the good news about Christ's saving grace be made known to others.

B. The Fullness of the Spirit and Courage

When Peter and John were dragged before the Sanhedrin after healing a lame man in the name of Jesus, Peter, "filled with the Holy Spirit" (Acts 4:8), addressed this angry court in a powerful, impromptu testimony to his Lord. As on the day of Pentecost, Peter was filled with the Spirit again for a special situation. The

Spirit gave him the courage to witness in a dangerous situation. Only several weeks before, this same Jewish court had condemned his Lord to death and they might very well have made an end of Peter's life, too.

Meanwhile some disciples were at home praying for Peter and John; when the two were finally released from prison, they returned to this praying community. Luke then reports that all of them were "filled with the Holy Spirit and [they] spoke the word of God with boldness" (Acts 4:31—another "fullness" passage).

It is not accidental that the word "boldness" occurs some twelve times in Acts (either as a noun, *parrhesia*, or as verb, *parrhesiazomai*). In Greek politics *parrhesia* stood generally for freedom of speech, the openness which is the right of every free citizen of the *polis*. In private life it stood for that feeling of relaxed openness with which friends share each other's interests. In the presence of God it means "confidence." In the face of opposition it means "boldness," or "courage."[6]

In the book of Acts the word is used only with reference to the church's witness to either Jews or Gentiles. It signifies the freedom and the boldness to speak even when it is dangerous to do so. *Parrhesia* is not something we develop through practice; it is not something under our control. It is the fruit of the Spirit's work in a person's life—something that has to be sought again and again.[7]

No one reading the book of Acts can help but be impressed by the courage of the early believers. They lived for the most part precariously. They had to endure hatred and opposition. They were often ostracized by society. Many suffered financial ruin because of economic boycotts against them. And what was the secret of their courage? The fullness of the Spirit.

Another instance of the fullness of the Spirit being related to courage was when Stephen challenged the basic structures of Judaism by questioning its most sacred values: the law and the temple—and this in the face of a threatening mob. Speaking against the temple was a very serious crime (Jesus was charged—falsely, of course—with this crime). Paul was later captured when charged (again falsely) with bringing a Gentile, Trophimus, into the temple. The Romans guaranteed the protection of the temple and any assault on the temple had serious consequences.

Stephen had earlier been chosen to serve at tables and now we find him preaching with great courage. Twice it is said of him that he was full of the Spirit (Acts 6:5; 7:55). Luke says: "He, full of the Holy Spirit, gazed into heaven." God's Spirit took away his fear of death and he became the first Christian martyr.

It was Stephen, a man filled with the Spirit, who in that awful moment of agony prayed for his enemies, "Lord, do not lay this sin to their charge." The presence of the Spirit of Jesus in his life gave him the grace to forgive his enemies, as Jesus had done; and with a prayer reminiscent of Jewish bedtime prayers, "Lord Jesus, receive my spirit," he fell asleep.

One more passage in which the fullness of the Spirit is related to courage is Acts 13:9. (It should be noticed, of course, that in all these passages it is the courage to witness in the face of great odds, and so one could see also in all of these passages the relationship of Spirit to witness.) On his first missionary journey, Paul, accompanied by Barnabas and John Mark, went to Paphos on the island of Cyprus, the seat of the Roman proconsul, Sergius Paulus. Here the magician Elymas, who evidently was part of the proconsul's entourage, tried to keep the governor from the faith. But Paul, "filled with the Holy Spirit," confronted him courageously in the name of Jesus, and Elymas was smitten with blindness—a risky thing to do to a court magician. The fullness of God's Spirit gave Paul the courage to confront the power of evil.

We should not think that courage came to these early Christian witnesses easily. It was not part of their nature anymore than it is of ours. But there was a new Spirit in their lives—the Spirit of Jesus—which assured them of ultimate victory over all evil powers. This courage was not lost when the church ran into stiff opposition in the first two centuries of its existence. What amazing courage both men and women displayed during the awful persecutions that were to come upon them in the decades ahead.

"Sunshiny" faces are not necessarily a sign of the fullness of the Spirit, but the courage to be true to Jesus, to confess him, even in the face of suffering and death, is a sure sign of the Spirit's fullness.

C. The Fullness of the Spirit and Service

Because the members of the church in Jerusalem came from different backgrounds, tension arose between the Hellenists and the Hebraists. The complaint was that the Hellenist widows were being overlooked in the distribution of charity. The apostles very wisely solved the problem by asking the believers to elect those who would attend to the needy. In this way the apostles could give themselves to the ministry of teaching and preaching.

But what kind of people were they to look for? What kind of people would be qualified best for this ministry to the needy? Perhaps it comes as a surprise to us to read, "Therefore, brethren, pick out from among you seven men of good repute, full of the Spirit and of wisdom, whom we may appoint to this duty" (Acts 6:3). We can understand that the apostles needed to be filled with the Holy Spirit in order to proclaim the gospel effectively, but here the fullness of the Spirit is a requirement for serving at tables and for performing financial duties.

It seems certain that people did not go about asking members of the church whether they were full of the Spirit in order to report their names to the apostles. It is significant that the fullness of the Spirit is only one of three requirements; they were also to be men of good reputation and full of wisdom. No doubt it was by their good reputation, and by the wisdom they had displayed in the life of the community, that others got the impression they were full of the Spirit of Christ.

The choosing of the seven indicates that we need the filling of the Spirit for the humblest tasks in the kingdom of God. In fact it may be that the unseen, unpublicized, and often thankless tasks call for a greater measure of the Spirit of God.

There was good Old Testament precedent for requiring the fullness of the Spirit for an undertaking that was rather mundane. When God ordered the building of the tabernacle, he assured Israel that Bezalel, who was to direct the building, was equipped not only with skills for the job but, as God says, "I have filled him with the Spirit of God" (Ex. 31:2, 3).

How often the spiritual equipment of those who serve in the church is overlooked! It is assumed that the treasurer of a congregation should have at least some knowledge of financial matters. But that is not enough. All who serve in Christ's kingdom must be equipped by the Spirit to do their work.

It is significant that the spiritual gifts listed in 1 Corinthians 12 includes not only knowledge and teaching, but also the gifts of "helping" and "administration." By listing these gifts with other *charismata* (gifts), it is obvious that even ordinary tasks in God's kingdom demand the help of the Spirit. All who serve in God's cause must constantly pray that he might fill them with his Spirit in order to accomplish their tasks.

D. The Fullness of the Spirit and Christian Character

The fullness of the Spirit is not manifested so much in ecstasy as it is in a Christlike character. By discussing the ethical dimensions of the fullness of the Spirit last, we are not suggesting that these are less important than witnessing or serving. In practice, of course, it is hard to distinguish being, doing, and speaking, but unless the Spirit produces a Christlike character in us, all our religious activities and our pious talk will lack the ring of authenticity.

So then, when we speak of character, it is not what we are born with that we have in mind, or what we have become by virtue of a Christian upbringing. It is much more that which God's Spirit impresses upon a person's life.

1. A Blameless Life

The fullness of the Spirit is linked in Acts 6:3 with a blameless life. The church was to look for persons with a good reputation who were full of the Spirit. The meaning of a word or phrase can often be determined by its association with other words or phrases. "Men of good report" and "full of the Holy Spirit" stand side by side and share in each other's meaning. The one defines the other and vice versa.

Acts 11:24 also connects the fullness of the Spirit with a godly life. There it is said of Barnabas that "he was a good man, full of the Holy Spirit." We need not read into the book of Acts too far before we discover the sterling qualities of this man. He comes upon the scene as one who, in an act of amazing generosity, sells his land and gives the proceeds to the church. Then he introduces the converted persecutor of Christians, Paul, to the Jerusalem church, when everyone feared to come close to the man who had formerly tried to devastate the church. Years later Barnabas was in Cilicia in search of Paul, whom he then took to Antioch as a teacher. Together with Paul he took famine relief to Jerusalem and finally accompanied him on his first missionary journey. "A good man, full of the Holy Spirit."

2. Faith

There is another aspect of Christian character that is related to the fullness of the Spirit and that is "faith." We ask, Do not all Christians have faith? Yes, indeed, for "by grace are you saved through faith." However, there are at least two people mentioned in the book of Acts of whom it is explicitly stated that they were "full of the Holy Spirit and of faith." They are Stephen and Barnabas (Acts 6:5 and 11:24, respectively). Faith in these passages certainly does not mean simply saving faith. Nor does it mean doctrine as the word "faith" seems to mean in Jude's exhortation to "contend for the faith which was once for all delivered to the saints" (v. 3).

It is possible that the expression "full of faith" refers to the gift of faith (1 Cor. 12:9). This is a gift, as Paul explains in 1 Corinthians 13:2, whereby people can "move mountains." The gift of faith is given by God to certain people who are called to do the seemingly impossible, that which is clearly unusual, in the kingdom of God.

It is not exactly clear that Luke meant to say Stephen and Barnabas had this special *charisma* of faith. (No doubt there were others who had it.) To be "full of faith" may mean that these persons had a deep trust and confidence in God. Their faith had been tested and tried in the vicissitudes of life. Theirs was a mature faith. They had learned to trust God in the dark, in the midst of great trials and adversity. In that sense, to be full of faith is not too different from being full of the Spirit, and the two expressions may be understood as an example of hendiadys.

The life of Barnabas gives the impression that to be full of the Spirit and of faith includes also confidence and trust in people. When no one trusted Paul, Barnabas accepted him and drew him into the Jerusalem community. When Paul gave up on John Mark, who had cut short his ministry on the first missionary journey, Barnabas took him along on another missionary venture; later even Paul had to acknowledge Mark's worth (2 Tim. 4:11). In his great hymn on love (1 Cor. 13), Paul says that "love . . . believes all things" (v. 7). Surely he does not mean that love is gullible. But love is trusting; it is not full of suspicion. At times when we trust people, they disappoint us and even deceive us. But it is certainly not a sign of being full of the Spirit when we treat people with suspicion rather than with trust.

To be full of the Spirit, however, should not be understood to mean that a person never makes mistakes. Though Paul and Barnabas were full of the Spirit, yet at one point they had a very deep quarrel, which led to the parting of their ways. Of course they forgave each other, but one wonders whether it could be said of these two good men that they were full of the Spirit when they fell out with each other. Christian people, full of the Spirit and faith, are not perfect; they also fail and make mistakes. But God's Spirit reproves, corrects, heals, and fills persons afresh.

3. *Joy*

There is a third aspect of Christian character that is related to the fullness of the Spirit, and that is joy. After making converts in Antioch of Pisidia, Paul and Barnabas were thrust out of the city. The believers were not discouraged but they "were filled with joy and with the Holy Spirit" (Acts 13:52). The Holy Spirit is supremely a Spirit of joy (Gal. 5:22; Rom. 14:17), and the note of joy is sounded throughout the book of Acts.

Interestingly, in the one passage where the fullness of the Spirit and joy are coordinated, joy springs from the hearts of suffering saints. This paradox of suffering and joy is found on several occasions in the letters of Paul. Of the Thessalonians Paul said that they "received the word in much affliction with joy in the Holy Spirit" (1 Thes. 1:6). He himself wrote a letter of joy (Philippians) from a Roman prison (the word "joy" in one form or another occurs some sixteen times in four chapters). Christian joy is not a euphoria that springs from pleasant circumstances. It is a joy that springs from the Holy Spirit even in adverse surroundings. On the other hand, life in the Spirit is not a staid affair either. While fanaticism must be discouraged, a church without joy will hardly attract those who are outside of Christ.

A question that naturally comes to mind when we read of people who were full of the Holy Spirit is: How can *we* be filled with the Spirit? Many books on the market outline steps that supposedly lead to this desired fullness. I have an aversion for "how to" books when it comes to the deeper Christian life. One cannot attain to the fullness of the Spirit through six easy lessons. Some authors, on the other hand, make the process quite complicated, and I think we ought to reject every attempt to make the Christian life complicated. Christian discipleship is not easy, but we should not make it complicated.

Obviously there can be no fullness of the Spirit without cleansing from sin, obedience to Christ's commands, and willingness to serve others. Then, too, we should not forget our Lord's encouraging promise that the heavenly Father will give "the Holy Spirit to those who ask him!" (Lk. 11:13). However, there is no such thing as a once-for-all fullness. The baptism of the Holy Spirit is a once-for-all transaction which takes place at the moment of salvation. It does not need to be repeated and we have no command to be baptized with the Spirit. The fullness of the Spirit, however, is something that must be repeated. We must keep on being "filled with the Spirit" (Eph. 5:18).

CHAPTER 8

The Presence of the Spirit in the Church's Pioneer Days

The Acts of the Apostles could just as well be called the Acts of the Holy Spirit. The word "spirit" *(pneuma)* occurs some 71 times in Acts; in 57 of these uses the divine Spirit is meant.[1]

The Gospels were all written after Pentecost, yet they contain relatively few references to the Holy Spirit. That is good evidence for their historical trustworthiness. Acts, on the other hand, describes a post-Pentecost situation and so we should not be surprised to find an average of two references to the Holy Spirit per chapter.

We have already discussed the coming of the Spirit at Pentecost and how, as the gospel spread, people were initiated into the family of God—"baptized" by the Spirit into the body of Christ. We have also traced the "fullness" passages in Acts to see how the Spirit worked in the lives of individuals and groups in the days and years following Pentecost. This chapter picks up several strands of teaching which were left aside in the earlier surveys. The first observation is that the Spirit creates anew a people of God, a "community of the Spirit," and that he continues to work in this community.

A. Spirit and the Creation of the Christian Community

The question "When did the church begin?" has been answered in different ways. Some, who wish to stress the continuity between the old and new people of God, have suggested that the church had its beginning with Abraham, the father of all believers. It is possible, however, to hold to the continuity of God's people and still insist that the church is a New Testament concept. But where does one place the beginning of the church in the New Testament? Some locate the origin of the church in Jesus' call to discipleship. The twelve must be viewed as the church's "founding fathers"; however, strictly speaking, the church was constituted when the risen Lord poured out his Spirit at Pentecost.[2] Dunn makes the observation that

> the Church properly conceived did not come into existence until Pentecost. Apart from everything else, the vital experience and possession of the Spirit, the constitutive life principle and hall mark of the early Church, was lacking. And as one cannot say "Christ" without also saying "Church," since a Christian is by definition a member of the Church, non-existence of the Church prior to Pentecost means that there were no Christians (properly speaking) prior to Pentecost.[3]

Since Pentecost is the church's birthday, the church can be described as "the fellowship of the Holy Spirit" (2 Cor. 13:14), to use a Pauline phrase. "Fellowship" (koinonia) has both a vertical (participating in Christ and in his Spirit) and a horizontal dimension (sharing one's life with other Christians). This fellowship is a creation of the Spirit of God.

The word "fellowship" (koinonia) occurs only once in Acts to describe the common life of the early church (2:42). Luke has other ways of impressing us with the deep sense of mutuality which characterized the early community of believers. Those who responded to the message of the gospel in repentance, faith, and baptism received the gift of the Spirit. There is no doubt that Luke wants us to understand the life of the new people of God, as described in Acts 2:41-47, as the direct and immediate result of the Spirit's coming. Taylor writes:

At the heart of this ferment of new life and new meaning was an unheard-of relationship with the Holy Spirit. It could only be described as the outpouring or fulness of the Spirit. It happened as a direct result of the glorification of Jesus Christ—his death, resurrection and ascension—and it brought into being a distinctive and unique society with a common life, love and unity of completely different sort.[4]

There are a number of marks of this early Christian community, this "fellowship of the Spirit."

1. A Believing Community

"All who believed were together" (Acts 2:44). They had believed the gospel as Peter had proclaimed it. In the hearing of a vast multitude on that Jewish festival of Pentecost, Peter had recounted the saving acts of God. Much of what he said was familiar to Jewish hearers—the prophecies of Joel, the Psalms of David, and other references to the Old Testament.

What struck them, however, was the fact that these had all been fulfilled in Christ. From the standpoint of the cross and the resurrection, these old familiar truths began to shine with a new light. The whole past of redemption history began to glow with a new luster. The great events of Israel's sacred story that lay on the other side of the empty tomb began to flicker and to burn, fanned into flame, as it were, by the wind of the Spirit. Men and women who had come from the vast borderlands of the Roman world to celebrate Pentecost, perked up their ears. Here was an authentic word from God. And the word hit home; it stung and pierced their hearts. Luke used some rather violent vocabulary in Acts to describe the effects of apostolic preaching. The words jab and stab and cut like two-edged swords.

Three thousand of those who listened to Peter's message "received his word" (Acts 2:41). That's another way of saying that they believed and obeyed the gospel. Through baptism they were publicly initiated into the new community, the body of Christ, as Paul calls it. And this new community created by the Spirit is described as "all those who believed" (v. 44). Often in Acts, Christians are called simply "the believers" (e.g., 4:32; 5:14).

The word "believe" has a variety of meanings in the New Testament. Basically it means trust and confidence in and commitment to Jesus Christ. It means to surrender one's life to him, to abandon oneself utterly to the grace and mercy of God offered in the gospel. Faith is a person's response to God's offer of salvation; it is his Yes! to God's call. By faith a person encounters the one who died and rose again.

The early church was a believing community. They knew not only *whom* they believed but also *what* they believed. The New Testament speaks not only of "faith" but also of "the faith," a body of doctrine. This is suggested in Luke's report that those who believed and were baptized "devoted themselves to the apostles' teaching" (v. 42). The apostles had been in the company of Jesus; later they communicated his teachings to the church. Whereas this kind of instruction was oral to begin with, the teaching of the apostles took written shape in the New Testament Scriptures.[5]

The church "was built upon the foundation of the apostles and prophets" (Eph. 2:20); only those churches that adhere to the teachings of the apostles can be called churches in the New Testament sense. This needs to be stressed in a day when there is so much confusion in doctrine and ethics. So much Christian literature on the market today is experience-centered, and our generation tends to be impatient with those who are concerned about the content of the Christian faith. Dorothy Sayers writes quite perceptively:

> We are constantly assured that churches are empty because preachers insist too much upon doctrine—dull dogma, as people call it. The fact is the precise opposite. It is the neglect of dogma that makes for dullness. The Christian faith is the most exciting drama that ever staggered the imagination of man—and the dogma is the drama.[6]

There is a body of truth to which the church must adhere. It's tragically possible to be correct doctrinally and to be spiritually dead, of course, but that is no argument against the importance of having a good grasp of the teachings of the apostles. If the early church had been a society of freethinkers, in which everyone was at liberty to believe what he or she liked, what a confusing mumbo jumbo the New Testament would have been. Adherence to a basic core of doctrinal and ethical teaching was a mark of the early church—and still is today. It is described elsewhere as "the pattern of the sound words" (2 Tim. 1:13), "the truth of the gospel" (Gal. 2:5), "the standard of teaching" (Rom. 6:17), "traditions" (1 Cor. 11:2). We get some idea of what the teaching of the apostles included if we look at the outline of Peter's sermon in Acts 10:36-43. Or, we may appeal to 1 Corinthians 15:3-5, which seems to be an early confession of faith.[7]

However, the early church was not only a believing community; it was also a worshiping community.

2. A Worshiping Community

The early church gave itself to prayer. The definite article with the word "prayers" (Acts 2:42) suggests an observance of Jewish prayer times in the temple. That early Christians continued to observe these can be seen from Acts 3:1-10, where Peter and John went to the temple for afternoon prayer. Jesus had taught the importance of private prayer (Mt. 6:6), but that did not rule out corporate praying. Repeatedly in the book of Acts the believers are seen gathering together for prayer. Several prayers of the early church have been preserved for us in the New Testament (e.g., Acts 4:24-26). The early church knew that it could not stand in its own strength. What is unique about the prayers of these new believers is that they were made in Jesus' name, in keeping with Christ's promise (Jn. 16:23, 24).

The fellowship of the early Christian community found expression also in common meals. They broke bread together. To begin with, the Lord's supper was a regular meal through which Christ's death was remembered. It was a joyous occasion, as Acts 2:46 indicates: "breaking bread in their homes, they partook of food with glad and generous hearts." When they ate together they seem to have rehearsed what happened at Calvary; they celebrated the presence of the risen Christ in their midst, and they anticipated the glorious coming of the Lord at the end of the age.

The exact relationship between these love meals and the solemn communion services of a later day is not quite clear. Evidently because of excesses at these common meals (1 Cor. 11:17-22, 33, 34), the Lord's supper became but a "token" meal, and greater emphasis was put on self-examination (1 Cor. 11:28, 29).

There were other aspects of the worship of the early church which Luke quite obviously omits, but enough is said to suggest that the early church was a worshiping community. This doesn't mean the Jerusalem church was a passive, pious enclave. "Fellowship" was more than togetherness; it had practical dimensions as well. Those who believed "were together and had all things in common; and they sold their possessions and goods and distributed them to all as they had need" (Acts 2:44, 45). They cared for each other.

3. A Caring Community

Jerusalem did not have a prospering economy (aside from the temple cult to which Jews all over the empire contributed). There were always many poor people in the holy city and the Jews had developed relief agencies. Christians, however, would hardly be eligible for such material aid, and so the believers found new ways of coping with the needs of the poor. We are told that those who had property sold it and in this way alleviated the needs of the destitute. In the case of Barnabas, we have an example of a wholesale liquidation; in other cases, it seems they did this as the need arose.

This made a deep impression on those still outside the church (2:47), and it still does. Those who limit their witness to the verbal expression of the gospel hardly stand in the tradition of Jesus and the early church, where concern for the poor and needy went hand in hand with the gospel that offered salvation from sin and death. Before Paul and Barnabas were sent on a mission of evangelism, they were commissioned to bring relief to the poor of Jerusalem (Acts 11:30; 13:1f.). Paul never forgot the poor even while he preached the gospel in the western empire.

The question remains whether the Jerusalem community is the model for the church for all times. Some Bible students are of the opinion that every change from the pattern of early church life is a departure from the New Testament ideal. Others allow for development under the guidance of the Holy Spirit. What is often overlooked is the fact that there is development even within the church of the New Testament. In its essentials the early church remains the model for the church as long as it continues here on earth. When it comes to producing a replica of the early church, however, that is not very easily possible. In many respects the church, founded at Pentecost, is unique and cannot be imitated in detail. We can never go back in time and relive the founding of the church in the days of the apostles. That would be something like a wealthy American purchasing an old mansion in England and transplanting it piece by piece in a totally different context. The Holy Spirit does not allow us to do that with the church. It is, therefore, presumptuous for one religious body to claim that it is closer to the New Testament model than any other. F. F. Bruce writes:

> The one uniform pattern which can indeed be discerned in the New Testament is the pattern of flexibility which facilitates instead of impeding the free movement of the Spirit as he makes provision for the churches and their members as and when the need arises.[8]

Having said that, it needs to be added that we cannot remain true to the New Testament if we disregard the example set for us by the early church. Unless we are a believing, worshiping, and caring community, we hardly have the right to claim that we are in the tradition of the New Testament church.

B. The Spirit and the Problems of the Early Church

It was soon discovered after Pentecost that the new community was comprised of fallible human beings. The fact that the Spirit had created a new people of God out of very diverse elements called for constant vigilance. After describing for us the vibrant Christian community which the Spirit had created in

Jerusalem (Acts 2 and 4), Luke goes on to report a shocking incident (Acts 5). Those who accuse Luke of painting an idealized picture of the early church should take special note of this account. It is a story of deception and hypocrisy by two members of the Jerusalem community.

1. The Problem of Hypocrisy

Ananias and Sapphira, Luke says, "lied to the Holy Spirit" (Acts 5:3), and agreed together to "tempt the Spirit of the Lord" (v. 9).

Against the background of the amazing generosity of Barnabas, who sold all he had and gave it to the church, Luke paints a rather dark picture of a couple who wanted to be known for their generosity but got entangled in the sin of Achan. Bruce is probably right in his observation that "it is idle to ask if Ananias and Sapphira were genuine believers or not,"[9] but the church no doubt believed that they too had received the gift of the Spirit. Membership in the church, however, did not prevent Satan from filling their hearts so that they lied to the Holy Spirit (which, according to verse 4, is a lie to God).

Like Achan of old (Josh. 22:20), this Christian couple withheld part of the property they had ostensibly given to the Lord. This was, according to Peter's interpretation, an effort to "tempt" the Spirit of the Lord—a phrase which is reminiscent of ancient Israel's sin, when they "tempted" God to see how much they could get away with. So real was the presence of the Spirit in the early church that to lie to the church was to lie to the Holy Spirit.

Ananias and Sapphira were under no compulsion to give all the money realized from the sale of their property to the church. But having given it, it was a deceitful act to withhold part of it.

It is not said that they committed the unpardonable sin against the Holy Spirit, and one cannot say that, because they died physically, they now suffer eternal death also. That judgment we leave to God. We must take this sad story to heart, however, for we too are tempted at times to seek a higher reputation than we deserve. Where the Spirit is present in power, the church is concerned about cleansing itself from all that grieves the Holy Spirit.

2. *The Problem of Disunity*

Since the potential for discord was present in the early church, it had to strive to keep "the unity of the Spirit in the bond of peace" (Eph. 4:3).

Luke reports that the Hellenist members of the Jerusalem congregation began to grumble because their widows were being overlooked by the Hebraists in the daily distribution of relief (Acts 6:1-6). To prevent a rift in the Christian community, the apostles instructed the congregation to find seven men "full of the Spirit" who might devote themselves to the administration of relief for the poor. The seven who were chosen happen to have Hellenistic names, and it may be that the Hebraists graciously relinquished their leadership in this ministry to offset a division along cultural and linguistic lines.

The potential for hurt is always present in the church—composed, as it is, of members who are far from perfect. Where there are those in the ranks of the church who are full of the Spirit, the unity of the Spirit can be maintained.

When the Samaritans received the Word of God and were baptized, the possibility of a Samaritan church emerging as a Christian community independent of the mother church was real. In God's providence, however, the gift of the Spirit was delayed until Peter and John came down and laid hands on these new believers and prayed for them (Acts 8:14-16). In this way the Samaritans were welcomed into the fellowship of the Jerusalem church by its representatives and the unity of the Spirit was established. The Holy Spirit always finds ways of bridging the gaps between the different social, ethnic, and economic groups in the church.

Peter could easily have torn the Jerusalem church apart if he had not handled his visit to the house of Cornelius wisely. When Jerusalem heard that the Gentiles had received the Word of God, the circumcision party was very critical of Peter for having entered and eaten in a Gentile home. They demanded an explanation (Acts 11:1-18).

Peter then explained that it was the Spirit that told him to go and to make no distinction between Jews and Gentiles (11:12). Moreover, when he preached to the Gentiles, he reported, the Holy Spirit fell on them just as it had fallen on Jews at Pentecost (11:15). In fact when he saw that the Gentiles had received the gift of the Spirit, he had been reminded of Jesus' words, "John baptized with water, but you shall be baptized with the Holy Spirit" (11:16).

The whole matter was to come to a head at the Jerusalem Council meeting, where the question whether Gentiles should be received into the church without circumcision threatened to divide the church into a Jewish and a Gentile faction (Acts 15:1-29).

Peter, profiting perhaps from Paul's recent rebuke (Gal. 2:11ff.), argued that Gentile believers should be accepted as equals with Jewish Christians on the grounds that God had given them the Holy Spirit just as he had to Jewish saints (15:8). With support from Paul and Barnabas, and the presiding elder, James, upon whom the circumcision party relied for support, the Holy Spirit guided the church through some treacherous waters. With the proviso that Gentile Christians respect Jewish sensitivities in such areas as sexual ethics, idolatry, and certain food laws, a *modus vivendi* was found which "seemed good to the Holy Spirit and to us" (15:28).

It was the presence of the Holy Spirit in the church that preserved the unity of the Christian community at critical moments in its history. Whenever the church's unity was threatened by cultural and linguistic differences, personal hurts, misunderstandings in religious practice, conscience scruples, or doctrinal questions, the Holy Spirit was present, bringing the discordant elements together. This continues to be the work of the Spirit even today, and the Spirit must be grieved no end at all the infighting that goes on both in local congregations and religious denominations, not to mention interdenominational misunderstandings, tensions, and feuds.

3. The Problem of Opposition

The early church faced the problems within its ranks by the power of the Holy Spirit; but it also was completely dependent on the Spirit in its confrontation with evil powers from without, powers that sought to crush God's little flock. To begin with, the church had to face fierce opposition from Jewish religious leaders. The bitter animosity which these leaders had manifested toward the prophet from Galilee was quickly transferred to his followers when they proclaimed the resurrection of Jesus and did powerful deeds in his name. When Peter and John were brought to trial before the Sanhedrin and Peter, "filled with the Spirit" (Acts 4:8), gave so powerful a testimony, the members of the high court were amazed at the "boldness" of Peter and John (Acts 4:13).

At their second arraignment before the Sanhedrin, Peter again showed great courage in his witness to Christ. In fact he linked the witness of the apostles with that of the Holy Spirit. "We are witnesses to these things, and so is the Holy Spirit whom God has given to those who obey him" (Acts 5:32). The apostles were so conscious of the possession of the Holy Spirit that they looked upon themselves as organs through which the Holy Spirit expressed himself.[10] What Jesus had predicted of the Paraclete, the Spirit of truth—that "he will bear witness to me; and you also are witnesses" (Jn. 15:26)—was now fulfilled.

The gift of the Holy Spirit, Peter explained, was given by God "to those who obey him," and that implies that the members of the Sanhedrin, who refused to "obey" the gospel and rejected Jesus as God's Messiah, were opponents of God's Spirit. Had it not been for the wise counsel of Gamaliel, the court might have made short shrift of the apostles. As it turned out, they continued to proclaim the gospel with great effect.

When, however, Stephen, representing the Hellenist wing of Jewish Christianity, laid the ax at the very roots of the tree of Judaism (the law and the temple), violent opposition flared up again. But, as Luke reports, his opponents "could not withstand the wisdom and the Spirit" with which Stephen spoke (6:10). This opposition, as Stephen later insisted, was not simply against him

and the Christians whom he represented, but against the Holy
Spirit. "You stiff-necked people, uncircumcised in heart and ears,
you always resist the Holy Spirit. As your fathers did, so do you"
(Acts 7:51). Just as their rebellious forefathers had resisted God's
Spirit by which he spoke through the prophets, so now unbelieving Judaism resisted (the Greek verb *antipipto* means literally to
"fall against") the Holy Spirit in the witness of Stephen. Stephen,
"full of the Holy Spirit" (7:55), died, but God's cause triumphed.

The conversion of Paul brought the persecution of the
church to an end and gave it a new lease on life. By then the
gospel had spread beyond Jerusalem to Samaria and even to
Galilee (although Luke does not tell us about Galilean Christianity). As a new chapter in the life of the church opened, Luke
gave a brief progress report: "So the church throughout all Judea
and Galilee and Samaria had peace and was built up; and walking
in the fear of the Lord and in the comfort of the Holy Spirit it was
multiplied" (Acts 9:31).

Precisely what Luke means with the "comfort" *(paraklesis)*
of the Holy Spirit is hard to say. If "comfort" is the proper translation, then, perhaps, we must understand it in its original sense of
"strengthening." Luke may have meant that the Holy Spirit
comforted the hearts of those who had been harassed and who
had lost loved ones in the persecution. Lake and Cadbury take
paraklesis to mean the "exhortation" of the Holy Spirit which
came to the church through preaching.[11] Haenchen, however,
suggests that *paraklesis* is used here in the sense that the church
enjoyed the protection of the Holy Spirit when the persecution
was over.[12] Hull says the church was "upheld by the Holy
Spirit."[13] We might have expected Luke to say that the church
was upheld by the Spirit when it was persecuted and not when it
was at peace. Did Luke realize that the *paraklesis* of the Spirit is
perhaps needed even more in times of peace than in times of
persecution? Certainly the church in the free world today needs
the exhortation and protection of the Holy Spirit as much as the
suffering church needs the Spirit's comfort. Without the Spirit's
gracious activity in the church, it cannot grow and be built up.

The early church faced opposition not only from the ranks of its Jewish opponents, but it also had to face the power of the evil one in the pagan world. Before Philip took the gospel to the Samaritans, a certain Simon, who was held in high repute by the Samaritans, had mesmerized the populace with his magical tricks. When his followers believed the gospel and were baptized, Simon, possibly because he had lost his adherents, also asked for baptism (Acts 8:9-13). Thinking perhaps that the apostles had the gift of religious magic, for the Samaritans received the Holy Spirit when the apostle laid hands on them, Simon begged them for the same power and offered to pay them for this remarkable gift (Acts 8:14-20).

Peter then, mincing no words, told Simon "to go to hell" (as the Greek has it), together with his money.[14] The Holy Spirit, Peter explained, is not for human trafficking. Peter may have thought that Simon had come close to committing the sin against the Holy Spirit, yet he held out the offer of forgiveness, if Simon would turn from the iniquity of his ways (Acts 8:21-24). He is not mentioned again in the New Testament. Clearly Simon had no understanding of the work of the Holy Spirit.

As is typical of Acts, Luke balances the acts of Peter with those of Paul,[15] and so we have a confrontation between Paul and another sorcerer recorded in Acts 13:4-12. In the city of Paphos Paul encountered a renegade Jew, Elymas, who was a "magician." Like Simon he traded on the popular superstitions of that day. Evidently the proconsul, Sergius Paulus, had come under his influence, and when the latter expressed interest in the gospel, Elymas did all in his power to prevent him from becoming a believer. Paul, then, "filled with the Holy Spirit" (Acts 13:9), withstood this evil power and Elymas was smitten with blindness and the opposition melted away.

Opposition from within the ranks of the church's membership, from the ruling authorities, and from representatives of the realm of superstition and the demonic could not stop the work of God begun and empowered by the Holy Spirit. This should give the church today great courage and confidence.

In spite of difficulties within the church and harassment from without, the church carried out its mission.

C. The Spirit and Mission of the Church

That Acts 1:8 is the "contents page" for the book of Acts hardly needs to be mentioned.[16] "But you shall receive power when the Holy Spirit has come upon you; and you shall be my witnesses in Jerusalem and in all Judea and Samaria and to the end of the earth" (Acts 1:8). The church's mandate to engage in a worldwide mission was given simultaneously with the gift of the Spirit.

The disciples had just asked Jesus whether Israel was to be restored to national independence at this time, since the Spirit was to be the mark of the age to come. His response was that such matters must be left to the Father (v. 7). Whatever God's plans for national Israel might be, political aspirations were not for them; they were to be Christ's witnesses, once the Spirit had come.

The world mission of the church lay beyond Pentecost. This mission was to begin in Jerusalem and expand to the "end of the earth." Acts 1:8, then, speaks not only of the power *(dunamis)* and practice *(martus*—witness) of mission, but also of the program of mission. Let us look at each of these briefly in the context of the book of Acts, before we say something about several of the early church's pioneers in mission.

1. The Power for Mission

In his first volume Luke records the command of Jesus to his disciples to remain in Jerusalem until they "are clothed with power from on high" (Lk. 24:49). Acts 1:8 may be thought of as a connecting link between Luke's Gospel and the Acts, for it reiterates the promise of the risen Christ that the disciples would receive power when the Holy Spirit came upon them. And when the day of Pentecost finally came, the same disciples, who had fled in terror when Jesus was captured, and who later cowered behind locked doors for fear of the Jews, were suddenly endowed with power for preaching and for working miracles.

The word *dunamis* (power) can, of course, suggest a blind, impersonal force; but that is not necessarily how the power of the Holy Spirit should be understood. The love of money can be a driving force in a person's life—an impersonal but very real power. On the other hand, the driving force behind a man's life might be a loving wife—very real, but personal.[17]

The Holy Spirit that empowered the early church's mission was the Spirit of the risen Christ. That power *(dunamis)* as used in Acts is almost an equivalent for the Holy Spirit can be seen, for example, from Acts 10:38, where Peter recalls that God "anointed Jesus of Nazareth with the Holy Spirit and with power" to carry out his mission.[18] Jesus was the prototype for the church in that he carried out his messianic calling by the power of the Spirit. The church could do no less.

When we speak of the power which the Holy Spirit supplies, we should remember that God's power is made known through weakness (2 Cor. 12:9, 10). The early disciples were weak in every respect; they had no economic power, nor social and educational advantages. Through the gift of the Holy Spirit, however, the power of the risen Christ was with them, enabling his followers to witness. David Watson writes: "Thus the church that is spiritually alive must be profoundly concerned with the work of communicating Christ; it cannot do otherwise when the Spirit is present in power."[19]

When the Holy Spirit is seen primarily as the power for sanctification or the source of charismatic gifts, and not equally as the power for witness, we overlook an important aspect of the Spirit's activity in the church. To speak figuratively, the emphasis in our use of the "Holy Spirit" is more often on the "holy," and less on the "spirit," the dynamic for mission. This can turn the church in on itself, rather than out to the world.[20] It is possible for a person or even a congregation to spend all its energies on keeping the body of Christ pure and to forget its apostolic calling. To be sure, where the Spirit's sanctifying work is not known, there will also be little power for witness, but where the presence of the Spirit is real in a congregation, there will be power for missions and evangelism. All the planning and organizing for evangelism, all the techniques and methods in the world will not lead to effective evangelism without the enablement of the Holy Spirit.

2. The Practice of Mission

The promise of Jesus that the Holy Spirit would supply his followers with a new power is closely related to their calling to be his witnesses. "You shall receive power . . . and you shall be my witnesses" (Acts 1:8). Luke uses the word "witness" (*martus*) some thirteen times. The twelve apostles are called witnesses (Acts 1:8, 22; 2:32; 3:15; 5:32; 10:39, 41; 13:31) as is Paul (22:15; 26:16) and Stephen (22:20). If, however, one adds to the noun witness all those words which have the same root, we have at least 30 passages in Acts which speak of witness.

The legal meaning of the word witness, common to classical Greek and the Septuagint, is not found in Acts, other than in the two references to false witnesses (Acts 6:13; 7:58). Several times the verb *martureo* ("to witness," "to testify") is used in the sense of human attestation of good conduct (Acts 6:3; 10:22; 16:2; 22:5, 12; 26:5). What is new in Acts is the use of witness for the proclamation of the gospel. Frequently the witness of the apostles is to the resurrection of Jesus (cf. Acts 2:32; 3:15; 13:31; 26:16), but the verb *martureo* is also used without an object in the sense of proclaiming the gospel of Christ (cf. Acts 23:11). Frequently Luke uses the compound *diamarturomai* for the "urgently wooing address of the gospel of Christ" (Acts 2:40; 8:25; 10:42; 18:5; 20:21, 24; 28:23).[21] The word "witness" in Acts does not yet mean "martyr" (which is derived from the Greek word *martus*), although there are indications that the meaning of the word is moving in that direction. Paul confesses later his approval when the "blood of Stephen thy witness was shed" (Acts 22:20). The sufferings which Christ's witnesses had to endure eventually lead to the equation of "witness" and "martyrdom."

By the power of the Holy Spirit the apostles witnessed to a vast multitude of Pentecost visitors (Acts 2:4ff.). Filled with the Holy Spirit, Peter witnessed to the Sanhedrin (4:8). So conscious were the early witnesses of the presence of the Spirit in their lives that they spoke of their witness as a joint witness with that of the Holy Spirit (5:32). There was such power in the witness of God's servants that the enemies of the church could not stand against "the wisdom and the Spirit" with which, for example, Stephen spoke (6:10). When Paul was called by God's grace to be a witness "of what you have seen and heard" (22:15), he was filled with the Holy Spirit (9:17) for his apostolic ministry. This witness of the early Christians is also called the "Word."

The "Word" is as common in Acts as the "Spirit," and the two belong together in the church's missionary practice.[22] Wherever early Christians went they carried the Word with them (Acts 8:4). Just as the Word had increased in Judea (6:7), so it spread in Samaria (8:14) and among the Gentiles (13:49). During the two years that Paul labored in Ephesus, "all the residents of Asia heard the word of the Lord" (19:10). The Word is the prime tool of the Spirit of God to change people's lives and to advance the kingdom of God.[23]

We should not, however, limit the witness of the early church to the apostles and a few outstanding leaders, although Luke quite naturally focuses on the founders of the Christian church. The church in the New Testament "does not know a witness by the apostles that ignores or has little appreciation for the witness of the individual members of the church. It does not know a witness by the members of the Church that does not recognize the authority of the apostles."[24]

All believers thought of themselves as witnesses as is suggested in a number of places in the book of Acts. For example, when the apostles were released by the Sanhedrin, they came to a praying multitude of whom it is said that "they were all filled with the Holy Spirit and spoke the word of God with boldness" (Acts 4:31). Ordinary Christians who were scattered because of the persecution that broke out in Jerusalem "went about preaching the word" (Acts 8:4). But even before the persecution there were Christians in Damascus (Ananias, for example; Acts 9:12). Nameless witnesses took the gospel to Phoenicia and Cyprus; men of

Cyprus and Cyrene took it to Antioch (Acts 11:19, 20). Harnack was perfectly right when he wrote, "We cannot hesitate to believe that the great mission of Christianity was in reality accomplished by means of informal missionaries."[25]

The witness of the early church, moreover, was given not only in word, but also in deed. By the power of the Spirit the apostles performed miracles. A considerable portion of Acts is taken up with the recounting of the "many wonders and signs" done through the apostles (Acts 2:43). The apostles make it very plain that healings and other miracles did not take place because they had any power in themselves (Acts 3:12; 4:7); it was by the power of the risen Christ, who was present by his Spirit. Stephen, too, was "full of grace and power" (6:8) and worked great wonders and signs among the people, as also did Philip in Samaria (8:13). It has often been pointed out by students of Acts that Luke balances Peter's deeds of power with those of Paul: both heal a cripple (3:2; 14:8ff.); both confront a sorcerer (8:18; 13:6); both raise someone from the dead (9:36; 20:9); both experience a miraculous release from prison (12:7; 16:27). Luke does not create these parallels, but selects them from his sources, perhaps for apologetic purposes.

Admittedly these deeds of power are not directly attributed to the Holy Spirit, but are done in Jesus' name. However, as Hull observes:

> It was only natural that the name of Jesus should be used in the working of miracles. . . . Luke knew whence He had acquired His power and that His followers had received it in such measure only because they were filled with His Spirit.[26]

3. The Program of Mission

Acts 1:8 informs us that the Holy Spirit not only supplies the power for the mission of the church and directs its missionary practice; it also spells out the ground plan for the church's outreach into the world. "You shall be my witnesses in Jerusalem and in all Judea and Samaria and to the end of the earth."

Old Testament prophets had foreseen the day when salvation would go out from Jerusalem to the ends of the earth. This explains why Jesus went to Jerusalem to die, and why the disciples were ordered to remain in Jerusalem until the Spirit was poured out. On the day of Pentecost the mission of the church was launched.

It is not without significance that Luke lets the Pentecost visitors, who heard the apostles proclaim the gospel in other tongues, enumerate the many lands from which they had come to Jerusalem for the festival. In a sense the program of missions (from Jerusalem to the end of the earth) could be seen in a nutshell on the day of Pentecost. The geographical list (Acts 2:9-11) focuses on the Near East and only Rome is given as representing the European continent. But it may be that Luke deliberately ended the main list with Rome (v. 10), since that's where the book of Acts ends.

We should not rule out the possibility that Luke used a standard geographical list and adapted it to his purposes under the Spirit's guidance.[27] The world was present at Pentecost, and the representatives of the known world pointed the church to its missionary task. The fact that they all heard the gospel in their mother tongues was another sign to the church that it must take the gospel to all nations in their own languages.

Some 3000 Pentecost visitors embraced the Christian faith on the day the Spirit was poured out. Their number soon grew to 5000. Then the good news spilled over into Judea and Samaria and the Holy Spirit took the initiative at every instance.

Eduard Schweizer writes, "The greatness of Luke's view lies in his showing more impressively than anyone else that the church can live only by evangelizing, and by following whatever new paths the Spirit indicates."[28] "The chief actor," writes John Taylor, "in the historic mission of the Christian church is the Holy Spirit. He is the director of the whole enterprise. The mission consists of the things he is doing in the world."[29] Let us see what evidence there is in Acts for the fact that the Spirit directs the missionary program of the church!

a. The Spirit Points to Opportunities for Mission. When Philip, one of the seven deacons who had been driven from Jerusalem when persecution broke out, was on his way to Gaza, the Spirit told him to join the chariot in which the Ethiopian was traveling (Acts 8:29). Earlier an angel of the Lord had directed him to go this road; that leads us to suspect that there is no great difference between the guidance of an angel and the guidance of the Spirit.[30] Perhaps in this instance, since Philip seems to have been alone, the Spirit spoke by an inner voice, nudging Philip on. Philip may not even have been conscious of the fact that it was the Holy Spirit speaking to him, but somehow he felt moved to witness to the Ethiopian official. Luke, in retrospect, could say that it was the voice of the Holy Spirit. It is a bit precarious to attribute every urge to speak or to act as the voice of the Holy Spirit. On the other hand, we must learn to be sensitive to the Spirit's voice. David Watson warns against two opposite mistakes about the guidance of the Spirit: one, the over-eager desire to ascribe almost every prompting and feeling to the direct intervention of the Spirit; the other, the denial of all such activity of the Spirit, reducing guidance to what he calls "that much overworked phrase 'sanctified commonsense.' "[31]

After Philip had led the Ethiopian to the Lord and baptized him, "the Spirit of the Lord caught up Philip" (Acts 8:39). Luke's language here is reminiscent of 2 Kings 2:11, where Elijah is whisked away by God's Spirit. The Western text of Acts has it that the "angel of the Lord" snatched Philip up, while the "Spirit of the Lord" fell upon the Ethiopian. Very likely this represents a scribal change in order to bring back at the end of the story the angel who had initiated the mission. More importantly, it must have struck early copyists as strange that nothing is said about the bestowal of the Holy Spirit on a man who had been converted and baptized.[32] That he had received the Holy Spirit is clearly suggested in Luke's report, for "he went on his way rejoicing" (v. 29). Joy is the fruit of the Spirit. While it is not made explicit in what sense the Spirit caught up Philip, the incident, from beginning to end, witnesses to the guidance of the Holy Spirit.

When Peter was praying on the roof top of Simon the tanner in Joppa, he had a vision of clean and unclean animals which he was asked to kill and eat. In this way God prepared his servant for the mission to the Gentiles. Meantime, the messengers of Cornelius stood at the door and asked for Peter. "And while Peter was pondering the vision, the Spirit said to him, 'Behold, three men are looking for you. Rise and go down, and accompany them without hesitation; for I have sent them' " (Acts 10:19, 20).

Interestingly the narrative resembles the previous story, in which the angel of the Lord takes the initiative, and the Spirit continues to guide Philip. Here the angel of God speaks to Cornelius (v. 3) and the Spirit speaks to Peter. The difference lies in the fact that Cornelius sees the angel in a vision, whereas Peter hears the voice of the Spirit. Just how the Spirit spoke to Peter is not stated. Did he actually hear a voice from outside? or was it an inner urge which he understood to be the voice of the Spirit? In any case, Peter was guided by the Spirit to take the gospel to the Gentiles. That he was sure of this is clearly stated later in his defense before his critics in Jerusalem: "The Spirit told me to go" (Acts 11:12).

The Holy Spirit also guided the Antiochian church to prepare itself for sharing its material possessions with the needy Jerusalem brothers, when Agabus predicted a famine. "Agabus stood up and foretold by the Spirit that there would be a great famine over all the world" (Acts 11:28). (According to the Western text of Acts, Luke was present when Agabus uttered this prophecy, for it reads: "When we were gathered together.")[33]

While the word *semaino* (signify) could refer to an oracular utterance, or even a symbolic action (as at 21:11), it seems best in this passage to take it in the sense of "foretell." It was a prophecy prompted by the Spirit. We should not, however, on the basis of this incident, simply equate prophecy with prediction; but certainly it was one form of prophecy in the early church, and it was highly regarded.

The early church experienced the guidance of the Spirit through prophets; this can be seen also by the way the Antiochian

church launched its mission to Cyprus and the lower Asiatic main-
land. Through the ministry of prophets and teachers, the church
had been prepared to hear the voice of the Spirit. As the church
worshiped and fasted, the Holy Spirit said, "Set apart for me
Barnabas and Saul for the work to which I have called them"
(Acts 13:2).

How did the Spirit speak to the church? Haenchen says:
"Naturally it was one of the 'prophets' who gave utterance to the
Spirit's direction."[34] Most commentators agree that someone with
the gift of prophecy became the agent of the Holy Spirit by which
the church was instructed to send forth several of its leading men
to proclaim the gospel in other lands.

When Paul, and Barnabas, and Mark left on their mission,
Luke says boldly that they were sent forth by the Holy Spirit
(13:4). The church was so conscious of the Spirit's guidance in this
matter that they saw little difference between being sent by the
church (v. 3) or by the Spirit (v. 4).

That this has been a pattern for the church throughout the
history of Christian missions can easily be verified. Often when
the church did not hear the voice of the Holy Spirit concerning its
mission responsibility, it was because of a lack of teaching,
prophecy, worship, and fasting.

b. *The Holy Spirit Closes and Opens Doors.* After the
Jerusalem Council meeting, Paul and Silas were sent out by the
Antiochian church to revisit the churches that had been founded
on the first missionary journey. At some point on this second
journey, the missioners decided to press westward into the
province of Asia. The *Via Egnatia* led to Ephesus—an unrivaled
field for preaching the gospel.[35]

For some reason, however, the Holy Spirit forbade them "to
speak the word in Asia" (Acts 16:6). When they came to Mysia,
they attempted to go into Bithynia, "but the Spirit of Jesus did not
allow them" (v. 7). Interestingly, in both cases the guidance of the
Spirit was negative, keeping the missioners from false moves, but
not really pointing out the place to which they should go.
Guidance by the Spirit should not be understood as ruling out

human planning. Indeed, one may ask the question whether God can direct us by his Spirit if we do nothing. Our plans to serve Christ may at times be thwarted, but the Holy Spirit uses these frustrated desires to lead us where God wants us. In the case of Paul and Silas (Timothy had by now also joined the party), the Spirit was directing them to a great harvest field in Europe.

Just how the Holy Spirit forbade the missioners to carry out their plans of evangelism is not stated. Williams suggests: "Possibly a prophet speaking in Jesus' name, possibly a vision of the risen Lord himself, or a blinding flash of inward illumination was the medium of revelation."[36] It is possible, also, that the Spirit spoke through a set of circumstances about which we are not informed. Perhaps the Spirit did not speak in the same way on the two occasions mentioned; that may be the reason why Luke speaks once of "the Holy Spirit" (v. 6) and then of "the Spirit of Jesus" (v. 7). However, it would be unwise to try to distinguish between these two.

Leslie Newbigin comments on the Holy Spirit's part in directing the early mission of the church in this way:

> Here it is enough to say that the picture given in the Acts is one that is constantly being reproduced in the missionary experience of the church. It is the Holy Spirit who leads the way, opening a door here which the church must then obediently enter, kindling a flame there which the church must lovingly tend. My own experience as a missionary has been that the significant advances of the church have not been the result of our own decisions, about the mobilizing and allocating of "resources." This kind of language, appropriate for a military campaign or a commerical enterprise, is not appropriate here. The significant advances in my experiences have come through happenings of which the story of Peter and Cornelius is a paradigm.... It was the free and sovereign deed of God who goes before his church.[37]

c. The Holy Spirit Directs the Lives of the Individual Missioners. After establishing Christianity on both shores of the Aegean, "Paul resolved in the Spirit to pass through Macedonia and Achaia and go to Jerusalem" (Acts 19:21). No doubt he wanted to hand over the monetary gifts of the Gentile churches to the Jerusalem community, and then sail for Rome, with the ultimate purpose of going on to Spain (Rom. 15:20, 24).

It is possible to read Acts 19:21 as a decision which Paul reached in his own spirit. This may also be the case in Acts 20:22, where Paul explains that he is going to Jerusalem "bound in the Spirit." Perhaps the phrases are designed simply to stress the intense earnestness of Paul's purpose.[38] On the other hand, Paul's spirit could be viewed as being so completely under the control of the Holy Spirit that Luke does not allow us to distinguish between the human spirit and the divine. Dupont and several other commentators argue, however, that *pneuma* in these instances does in fact mean the Holy Spirit.[39] The suggestion that the journey to Jerusalem was a bad mistake and that Paul should have listened to the Spirit as he spoke through Paul's friends, rather than simply deciding on this path in his own spirit, has no support. Paul is nowhere rebuked for having gone to Jerusalem.

In his farewell words to the Ephesian elders, Paul anticipates imprisonment and affliction, for that is what "the Holy Spirit testifies to me in every city" (Acts 20:23). Presumably the Spirit spoke to Paul through the mouth of Christian prophets; at least that was the case at Tyre and Caesarea (21:4, 11).

What makes this whole matter of guidance by the Spirit somewhat complicated at this point is the fact that some prophets at Tyre told Paul "through the Spirit" (21:4) not to go to Jerusalem. Luke makes no attempt to reconcile Paul's persistence in going to Jerusalem and the warnings of these prophets. It would not be wise to conclude that Paul disobeyed the Spirit by going to Jerusalem. Perhaps we have an example here of what Paul meant when he told the Thessalonians not to despise prophecy but to "test everything" (1 Thes. 5:20, 21). Evidently Paul was not convinced that these prophets were conveying God's will to him. Or else, as A. T. Robertson suggests, Paul interpreted what they said as information and warning and not as a prohibition.[40]

At Caesarea, Agabus, by symbolic action and by the voice of the Holy Spirit, predicts Paul's captivity. In contrast to the prophets at Tyre, Agabus does not tell Paul not to go to Jerusalem, but simply predicts the outcome (21:11). Paul's friends, however, did beg him not to go (v. 12). But Paul, like his master, whom his friends also tried to deter when he set his face to go to Jerusalem (Lk. 9:51), would not be dissuaded. "Some may label it stubbornness; but before doing that, it is well to reflect that he was not doing it in his own strength, but was bound in the Spirit" (20:22).[41]

In the matter of guidance, Luke makes clear that not only entire congregations but also individual members were guided by the Spirit in the decisions which they made concerning the work of God's kingdom. We should not infer from this, however, that the early church experienced the Spirit's guidance only in matters pertaining to the life of the church and its mission. No doubt the guidance of the Spirit was experienced also in the more mundane affairs of daily life. Acts is, after all, a record of how the gospel moved from Jerusalem to Rome, and Luke wants to show that the Holy Spirit guided the church and its messengers in its evangelistic concerns.

Just because Luke does not take his account of the mission of the church beyond Rome does not mean that its mission was now complete, but the gospel had come, as it were, to "the end of the earth." (There is some evidence that Rome was meant by "the end of the earth.")[42] Bruce writes:

> When at the end of the book, Paul has been brought to Rome and spends his two years under house arrest "preaching the kingdom of God and teaching about the Lord Jesus Christ quite openly and unhindered" in the heart of the Roman Empire, the impression with which we are left is not that the Holy Spirit has finished, or nearly finished, his work in the world. Rather, having brought the gospel thus far from its earlier bases in Jerusalem, Syrian Antioch, and Ephesus, he will continue to advance it in increasing measure from its new base in Rome. The future belongs to the Spirit, and thanks to him the gospel cannot be stopped.[43]

PART THREE

The Spirit in the Life of
the Believer

CHAPTER 9

The Spirit and the Foundations of the New Life

In the epistolary literature of the New Testament it is obvious that no writer has so much to say about the Holy Spirit as the apostle Paul. The word *pneuma* occurs some 146 times in his letters and most of these references are to the divine Spirit (sometimes the word *pneuma* refers to the human spirit or even to the evil spirit).

It has not always been recognized in the past that the doctrine of the Holy Spirit is one of the central teachings of Paul. Hermann Gunkel had pointed this out as early as 1899,[1] but as long as the marrow of Paulinism was thought to be found in Romans and Galatians, the Reformation doctrine of justification by faith held center stage. Nonetheless, it is in these two epistles that Paul says more about the Spirit than in his other writings, with the exception, perhaps, of 1 Corinthians.

In 1928 H. W. Robinson wrote: "The increasing recognition that the doctrine of the Holy Spirit is central in the Christian thought of the Apostle Paul (rather than the Rabbinical doctrine of justification) marks a great advance in the interpretation of his Gospel."[2] More recently E. W. Hunt declared: "The doctrine of the Spirit is one of the salient doctrines of Paul's theology; indeed, some would argue that it was the core of it."[3]

We should not give the impression, however, that other New Testament writers, such as Peter, John, and the author of Hebrews, are less interested in the doctrine of the Holy Spirit than Paul. By and large they agree with Paul in his teaching on the Spirit, but since they say relatively less about the Spirit, we shall treat the epistolary literature as a unit.

The caption for this section of our study, "The Spirit in the Life of the Believer," should not be construed to mean the apostolic letter writers fostered an individualism that runs counter to the emphasis on the corporate life of the community. The believer is always seen as part of the Christian community; but one cannot have a community of the Holy Spirit unless the individuals who make up this community possess the Spirit of Christ.

Since the church, the new people of God, is built on the foundation of the apostles and prophets (Eph. 2:20), it is only proper that we comment on how the apostles relate the Holy Spirit to the church's spiritual foundations. We begin with God's revelation which came to be recorded in the Scriptures.

A. The Spirit and Revelation

If God had not chosen to make his saving purposes known to humankind, humanity would be forever lost in the darkness of its sin. In his infinite wisdom and grace, however, God revealed his salvation plans, first to Israel and ultimately in Jesus Christ. Peter explains that "no prophecy ever came by the impulse of man, but men moved by the Holy Spirit spoke from God" (2 Pet. 1:21).

False prophets spoke the "visions of their own minds" (Jer. 23:16), but true prophets were "carried along" by the Holy Spirit when they spoke God's Word. The prophetic Scriptures consequently are entirely trustworthy, since God's prophets were inspired by the Spirit to convey God's message. Michael Green suggests that Peter uses a nautical term here (*pheromene* is used of a ship carried along by the wind). "The prophets raised their sails, so to speak (they were obedient and receptive), and the Holy

Spirit filled them and carried their craft along in the direction He wished. Men spoke: God spoke."[4]

The writers of Scripture were not simply assisted by the Holy Spirit to express their own thoughts; they were guided in such a way as to ensure a trustworthy witness to God's revelation in the events of biblical history culminating in Jesus Christ.[5]

Since the prophets were inspired by the Spirit of God, the writer to the Hebrews can quote an Old Testament passage and say, "The Holy Spirit says" (Heb. 3:7). The writer uses the present tense as if to suggest that the Holy Spirit was still speaking through the ancient psalm which he quotes, since the psalm was inspired by the Spirit. That the author of Hebrews thinks of the Holy Spirit as still speaking through the Old Testament Scriptures is clearly indicated in 9:8. After describing the tabernacle arrangements and the Levitical offerings, he says, "By this the Holy Spirit indicates that the way into the sanctuary is not yet opened as long as the outer tent is still standing." In other words, the Holy Spirit has lessons to teach from the Old Testament. Also, in Hebrews 10:15, the Holy Spirit is represented as bearing witness to the readers; the author then proceeds to quote Old Testament promises of a new covenant (vv. 16, 17). Bruce comments: "These words, spoken by the prophet under inspiration, are naturally quoted as the words of the Holy Spirit, and they are viewed as the Holy Spirit's confirmation of the conclusion to which our author's argument has just led them."[6]

Whereas Paul does not mention the Holy Spirit in connection with the inspiration of the Old Testament Scriptures, he stresses that they are God-inbreathed *(theopneustos)*. "All scripture is inspired by God and profitable for teaching, for reproof, for correction, and for training in righteousness, that the man of God may be complete, equipped for every good work" (2 Tim. 3:16).

"All scripture," whether in its parts or as a whole, refers specifically to the Old Testament, for when Paul wrote, the New Testament books had not yet been collected; in fact, some had not yet been written. However, we would not be wrong if we included the New Testament writings in the phrase "all scripture."

Paul can combine a passage from Deuteronomy (25:4) with a saying of Jesus (Lk. 10:7) and call both alike "Scripture" (1 Tim. 5:18). Moreover, Paul claims to speak or write with the authority of Christ (2 Cor. 2:17; 13:3; Gal. 4:14), and calls his message "the word of God" (1 Thes. 2:13), and orders that his writings be read in the churches (Col. 4:16). He challenges those who thought they were "inspired" to recognize and abide by what he said (1 Cor. 14:38). Peter certainly regarded Paul's letters as Scripture (2 Pet. 3:16).[7] Donald Bloesch writes:

> When it is said that "all scripture is inspired by God," the reference is not only to the Old Testament documents but also those of the New Testament, some of which were even then circulating in written form. . . . To be sure, the canon of the sacred writings had not yet been determined, but the church has wisely interpreted 2 Timothy 3:16 as covering the whole of the canon.[8]

While the apostles affirmed that the Holy Spirit inspired the Old Testament prophets, they did not insist that the prophets always understood fully the implications of what they were saying. Peter wrote that "the prophets . . . inquired what person or time was indicated by the Spirit of Christ within them when predicting the sufferings of Christ and the subsequent glory" (1 Pet. 1:10, 11).

It is possible that Peter thought of Christ as active in the period prior to his incarnation, with his Spirit inspiring the prophets about himself. On the other hand, it may be that he made no distinction between the Spirit of God, the Holy Spirit, and the Spirit of Christ.[9] That same Holy Spirit who inspired the prophets of old, now equips the New Testament witnesses to preach the good news ("who preached the good news to you through the Holy Spirit sent from heaven," 1 Pet. 1:12).[10] "So there is a Spirit-inspired unity in the testimony of Old Testament prophets and New Testament apostles or gospel missionaries. It is through their combined witness that men embrace God's saving grace in Christ, and His Church is built" (see Eph. 2:18-22).[11]

Neither Peter nor Paul made any attempt to define the inspiration of the Scriptures for us; all such attempts, ancient or modern, are more or less inadequate. In speaking of the divine inspiration of the Scriptures, we are on holy ground and we do best to take off our shoes in the presence of this great mystery. Nevertheless, we must boldly join the apostles in everything they affirm about the inspiration of the Word of God.

There is no suggestion that the personality or individuality of the writer was suppressed by the Spirit's inspiration. Neither the writer's linguistic nor creative faculties were pushed aside; even the diligent research into available sources on the part of the writers was used by the Holy Spirit to give us a trustworthy Word from God. The Spirit inspired these human authors in such a way that they were kept from error, and what they wrote remains for all times the supreme authority for the people of God.[12]

When the church was born at Pentecost, it had God's written revelation, as this was found in what we now call the Old Testament Scriptures. However, they also had an inspired oral tradition going back to Jesus and guaranteed by the faithful witness of the apostles. Nor did the Spirit cease from giving new "revelations" to the early apostles. Paul, for example, claims that there were things not known to earlier generations which God had now revealed "to his holy apostles and prophets by the Spirit" (Eph. 3:5). Specifically, the concept of the church as the body of Christ, comprised of Jew and Gentile, was a mystery which Paul claims was revealed to him in a special way (v. 6). When Paul speaks of the "mystery" which has been revealed to him, he does not mean that other believers do not have access to this new insight which the Spirit of God gave him; he means that this is a truth that is beyond human discovery which God in his grace has chosen to reveal.

The Old Testament is the record of what God revealed by his Spirit to the prophets of old; the New Testament, which was probably circulating more or less in the form that we have it today by the end of the first century, witnesses to God's final revelation in Jesus Christ. The source of all divine revelation, both old and new, is the Holy Spirit.

But to say that we have an inspired book does not mean that

when the message of the Bible is proclaimed, or when people read these foundation documents of the church, they always understand the message of this book. It is very important, therefore, that we comment on the work of the Holy Spirit in illuminating people's minds.

B. The Spirit and Illumination

The apostles are unanimous in their judgment that a person separated from God lives in darkness—a metaphor for sin, unbelief, ignorance, and death. Those who turn their backs on the true light have "their senseless minds" darkened (Rom. 1:21). Of the Gentiles Paul wrote: "They are darkened in their understanding, alienated from the life of God" (Eph. 4:18). He reminded his Ephesian readers that before their conversion they "were darkness," but now they are "light in the Lord" (Eph. 5:8). Believers are exhorted to put on the whole armor of God since they are engaged in a struggle "against the world rulers of this present darkness" (Eph. 6:12). At the head of these powers of darkness stands Satan, the god of this world, who "has blinded the minds of the unbelievers, to keep them from seeing the light of the gospel of the glory of Christ" (2 Cor. 4:4).

By contrast, "God is light and in him is no darkness at all" (1 Jn. 1:5). It is only natural, then, that conversion should be described as a deliverance from the kingdom of darkness into Christ's kingdom (Col. 1:13). The new people of God, said Peter, have the vocation to "declare the wonderful deeds of him who called [them] . . . out of darkness into this marvelous light" (1 Pet. 2:9). By the gospel God calls people into "his" light. This light is so marvelous because it illumines the mind of those who believe so that they can grasp what God has done for them in Christ. The same God who at the beginning of the first creation said, "Let light shine out of darkness," shines into the dark recesses of fallen humanity to "give the light of the knowledge of the glory of God in the face of Christ" (2 Cor. 4:6). Conversion is thought of as illumination, and since baptism attended conversion in the early church, baptism came to be called "illumination."[13] Initiation into the Christian life is called "enlightenment," an enlightenment made possible only by the Holy Spirit.[14] The writer to the Hebrews speaks of people who had come to Christ as "those who have once been enlightened, who have tasted the heavenly gift, and have become partakers of the Holy Spirit" (Heb. 6:4), and were now in danger of apostatizing (v. 6).

Perhaps no passage brings out the illuminating work of the Holy Spirit as does 1 Corinthians 2. To grasp what God has done in Christ is just as much a work of the Holy Spirit as the renewal of persons themselves.[15] Of the *teleioi* (the "perfect"; presumably here the equivalent of the "spiritual" who have God's Spirit), Paul says that they have a wisdom which the rulers of this age do not have. It is a wisdom which only God can impart (1 Cor. 2:7). The rulers of this age acted foolishly in unbelief because their eyes were not open to what God was doing in Christ. Unaided by the Spirit of God, they were blind to God's saving acts. There is only one way in which a person can grasp this: "God has revealed [it] to us through the Spirit" (1 Cor. 2:10). The Christian can take no credit for grasping the meaning of what happened at Calvary, for it is a gift of God, a work of God's Spirit.[16]

To elaborate a bit on the illuminating activity of the Spirit, Paul says, "The Spirit searches all things" (1 Cor. 10).[17] God in his innermost reality is not accessible to us; only God's Spirit can make the "deep things of God," that is his revelation, available to us. By analogy, Paul adds, no one knows what goes on inside a person except the person himself (1 Cor. 2:11).[18] In the same way, he reasons, no one except God can know what is in God. The analogy is not perfect but it helps to illustrate the point. "Apart therefore from the Spirit of God, man remains in ignorance of God and of his wise purpose for this world."[19]

The believer, who has been given the Spirit of God, can understand the things graciously given to us by God (1 Cor. 2:12)—meaning perhaps the benefits of Christ's saving acts. Not only do unbelievers need the Spirit of God to understand what God has done for them in Christ, but believers need the help of the Spirit even to speak properly about the things of God. "The

Spirit also provides language that makes conversation about these truths possible."[20]

A person outside Christ, by contrast, is blind to the meaning of the Christ-event. To such persons, who do not have the Spirit of God, "the things of the Spirit of God" make no sense (1 Cor. 2:14), because they do not receive them. The "spiritual" person, however, who has the Spirit of God and the mind of Christ, has the God-given facility to grasp and understand God's revelation in Christ.

Unbelieving Jews, Paul insists, just like the Gentiles, are in darkness. They cannot understand their own Scriptures, for a veil lies upon their hearts. Only when they turn to Christ is this veil removed (2 Cor. 3:6). The Spirit does this by removing the veil from their darkened eyes and enabling them to understand the salvatory purposes of God as expressed in the Jewish Scriptures.

The Holy Spirit not only enlightens fallen persons in their darkness so that they can see what God has done for them in Christ; he continues to illuminate the saints, who have the Spirit of God. In Ephesians 1:17, 18, Paul prays that the "God of our Lord Jesus Christ, the Father of glory, may give you a spirit of wisdom and of revelation in the knowledge of him, having the eyes of your hearts enlightened that you may know . . . ." The knowledge which the Spirit gives the believer is defined as an understanding of the hope which comes from God's call in the gospel, the wealth of his glorious inheritance in the saints, and the immeasurable greatness of his power in us who believe (vv. 18, 19). Paul has that inward illumination of the believer in mind which comes by faith and love.[21] John Stott writes:

> Thus, when a person is newly born of the Spirit, his grasp of God's purpose for him is usually very limited and his experience is limited in proportion. But as the Holy Spirit enlightens the eyes of his heart, vistas begin to open up before him of which at first he had scarcely even dreamed. He begins to see and know the hope of God's calling, the riches of God's inheritance and the greatness of God's power. He is challenged to embrace by faith the fullness of God's purpose for him. The tragedy is that often our faith does not keep pace with our knowledge.[22]

Not all agree that the word *pneuma* in this passage refers to the Holy Spirit, but Abbott is probably right when he says "that the spirit of wisdom here is the effect of the Holy Spirit; [it] is naturally understood but not expressed."[23] One cannot possess the spirit of wisdom by which God's saving acts in Christ can be grasped without the help of the Spirit of God. By God's Spirit "the eyes of the heart" can be opened to perceive the realities of divine grace.

Paul had a similar thought in mind when he prayed that the Colossians "be filled with the knowledge of his will in all spiritual wisdom and understanding" (Col. 1:9). Here the apostle seemed to stress the need for illumination by the Spirit in ethical decision making, for it takes more than human intellect to know how to please God. It is not so much the mastery of a body of facts that the Spirit applies (although objective knowledge is not inimical to a knowledge of God), but the kind of knowledge that leads to right behavior.[24]

It is a source of great comfort and assurance for those who share the gospel with unbelievers that the Holy Spirit is at work in the hearts of unbelievers, seeking to remove the veil from their darkened eyes. Likewise, it makes the witness to the gospel totally dependent on the Spirit of God to bring about the illumination which is necessary for faith in Christ.

It is also very important for believers who have been illumined to see the light of the glorious gospel, that they be further enlightened by the Holy Spirit in order to grasp the great truths of God's revelation more firmly and to penetrate more deeply into their meaning and see their implications for daily living.

Without the Spirit of God to help us we can so easily misunderstand God's Word. Moreover, since the whole counsel of God is immeasurably rich, we need the help of the Spirit to hold the truths of divine revelation in balance. As much harm has been done through overemphasis of one truth at the expense of another as through misinterpretation of Scripture passages. The Spirit is needed also to bring truths to our attention which we may have forgotten, or to give us fresh insights into those truths which have become all too familiar. Also, the Spirit helps us to see the relevance of particular truths for today's situation, and in that way the Word is kept alive.[25]

Just as the Spirit who inspired the prophets and apostles did not rule out hard thought and study, so the enlightenment of the believer is often related to serious search and study. All insights that come to the individual believer should, however, be put to the test in the context of the Christian community and examined carefully in the light of the Scriptures. A new "revelation" that is contrary to the written Word of God must be rejected.

> The divine author of Scripture is an ever active divine agent who reveals the truths that he imparted in the biblical past to people of every age.... What the Spirit reveals is not a new word but the truth already proclaimed in Holy Scripture. Yet this truth would remain buried in the past unless the Spirit were active now bringing it to light in the consciousness of men and women.[26]

The revelation which came to the prophets and the apostles by the Holy Spirit, and the illumination which the Spirit gives to the unbeliever when he hears the gospel, may be called the foundation of the new life in Christ. It is important, therefore, that we see how the Spirit is related to the proclamation of the gospel.

C. The Spirit and Proclamation

The apostles recognized that between the resurrection (by which Jesus had been declared Lord "according to the Spirit of holiness," Rom. 1:4) and the parousia, the gospel was to be preached to the ends of the earth. "This missionary proclamation of the Church, its preaching of the gospel, gives to the period between Christ's resurrection and parousia its meaning for redemptive history."[27]

This mission of the church is possible only by the power of the Spirit. The church has received what Paul calls a "dispensation of the Spirit" (2 Cor. 3:8). Repeatedly in Paul's letters we find *pneuma* (often with *dunamis*—power) in contexts which deal with the missionary preaching of the apostle. In his reflections on the beginning of the gospel at Thessalonica, Paul confesses: "For our gospel came to you not only in word, but also in power and in the Holy Spirit and with full conviction. . . . For you received the word in much affliction, with joy inspired by the Holy Spirit" (1 Thes. 1:5, 6).

The preaching of the gospel in Thessalonica was attended by "power," "Spirit," and "assurance." None of these three had its source in Paul's eloquence or persuasive arguments.[28] All of them stand in contrast to "in word only." To be sure the gospel was proclaimed in "word," but this did not explain its effectiveness. Rhetoric could not account for the conversion of the Thessalonians from idolatry to the living God (1 Thes. 1:9). In some passages Paul says that the gospel itself is the power of God for salvation (Rom. 1:8; 1 Cor. 1:18), but here it is the power of the Spirit which worked through the preaching of the gospel.

Some commentators look upon the three expressions "in power," "in Spirit," and "in full assurance" as coordinate phrases to express what Delling calls "the great fulness of divine activity."[29] Mason relates the three as follows: The power was seen in the establishment of the Thessalonian community in a short period of time. The source of this power was the Holy Spirit, which gave the gospel its authority, its power to convince. In the bearers of the gospel this power was manifested in assurance, the assurance that they were borne up by a power beyond themselves.[30]

One might also view "power" and "Spirit" as hendiadys (two words used to express the same idea) and relate them to "full assurance" in the sense that, by the power of the Spirit, the messengers were convinced that God was at work and the hearers were assured that the gospel was truly God's Word of salvation for them. We should not restrict the meaning of *plerophoria* (assurance) to the preachers only. Perhaps it is not accidental that "Spirit" stands between "power" and "assurance." The Spirit gave the proclamation divine power, and the Spirit gave assurance to both preachers and hearers that God was at work in the hearts of the hearers, delivering them from the power of darkness and transferring them into the kingdom of Christ.

In 1 Thessalonians 1:6, Paul gives further evidence of the work of the Spirit among the Thessalonians. They had received the Word with much affliction but, paradoxically, with a joy (a fruit of the Spirit) which the Holy Spirit gave them. This joy, inspired by the Holy Spirit, could not be quenched by the pressure of the opposition; it was a foretaste of the age to come. The gospel preached by the power of the Spirit had created in the Thessalonians a faith that was sustained by the power of the Spirit, even in the midst of suffering. It is worth noticing that in both 1 Thessalonians and 1 Corinthians, the first time the Spirit is mentioned, it is in connection with the power which the Spirit supplies to the preachers of the gospel.

In 1 Corinthians 2:4, 5, Paul acknowledges that the miracle of founding the church in Corinth was due to the power of the Spirit and not to "the persuasive words of wisdom." Not that Paul had a quarrel with persuasive words as such, but he realized that when they reflect only worldly wisdom they cannot deliver persons from bondage. If, on the other hand, the Word is proclaimed "in demonstration of the Spirit and of power," as at Corinth, there is a solid foundation for the faith of hearers (1 Cor. 2:4, 5).

In the preaching of the gospel Paul saw a demonstration (*apodeixis* is a technical term of rhetoric)[31] of the power of the Spirit, as well as a demonstration which comes from the power of the Spirit that takes place in the preaching of the gospel. Whether Paul thought of miracles or certain gifts of the Spirit as evidence of the Spirit's power at this point, we do not know. That the gospel was confirmed by gifts of the Spirit is expressly stated in Hebrews 2:4. More likely Paul had the founding of the church in mind.[32] The reason he refused the clever manipulations of the rhetorician and trusted rather in God's Spirit to do the work of renewing hearts, was that he wanted the faith of his hearers to rest on God's power and not on human wisdom.

Paul had trembled when he faced wicked Corinth for the

first time (1 Cor. 2:1f.). This feeling of personal weakness arose
out of the conviction that the proclamation of the gospel calls for a
strength other than human. To convert the gospel into "human
wisdom" and to propagate it by purely human means meant an
"emptying" of the cross (1 Cor. 1:17). Whether we are to think of
popular philosophy, the religion of Judaism, or the secret wisdom
of the Gnostics, there is according to Paul a deep gulf between all
human wisdom and the gospel. And it is significant that Paul
reminds his readers that he had decided (v. 2) to know nothing
but Christ crucified among them. Paul thought of himself not as a
teacher of wisdom, but as a witness to the cross of Christ. This determined the form of his proclamation: not dialectical eloquence,
but the demonstration of the Spirit and power. As the proclamation of Christ was made, the Spirit of God made the Christ-
event—the death and exaltation of our Lord and the coming of
his Spirit—contemporary with the hearers,[33] and by the Spirit
they were enabled to stretch out the hand of faith and to accept
God's offer of salvation.

In Galatians 3:1-5, the preaching of the gospel, the work of
the Spirit, and the hearing attended by faith are related. Also, in
Romans 15:18, 19, the power of the Spirit is referred to as the
secret of success in Paul's Gentile mission. In his review of the success of his missionary labors, he confessed that he would not dare
speak of it if it were not Christ's work. Christ had worked signs
and wonders by his Spirit and so had validated Paul's preaching.
All this agrees essentially with what Paul says in 2 Corinthians 3
about the ministry of the new covenant, which is a ministry of the
Spirit.

In 2 Corinthians 6:6, the Spirit is not mentioned specifically
in connection with the preaching of the gospel, but it is related to
the apostolic mission of Paul. He introduced himself (and his co-
workers) as a herald of the good news of salvation. This "day of
salvation," as promised by the prophet (Is. 49:8), has now come.
What he wants to avoid, therefore, is to give anyone the occasion
for making his conduct as a minister of the gospel a ground for rejecting it;[34] so he commends himself by giving a list of his trials

which he had patiently borne (vv. 4, 5) and the spiritual graces which characterize him as servant of Christ (v. 6). Among these is "the Holy Spirit." Plummer finds it incredible that there should be a reference to the Holy Spirit in a list of human virtues, and that in a subordinate place (neither first nor last). Therefore, he renders it as "a spirit that is holy."[35] Allo takes it to mean the Holy Spirit in the sense of its supernatural gifts (revelations, miracles, etc.).[36] The majority of commentators, however, hold that it is the Holy Spirit, not the pious spirit of man, that Paul has in mind.[37] The Spirit of God helped Paul bear hardships which came to him in the course of his ministry. Moreover, it is worth noting that Paul went on to mention "the power of God" (v. 7); that would suggest that Paul may well have had in mind the power of the Spirit in his ministry of apostleship. It would appear, then, that "in Holy Spirit" speaks of the divine power which enabled Paul to proclaim the good news, to live without offense, and to suffer for the sake of the gospel in the Spirit of Christ.

About one thing we can be certain: Paul never took credit for his success in preaching the gospel. He always attributed it to the power of the Spirit of God. For this reason, too, he exhorts the readers of the Ephesian epistle to take hold of the "sword of the Spirit, which is the word of God" (Eph. 6:17). The "sword of the Spirit" is part of the equipment of the Christian soldier.

The genitive ("*of* the Spirit") is a bit elusive. If it is qualitative, then it means that the Word of God is a "spiritual sword," which of course it is. However, it is more likely to be a subjective genitive, with Spirit indicating the source of the sword: the sword which comes from the Spirit. "The sword is supplied by the Spirit," says George Johnston.[38]

That the Word of God is likened to a sword is not unusual in biblical language (e.g., Is. 49:2; Hos. 6:5; cf. Heb. 4:12). It has been suggested that the figure of speech used in Ephesians 6:17 is derived from Isaiah 11:4, where in the new age the messianic ruler is to smite the earth with the rod of his mouth and slay the wicked with the "breath *(ruach)* of his lips." The Torah also was likened to a sword in Judaism.[39] In Revelation 1:16 the sword which comes out of the mouth of the risen Christ is the Word of God.

A question that is not entirely easy to answer is how the sword of the Spirit is to be used by the Christian warrior. Did Paul think of the Word of God as the sword with which the besieged Christian is to defend himself, or did he urge taking the offensive against the "spiritual hosts of wickedness"? The word for "sword" (*machaira*—the daggerlike, short sword) does not settle the question. If the "sword of the Spirit" is an offensive weapon, then it would be the only one in the list of weapons in the Christian's armor, for all the other weapons are for defense and protection.

Perhaps we do best if we do not restrict the meaning unnecessarily and allow for both meanings. It is possible that Paul has the defense of the believer before human courts in mind.[40] If so, we may have a reference here to the promise of Jesus that the Holy Spirit would enable his followers to speak in defense of their faith in such a moment of need (Mk. 13:11). On the other hand, we could also think of attacks of the devil in the day-to-day life of Christ's followers in which their only defense is the Word of God, which the Holy Spirit supplies. We have a good example of this in our Lord, who defended the attacks of the evil one with God's Word (Mt. 4:1-10).

Since, however, the author went on to exhort his readers to pray for him that he might be enabled to proclaim the Word in *parrhesia* (freedom, boldness), it is more likely that Paul thought of the sword of the Spirit as the proclaimed Word of God. The Spirit gives the Word of God its cutting edge, as it were. It is, as the writer to the Hebrews put it, "living and active, sharper than any two-edged sword" (Heb. 4:12).

We should be careful when we read the text in this way, that we do not think of the Christian preacher as one who can knock down his enemies by quoting or by arguing from the Word of God. The writer has just said that the believer is to have his feet shod with the "gospel of peace" (v. 15); the Word which he proclaims is God's message of reconciliation. However, since the proclamation of the gospel is viewed as a military campaign against "principalities and powers," there is nothing inappropriate about the metaphor. As the Word of God is proclaimed, the Spirit takes that Word and illumines darkened minds, quickens a sluggish conscience, convicts and convinces, and leads the hearer to obey the call of the gospel. In this way the enemy of humankind is defeated and he is robbed of his goods. "Therefore, it is probable that the 'word of God,' which he calls a 'sword,' has to do most directly with the preaching of the gospel and with prayer,"[41] for the same Spirit who gives the Word, according to Ephesians 6:17, is also the source and the ground, the sphere and the instrument of prayer.[42]

It is significant that the Word of God and the Spirit are so closely tied together once again in our passage. Not that the Spirit is confined to the Word; he speaks to people in a great variety of ways apart from the Scriptures; but he never speaks at variance with the Scriptures.[43]

Certainly it was the Holy Spirit who gave the early disciples the power to proclaim Christ against great odds. It was the power of the Spirit that made them bold in the presence of their accusers and in the face of opposition and persecution. It was the power that brought conviction of sin, righteousness, and judgment, as Jesus had promised.

> If we lack this power of the Spirit, our preaching and our labors will all be in vain. He alone can make the written word the living word. Only the Spirit can quicken the conscience, illuminate the mind, reveal Christ, create the new birth, bring assurance of salvation, and instruct the believer. The preacher must seek for continuous renewal of the Holy Spirit in his own life before he can bring God's life to anyone else.[44]

The Holy Spirit, who was the source of divine revelation for the prophets of old, also enabled the evangelists who in the more recent past "preached the good news to you through the Holy Spirit sent from heaven" (1 Pet. 1:12). Because the Spirit was sent from heaven, the preachers of the gospel are now clothed with power and authority to announce God's salvation to the world.[45] There is no question in Peter's mind that the Holy Spirit assists and confirms the preaching of the gospel.[46] It is of the utmost significance, therefore, that all who proclaim the gospel be reminded that the Spirit is not only the source of all insight into God's saving truth, but he alone empowers the revealed Word of God. And so "we impart this in words not taught by human wisdom but taught by the Spirit" (1 Cor. 2:13).

The weakness of contemporary Christianity stems in part from the poverty of its preaching. Some ministers consider it a chore; many congregations complain that it lasts twenty minutes; surveys seek to demonstrate its ineffectiveness. But where the gospel is preached in the power of the Holy Spirit, it becomes life changing. Some theologians claim that the Bible *becomes* the Word of God when the Spirit uses the Word preached or read to create an encounter with the hearts of men; we may justifiably protest by saying that it *is* the Word of God; yet we all recognize the point that is being made.

At times it has been suggested that the careful preparation and presentation of the message of the gospel is inimical to the activity of the Spirit in preaching. This is patently false. The "foolishness of the gospel" by which God's power unto salvation is manifested (1 Cor. 1:18) is not the "preaching of foolishness." We all know that God can use the most poorly prepared sermon to point hearers to Christ, but this he does in spite of the ill-prepared message and not because of it. On the other hand, the most carefully prepared sermon may fall flat to the ground if preacher and sermon are not sustained and empowered by the Spirit of God.

But the gospel, proclaimed by the power of the Spirit, must be believed if its saving power is to be experienced, and so we must pursue further the relationship between the Spirit and faith.

CHAPTER 10

The Spirit and the New Life
in Christ

A. The Spirit and Faith

It would be quite accurate to say that the Christian life begins with the reception of the Spirit. As Paul put it, "Any one who does not have the Spirit of Christ does not belong to him" (Rom. 8:9). The gift of the Spirit is bestowed upon the person who puts his trust in Christ and his redemptive work. "Becoming a Christian is therefore essentially a matter of receiving the Spirit. And the Spirit is received by the exercise of the faith which the message of Christ stirs up. . . ."[1]

But one might ask, Is not saving faith itself a gift of the Holy Spirit? James Denney said some wise things on this relationship:

> Just as everything Christian can be defined in terms of the Spirit, when we refer it to God as its source, so everything Christian can be defined in terms of faith, when it is referred to man's response to God as its condition. It is natural, when we think (as we habitually do) of man's responsibility to God in connection with the gospel, to put faith in the forefront, and to make the reception of the Spirit depend upon faith, and often St. Paul does so himself. But, on the other hand, it is through the Spirit that the love of God which in Christ crucified makes its appeal to man is shed abroad in our hearts and to that love, faith is only the response. Hence it is hardly real to

argue about the relations of faith and the Spirit. They are alternative ways of describing all Christian experience, according as we regard them as explicable through man's abandonment of himself to God or through God's gracious and powerful operation on and in man.[2]

With this perspective, let us turn to those Pauline texts where faith and the Spirit are related. In Galatians 3:2 Paul asked the readers, who were in danger of falling back into legalism: "Did you receive the Spirit by works of the law, by hearing with faith?" The answer is implied. Negatively stated, a person does not receive the Spirit as a result of the works of the law. Positively stated, the Galatians had received the Spirit by "the hearing of faith." The expression "hearing of faith" is a bit difficult to grasp. It could be the hearing of the gospel which springs from faith (subjective genitive). If the genitive is understood as descriptive, one might translate: "faithful hearing," that is, the kind of hearing of the gospel that is attended by faith. It is the kind of hearing that welcomes the gospel and leads the listener to entrust his life to Christ. When this happens, God's Spirit comes into the heart of the listener. "We received the Spirit when we responded in faith as we listened to the gospel which God's grace offered to us through Christ."[3]

To be more specific than that only leads to endless quibbling about the order of Christian experience. The claim that the Spirit is received by faith could be countered by saying that without the Spirit there could be no faith.[4] Or, one might go a step further and ask: Does not the preaching of the gospel precede both faith and the reception of the Spirit?[5] But unless the Spirit quickens the words of the gospel, faith cannot be kindled (cf. 1 Cor. 2:1-5). This kind of precision is not very Pauline, nor is it the language of life. Denney again is helpful at this point:

> The faith which abandons itself to Christ is at the same time a receiving of the Spirit of Christ. . . . There are not two things here but one, though it can be represented in the two relations which the words faith and Spirit suggest. Where human responsibility is to be emphasized, it is naturally faith which is put to the front; where the gracious help of God is the main point, prominence is given to the Spirit.[6]

Returning to Galatians 3, Paul asks a second time how the Galatians received the Spirit (Gal. 3:5). His answer is essentially the same as the one given in Galatians 3:2. In the hour of their conversion, when they put their trust in Christ, they received the Holy Spirit. When the Galatians heard the gospel and believed it, they had nothing to offer to God in order to earn his gifts. They did not earn the gift of the Spirit; it was given to them gratuitously. No amount of effort on their part could bring them God's favor; all they could do was open up to the grace offered in the gospel.[7]

In Galatians 3:14 Paul argued that Christian believers are the true sons of Abraham, and that through Jesus Christ the blessing of Abraham has come upon them. This blessing of Abraham is the gift of the Spirit. And how is this gift received? By faith.

> The gift of the Spirit and justification are two sides of the one coin. The blessing of Abraham is equated with the latter in vv. 8f., and with the former in v. 14. Both times the means given is faith. . . . It follows that the gift of the Spirit is what makes us sons of Abraham, sons of God, and puts us *en Christo*. For the promise to Abraham has a double fulfillment. It is fulfilled both in Christ as the promised seed (v. 16), and in the reception of the Spirit by individuals (v. 14).[8]

Another passage in which Paul relates the Spirit and faith is 2 Thessalonians 2:13. Here "sanctification by the Spirit" and "belief in the truth" stand in parallel construction. There seems to be general agreement that "Spirit" here refers not to the human spirit but to the Holy Spirit, who effects the initial sanctification of the believer. It is said that the readers were chosen by God for salvation, and into this salvation they entered when the Holy Spirit set them apart for God. But there is another aspect: the response of faith to the preaching of the gospel. The "truth" they believed in is the gospel. The work of the Holy Spirit in setting the believer apart for God, and the response of faith to the truth concerning Christ, are dual aspects of Christian initiation. "When 'the Spirit set you apart'—that was God's side; and 'when you believed the truth'—that was your side."[9]

In Ephesians 1:13 the work of the Holy Spirit and "believing" also go hand in hand. Again (as in Gal. 3:2, 5, 14 and 2 Thes. 2:13) it doesn't refer to "believing" in general, but to faith in the "word of truth." The hearing of the word of truth (defined as the "gospel of salvation"), the response to that gospel in faith, and the sealing with the Holy Spirit was God's seal set on the faith of those who heard the gospel and accepted its message.

The rendering of this verse in the Authorized Version of 1611 ("after that ye believed, ye were sealed with that holy Spirit of promise") has been misconstrued by some interpreters to mean that Paul speaks to two quite independent Christian experiences: that of faith in Christ, and a subsequent sealing with the Spirit. The context, however, rules out such a reading of the text. It was in the moment when they put their faith in Christ that the Spirit was bestowed.[10]

According to Paul the hearing of the Word elicits faith (a work of the Holy Spirit), and in response to faith God gives us his Holy Spirit, who assures us that we are the children of God.

B. The Spirit and Life

When a person hears the gospel and puts his trust in Christ, he receives the gift of the Holy Spirit. The Spirit creates new life in the one who believes and, as a result, the manner of his life is also changed. "If we live by the Spirit, let us also walk by the Spirit" (Gal. 5:25). "Spirit" here quite obviously means the Spirit of God. The imperative to walk in (or by) the Spirit is based on the indicative, the fact that we have come to life by the Spirit. Since the "if clause" is true to fact—it affirms what already is—perhaps we should translate it, "*Since* we have come to life by the Spirit, let us walk by the Spirit." *The New English Bible* has given the verse a felicitous rendering: "If the Spirit is the source of our life, let the Spirit also direct our course." Before there can be a "walking" in the Spirit, there must be a new life in the Spirit.[11] The Spirit is the "go-between" who communicates the life of the risen Christ to those who put their trust in him.

In Romans 8 Paul develops this theme of life by the Spirit in

greater detail. So closely are "Spirit" and "life" related that
O. Michel can say that the two terms interpret each other.[12] The
chapter begins with the affirmation: "The law of the Spirit of life
in Christ Jesus has set me free from the law of sin and death"
(8:2). The power of the Spirit which gives life to the believer
makes him free from the rule of sin and death. What the Spirit of
life does, he does "in Christ Jesus." The Spirit takes the saving
benefits of Christ's death, applies them to the believer, and communicates the resurrection life of the exalted Lord to those who
put their trust in him.

Continuing the theme of "life in the Spirit," Paul says: "To
set the mind on the flesh is death, but to set the mind on the Spirit
is life and peace" (8:6). The gift of the Spirit is life and peace even
in this present age. The believer's body, however, is subject to
death because of sin; but the Holy Spirit supplies life-forces to the
believer and assures him of the resurrection (8:10). The presence
of the Spirit in his life assures the believer of the resurrection of his
mortal body.[13] He is raised with Christ by the Spirit to a new life,
and the Spirit is the guarantee that he shall live forever even when
his body decays. The Spirit is at work in his resurrection power in
anticipation of the day when "the mortal puts on immortality"
(1 Cor. 15:54).

In Romans 8:13 the antithetical issues of life after the flesh
and life after the Spirit are stated again: "For if you live according
to the flesh you will die, but if by the Spirit you put to death the
deeds of the body you will live." To live after the flesh is not true
life, for it leads to death. But where the reign of the flesh is broken
by the Spirit, there is fullness of life both now and in the age to
come.

That the Spirit is the source of the believer's life is stated also
in 2 Corinthians 3:6b: "The written code kills, but the Spirit gives
life." Chevallier thinks Ezekiel 37 may lie in the background of
this passage. There God's Spirit blows upon the valley of dry
bones and new life is created.[14] Paul is not denigrating the written
Word of God, the "letter," in contrast to free spiritual insight; nor
is he contrasting the literal interpretation of the Old Testament

with the spiritual, or allegorical, interpretation which became so popular in the Alexandrian school. Rather, he has in mind the deadly effect of the written law in contrast with the transforming power of the gospel, through which the Spirit of God acts to bring about "newness of life" (Rom. 6:4).[15]

The Mosaic law stated human duty, making humanity answerable to God, but since humanity failed to obey God's law, it became an agent of death; it condemned humanity. But now the new covenant is proclaimed in the gospel, and those who believe are made alive by the Spirit of God. Paul is not disparaging God's holy law. What makes the human situation so desperate is the fact that we do not live up to God's law and so the law condemns and kills us.[16] The gospel, by contrast, proclaims that Christ's life is now communicated by the Spirit to the sinner who turns in faith to Christ.

Paul himself had sought to observe the letter of the law; yet he was a lawbreaker.

> It was by faith in Christ alone and the operation of the Holy Spirit's grace in his heart that it became possible for him to conform inwardly, in spirit, as well as outwardly, in letter, to the demands of the law—or, as he puts it in another epistle, to "serve in newness of the Spirit, and not in the oldness of the letter" (Rom. 7:6).[17]

Without the Spirit, then, a person is not a Christian, for the Spirit alone can create the new life in Christ which God offers us in the gospel.

In the last of the "sure sayings" of the pastoral epistles, Paul may have been quoting from a baptismal hymn. His reference to the "washing of regeneration" makes this not improbable. What is significant for our discussion at this point is that regeneration is described as a renewal brought about by the Holy Spirit. "It is fairly certain that 'regeneration' *(palingenesia)* and 'renewal' *(anakainosis)* represent the same reality, although their derivations differ."[18]

This Spirit, Paul went on to say, has been "poured out upon us richly through Jesus Christ our Savior" (Tit. 3:6), enabling us to be justified by his grace. The verb "poured out" *(execheen)* is chosen because the writer thinks of the beginning of the new life in Christ as a washing. "It is the cleansing and purifying we experience when the Spirit is poured out upon us which brings about our regeneration and renewal."[19]

If we may speak of an order in the experience of becoming a member of the new people of God, perhaps we could say: When the gospel is proclaimed, the Holy Spirit illuminates our darkened minds to grasp the word of salvation; as we reach out in faith to receive God's grace, the Spirit creates in us a new life.

C. The Spirit and Assurance

When a person comes to life by the Spirit of God, it is very important that he have the assurance that he belongs to the new family of God. And that is just what the Spirit does.

Paul assured his Roman readers that those who "are led by the Spirit of God are sons of God" (Rom. 8:14). He went on to say that in the cry "Abba! Father!" the believer has the evidence that he belongs to God's family, for in this cry of recognition "the Spirit himself [bears] ... witness with our spirit that we are children of God" (8:16). Similarly, Paul writes to the Galatians: "Because you are sons, God has sent the Spirit of his Son into our hearts, crying, 'Abba! Father!' " (Gal. 4:6).

Through the Spirit, Paul had full assurance of his acceptance by God; his converts shared this certainty with the apostle. He reminded the Corinthians that he had brought them the gospel not in words of wisdom "but in demonstration of the Spirit and of power" (1 Cor. 2:4); the reason for this reminder was so that their faith would rest not in the wisdom of men but in the power of God. Paul was convinced that only the Spirit of God could assure his hearers of the trustworthiness of the gospel. This note of assurance rings in all of Paul's writings, and in his last letter he confessed: "I know whom I have believed, and I am sure that he is able to guard until that Day what has been entrusted to me" (2 Tim. 1:12). However, no New Testament writer has so much to say about assurance (which comes from the Spirit) as does John.

In 1 John 3:19, 20, John explained that when our hearts condemn us we can safely entrust ourselves to the judgment of God, who knows all about us. This gives peace to our hearts. Feeling guilty and inadequate does not shut us out from the assurance of divine acceptance. Confidence before God, he explained, comes from obedience to his commands (3:21-24a). But just as an accusing conscience may create doubts about our relationship to God, so our imperfect obedience to God's commands may shake our assurance. He then gave a further and more dependable source of confidence: "And by this we know that he abides in us, by the Spirit which he has given us" (1 Jn. 3:24b).

John did not explain how the Spirit does this, nor how this assurance manifests itself. Perhaps that was wise, lest we think of one particular kind of experience as the evidence of the Spirit's presence. It may be that the Spirit gives us the assurance that we are loved of God for, as Paul explained, the love of God is poured into our hearts by the Holy Spirit (Rom. 5:5); or the Spirit gives us the freedom to call God our Father, assuring us that we are his sons and daughters; or by creating in us what Paul called the fruit of the Spirit (Gal. 5:22); or by bestowing gifts of the Spirit upon us (1 Cor. 12—14).[20] There may be any number of ways in which the Spirit assures us that we belong to God.

Appeals to the witness of the Spirit are useless, however, if one does not know that it is actually the Spirit of God who bears testimony in our hearts. There are other spirits which are not from God (1 Jn. 4:1, 2). The mark of the Spirit of God is the confession that Jesus Christ has come in the flesh. A person who claims to be inspired by the Spirit can be tested by this confession. John, of course, had a particular historical situation in mind in which a faulty confession in the matter of Christ's incarnation was evidence that the Spirit of God was not present in a person's life. Needless to say, verbalizing a correct confession is not by itself proof of the presence of the Spirit of God.

One way of testing whether someone has the Spirit of truth, i.e., the Holy Spirit, is by the confession that Jesus has come in the flesh. Another test is the response of a person to the message of the church: "Whoever knows God listens to us.... By this we know the spirit of truth and the spirit of error" (4:6).

In a manner somewhat similar to that of 3:24b, John declared that we can know that we are in God and God in us by the fact that he has given us his Spirit (1 Jn. 4:13). The perfect tense *(dedoken)* emphasizes the continuous presence of the Spirit in the believer. By giving us a share of his Spirit, God has assured us that we are in God and God in us. Just how the Spirit works in our lives to give us the assurance that we belong to God is again not spelled out. "In any case it is important to recognize that the grounds of Christian assurance and the tests of the reality of Christian experience are multiple."[21]

In 1 John 5:6, 7 a somewhat different aspect of the Spirit's witness seems to be in focus. Here the Spirit is the witness to the truth about Christ. What the Spirit says can be trusted. John seems to be saying that the Spirit witnesses in the heart of the believer that Jesus is the Christ. This is in keeping with what Jesus said the Spirit would do, namely, testify to Jesus (Jn. 15:26).

In 1 John 5:8 John introduced a corrective. There is not one witness but three. These are identified as the Spirit, the water, and the blood. The implication is that one cannot accept the witness of the Spirit if one rejects the witness of the water and the blood to the true character of Jesus. The water is probably a reference to Christ's baptism and the blood to his death. Evidently John's opponents accepted the "water" but not the "blood." They held that the heavenly Christ descended on Jesus at his baptism but withdrew from him before his death, so that it was only the earthly Jesus that died. God by his Spirit testifies to the reality of Christ's incarnation and atoning death on the cross, leading those who accept the gospel by faith to put their trust in the saving benefits of Christ's death. "Jesus, the Christ, is the one who has come through the water of his baptism, through the blood of his cross, and is mediated to us through the Holy Spirit."[22]

D. The Spirit and Freedom

At the heart of the gospel message is the offer of freedom:

freedom from the bondage that sin brings. Life outside of Christ is frequently described as a life of servitude (e.g., Rom. 6:16, 17). Such language is reminiscent of Israel's deliverance from Egypt after being enslaved by the Pharaoh. As a freed people, Israel became God's covenant people. Similarly in the New Testament the watchword of God's people is: "For freedom Christ has set us free" (Gal. 5:1). Deliverance from the bondage of sin, death, and evil powers is usually related to Christ's death on the cross. But it should not be overlooked that the benefits of Christ's death are made available to the believer by the Holy Spirit, so it is not wrong to say that the Spirit sets us free. "Where the Spirit of the Lord is, there is freedom" (2 Cor. 3:17). In fact "Spirit" and "freedom" are so closely related that the two terms may be viewed as correlatives. [23]

The New Testament has nothing to say about political freedom. Also, it dissociates itself from the idea of freedom as the power to do with one's self and one's life whatever one wants. [24] Moreover, the concept of freedom is decidedly different from the Stoic teaching about the conscious, deliberate freedom of the soul from menacing external existence. The Stoic's view of freedom as self-mastery, freedom from passions, steadfastness, and the power to act of oneself, is all self-deception. No person can be free so long as he is in bondage to the flesh. "It is axiomatic to him that we must be given true liberty by God, for it is the divine *pneuma* that overcomes the *sarx*," says Schnackenburg. [25] True moral freedom is not independence of everything and everyone, but rather freedom from the power of sin, from the law, and from death. This kind of freedom the Spirit alone can bring.

1. Freedom from Sin

No New Testament writer has more to say about the power of sin than Paul. He uses the abstract noun *hamartia* some 60 times, not to mention the verb and other forms of the word. Whereas in classical Greek the word means literally "to miss the mark," "to fail," "to make a mistake," the translation of the Old Testament into Greek led to a deepening of the word: *hamartia* becomes a personal offense against a personal God. To sin is to break God's laws. Through its fall into sin, sin holds sway over humankind. The purpose of Christ's coming is to break the power of sin. This redemption from sin, which was accomplished through Christ's death and resurrection, is made real by the Holy Spirit. "The law of the Spirit of life in Christ Jesus has set me free from the law of sin and death" (Rom. 8:2). "Law" must be understood here as a regulating and actuating power. The lives of those outside of Christ are under the power of sin, which leads to death; those who are justified by faith are under a new power: the power of the Holy Spirit.[26]

This liberation from the power of sin by the Spirit is not, however, a magical security against the possibility of sinning or a false perfectionism; it is a deliverance by the Spirit from sin's dominion. Though the believer is freed from sin's rule when the Spirit applies the benefits of Christ's death to his life, he or she is still a sinner; the conflict with evil continues, yet the Spirit supplies the power to be victorious.[27] The evil power which operates in the life of sinful humanity is called the "flesh." One might think of the flesh as the base of operations for sin. Because of its many nuances, the term flesh can easily be misunderstood. Earthly existence, with its frailty and mortality, may be described as flesh. At times the human body is called the "flesh." It becomes a pejorative term when it describes humankind in its distance from and enmity against God—its desire for autonomous existence.[28] This sinful flesh is portrayed as a power which holds us captive, a power from which only the Spirit can make us free (Gal. 5:16-18).

It must be emphasized that the flesh is not a part of a human person; it's not the bodily or sensual side in contrast to the intellectual or the spiritual. The flesh is the whole person apart from Christ. Perhaps nowhere is the power of the sinful flesh described so poignantly as in Romans 7. "For I know that nothing good dwells within me, that is, in my flesh" (7:18). However, Paul did not stop with complaints about his bondage to the flesh; he went on to describe the freedom which the Holy Spirit brings from the flesh (chapter 8). This liberty through the Spirit is experienced only in measure in the here and now, but we have the promise of complete freedom from sin in the life of the age to come; during this interim between the resurrection and the parousia, the warfare between the flesh and the Spirit continues. "Conversion was the entry into man of a new principle and power, the law of the Spirit of life, which rose above and dethroned the old principle and power, the law of sin and death; conversion was the transfer from . . . domination by the flesh to domination by the Spirit."[29]

Galatians 5:8 may serve as a kind of summary for the discussion of freedom from sinful flesh. If the believer is led by the Spirit, says Paul, he is not spiritually impotent as he was under the law, for he has the Spirit of God, who gives him the power to do God's will. Burton observes that life in the Spirit constitutes for Paul a third way of life, distinct both from legalism and from that characterized by the flesh, lawlessness. "It is by no means a middle course between them, but a highway above them both."[30]

2. Freedom from the Law

To define the term "law" in Paul is very difficult, for he uses it in so many different ways. We need not pursue its many meanings at this point. Because we cannot keep God's law perfectly, the law condemns (Rom. 3:10; 8:1) and curses us (Gal. 3:10). On the cross, Jesus Christ, who had kept God's law perfectly, bore the curse of the law for us (Gal. 3:13). The law's sentence of condemnation on sin was experienced by Christ, our substitute, and now we are free. Yet the law is not abolished (Rom. 3:31); it is spiritual and holy (Rom. 7:12, 14). We have been freed from the law, yet we are obligated to do God's will, expressed in his law. How shall we resolve this paradox? It is precisely at this point that Paul's doctrine of the Holy Spirit helps us to cut the Gordian knot.

When viewed as a system of legalism—a way of earning merit before God—the Spirit stands in opposition to the law (Gal. 3:2-5). The law cannot give us life (Gal. 3:21). Those who are led by the Spirit are not under law (Gal. 5:18). On the other hand, the righteousness of the law is fulfilled in us "who walk not according to the flesh but according to the Spirit" (Rom. 8:4). "Law and

Spirit, we are apt to think," says Denney, "are mutually exclusive terms. The Christian lives in the Spirit, and therefore he is not under the law. But with all this disparagement of the law in certain relations or for certain purposes St. Paul never forgets that the law is of God."[31]

Freedom from the law should not be misconstrued then as license to sin (Gal. 5:13). The freedom to which we have been called (Gal. 5:1) is both a freedom from the law, in the sense of legalism, and a freedom to do what God demands in the law. We fulfill God's law if we live by the law of love (5:14). To bite and to devour one another (5:15) would be living "after the flesh." The freedom from legalism which Paul advocated does not give the flesh a "point of departure" (5:13), but leads to loving service (5:13). How is this possible? The answer is, by the power of the Spirit (5:16, 17). "Walk by the Spirit, and do not gratify the desires of the flesh." The Spirit delivers believers from the law as a system of merit—a method to attempt to gain standing before God by the works of the law. At the same time the Spirit makes it possible for the liberated believer to fulfill the law by a life of love and freedom from the flesh. It would not be altogether accurate to say that the Spirit in Paul has taken the place of the law; rather, by the Spirit we are set free to do God's law. This is not only clearly stated in Romans 8:4, but it is also suggested in Galatians 5:23, where, after listing the fruit of the Spirit (v. 22), Paul says: "Against such there is no law." This is a mild way of saying that these things fully meet the requirements of God's law. The law is thus both negated and affirmed by the Holy Spirit. Paul is not antinomian, for by the Spirit the believer is guided and enabled to do the will of God as made known in Christ. Nor must we conclude from Paul's statement that the whole law is fulfilled in the law of love (Gal. 5:14), that the law is superfluous. Cranfield points out that we still need the law to define for us what it means to love truly.[32]

In Romans 7:1-6 Paul compared the bondage to the law with the marriage bond which can be broken only by the death of one of the partners. If the husband dies the wife is free to marry another man. This death, Paul goes on to say, took place at the cross; we are now free from the law and are, as it were, married to Christ. "But now we are discharged from the law, dead to that which held us captive, so that we serve not under the old written code but in the new life of the Spirit" (7:6).

But the Spirit not only makes us free from the power of the flesh and from the burden of legalism, it also assures us of deliverance from death.

3. Freedom from Death

Death is viewed in the New Testament as a terrible enemy—the last enemy to be destroyed (1 Cor. 15:26). Death is not understood as a law of nature but rather as the penalty of sin (Rom. 5:12f.; 6:23). The destructive power of death rules people's lives. In fact fallen humanity is described as enslaved by the fear of death (Heb. 2:15). But Christ, by his triumph over the grave, has brought deliverance. Death has lost its sting (1 Cor. 15:55) because Christ has died for us (Rom. 5:6f.). For the believer the final destruction of death is present even now as a hope. By the Spirit the resurrection life of Christ is made available to all those who put their faith in Christ. The freedom from the power of death is experienced as a foretaste even now through the presence of the life-giving Spirit.

We have already mentioned Romans 8:2, where Paul explained that the law of the Spirit of life in Christ Jesus has made Christians free from the law of sin and death. Again in 8:6 the mind of the flesh is said to be death, but the mind of the Spirit is life and peace. In 8:10 we are informed that the body is dead because of sin, but the Spirit is "life" because of righteousness. Furthermore, in 8:11 the promise is given: "If the Spirit of him who raised Jesus from the dead dwells in you, he who raised Christ Jesus from the dead will give life to your mortal bodies also through his Spirit which dwells in you." Freedom from death is expressed also in Romans 8:13. "If you live according to the flesh you will die, but if by the Spirit you put to death the deeds of the body you will live."

Although the believer groans together with the rest of creation (8:22), he is sure of the redemption of his body (v. 23), because he has the firstfruits of the Spirit. A very similar thought is
expressed in 2 Corinthians 5:5, where, after sighing for immortality (v. 4), Paul expressed his confidence in victory over
death: "He who has prepared us for this very thing is God, who
has given us the Spirit as guarantee." Similarly, in Ephesians 4:30,
the sealing of the Spirit is for the day of redemption—an oblique
reference to the redemption of the body.

The gift of the Spirit is of course only an "earnest," only the
"first fruits" (Rom. 8:23; 2 Cor. 1:22; 5:5); the complete deliverance from death will not be experienced until the end. But we
know that since Christ broke the power of death by his resurrection and became a "life-giving spirit" (1 Cor. 15:45), his resurrection life is communicated to us by his Spirit. Because the Spirit is
the Spirit of the risen Lord who dwells in the believer, Paul can
identify the destiny of the believer with that of the risen Lord,
which means that he experiences "eternal life" both as a present
possession (Rom. 5:21; 6:22) and as a living hope (Gal. 6:8). The
Spirit is the power of Christ which reaches down into our finite
and mortal existence and unites us with the living Christ in his
eternal life. To be sure, the transformation of our earthly body
into the spiritual is reserved for the future, but the Spirit is already
at work in us. In the words of Cullmann: "Because we on the basis
of the resurrection of Christ and by faith in this redemptive fact
are able in the present to gain possession of the Holy Spirit, we
know that we may hope for the resurrection of the body, which is
effected through the same Spirit who dwells in us (Rom. 8:11)."[33]

In Christ the rule of sin, law, and death has been broken.
These spiritual freedoms are enjoyed by the church through the
work of the Holy Spirit. But the church never "arrives," because
the new age has not yet arrived in its fullness; the church,
therefore, is always on the way.

In this chapter, then, we have tried to show that the Holy
Spirit, who illumines our minds to understand the gospel, comes
into a believer's life when he puts his faith in Christ. The Spirit

makes him a child of God and gives him new life. The Spirit also assures him that he is a member of God's family. And when the Holy Spirit enters the heart of the believer, he delivers him from the bondage of evil powers.

All this is very personal. By the Spirit, however, we as individuals are baptized into the body of Christ. We become related to Christ personally, but we cannot live the Christian life alone. By the Spirit we are made members of a larger community, a "fellowship of the Holy Spirit" (2 Cor. 13:14).

CHAPTER 11

The Spirit and the Christian Community

The risen Lord, who by his resurrection became a life-giving Spirit (1 Cor. 15:45), now embraces in himself all those who put their trust in his saving work on the cross. "That the Holy Spirit is the bond which unites the ascended Lord to his followers and the agency through which they become his members, sharing in his Messianic unction, is the general teaching of the New Testament as a whole," says Professor Lampe.[1]

On the one hand, the apostles stress the continuity of the New Testament church with the Old Testament covenant people, at least with the faithful remnant. Christians are called "the Israel of God" (Gal. 6:16), the true circumcision (Phil. 3:3), the seed of Abraham (Gal. 3:29), true Jews (Rom. 2:28, 29), shoots grafted into the Abrahamic tree (Rom. 11:16-24). On the other hand, the church is a post-Easter, Pentecost creation. For Paul the church's realized existence "begins with the threefold element of the Cross, the Resurrection, and the descent of the Spirit."[2] Or, to put it differently, "as the Messianic Community the Church is inseparably linked in the thought of the New Testament writers with the Spirit. At Pentecost the New Israel was endowed with the Spirit

200

whom Joel had foretold would be the abiding possession of the *ecclesia* in the last days. . . ."[3]

What distinguishes the church from Judaism, including the Qumran community, to say nothing of paganism and its cults, is the consciousness of having received the Holy Spirit as the first-fruits and pledge of redemption.[4] "The Church is the sphere on earth of the incarnation of this Holy Spirit, a visible society with an invisible life, a divine-human phenomenon."[5] By the Spirit the church is constituted, and by the Spirit the life of the church is sustained.

A question we must now address is: How does one become a member of this new people of God? We have already answered that question in part by saying that it is through faith and the gift of the Spirit. But we must move from the individual to the corporate, and this calls for a brief discussion of the Spirit and baptism.

A. The Spirit and Baptism

In the early church baptism followed upon confession of faith in Christ. The practice of allowing for an extended interval between conversion and baptism for the purpose of testing or instructing new converts (however good this innovation was) belongs to a later period; the New Testament does not speak to this question directly. In a missionary situation when Gentile or Jew believed the good news and decided to join the Christian congregation, baptism followed upon conversion as the decisive act by which he was incorporated into the believing community.

Hearing the gospel, believing it, receiving the Spirit, and water-baptism are all different aspects of the same experience. Watson writes:

> The difficulty lies in the fact that Christian initiation, symbolized and sealed by water-baptism, is a united cluster of distinct concepts, including forgiveness, justification, regeneration, death, burial and resurrection with Christ, adoption, the gift and baptism of the Spirit. These concepts are not identical, in meaning or experience. Although they all form one united cluster which belongs to all those in Christ, they can be examined separately, and they may be experienced separately.[6]

It would not be fair, however, to say indiscriminately that salvation is either by baptism or by faith. Salvation is by faith; but the one who believes identifies with a Christian community by baptism. George Johnston writes: "For appropriation of salvation, baptism is less important than faith. God's sons are those led by the Spirit and this Spirit is received by faith and this depends, on the one hand on hearing God's call, on the other, on the hearing of faith."[7] Water-baptism is a visible, external witness to the baptism which the Spirit effects.

1. Baptism with the Spirit

Paul speaks of the baptism with the Spirit only once. In that passage he has the initiation of the new believer into the body of Christ in mind, and this is expressed publicly in water-baptism. When the New Testament contrasts water- and Spirit-baptism, it is always a contrast of John's water-baptism with Christian Spirit-baptism. The Christian community which was born at Pentecost retained water-baptism, but thought of Spirit-baptism as coincident with it. "For by one Spirit we were all baptized into one body—Jews or Greeks, slaves or free—and all were made to drink of one Spirit" (1 Cor. 12:13).

In the four Gospel passages (Mt. 3:11; Mk. 1:8; Lk. 3:16; Jn. 1:33) and the two passages in Acts (1:5; 11:16) in which the baptism with the Spirit is mentioned, the reference is to Pentecost, as we have shown earlier. In 1 Corinthians 12:13, the only passage in the New Testament epistles which refers to the baptism with the Spirit, the reference is not to Pentecost, for neither Paul nor the Corinthians were present when the Spirit was poured out. But as in the other passages which describe the inauguration of the new age and the establishment of the church as a baptism of the Spirit, here too it describes an initiatory process, for it is by Spirit-baptism that the Corinthian believers had become members of the body of Christ.

Some see in this passage a reference to a post-conversion experience by which the believer is lifted up to a new level of existence by a special effusion of the Spirit. This overlooks the fact that the text says that "all" the Corinthians were baptized by the Spirit into the body of Christ. The baptism of the Spirit, then, does not divide the church into the "haves" and the "have-nots," but it is the great uniting factor, for all believers have been baptized by the Spirit. It is the only way persons can become members of Christ's body. To be baptized into Christ's body means to be united with one another in this body.

It is overly subtle to distinguish between a baptism "by" the Spirit and a baptism "with" or "in" the Spirit. One hears it said at times that all believers are baptized "by" the Spirit into the body of Christ, but not all believers are baptized "with" the Spirit. But the Greek expression is the same in all seven passages in which Spirit-baptism is referred to. Also, it is unnatural to make Jesus Christ the baptizer in the other six passages and the Holy Spirit the baptizer in 1 Corinthians 12:13. John R. Stott writes:

> If we put the seven references to this baptism together, we learn that Jesus Christ is the baptizer, as John the Baptist clearly foretold. According to 1 Corinthians 12:13 the baptized are "we all." The Holy Spirit is himself the "element" with, or in *(en)* which the baptism takes place (if one may so describe the Third Person of the trinity; the analogy between baptism with water and baptism with the Spirit seems to make it legitimate). And the purpose of this baptism is incorporation "into *(eis)* one body," namely the body of Christ, the church.[8]

The body of Christ was constituted at Pentecost. By the Spirit the individual members are incorporated into this body. To be incorporated into Christ's body implies that one participates in the Spirit by which it was constituted.

The baptism of the believer into the body of Christ by the Spirit is illustrated by water-baptism. Michael Green writes:

> There are three strands which taken together make a man a Christian. There is the human side—repentance and faith. There is the divine side—reception of the Spirit, adoption into the family of God, forgiveness of sins, justification. There is the churchly side—baptism into the body of believers. And all three belong together and are necessary parts of initiation.[9]

The latter half of 1 Corinthians 12:13 seems to underscore

the first half: "And all were made to drink of one Spirit." Some commentators see in this a reference to the Eucharist, since the first part refers to baptism. Moreover, the drinking of the Spirit can hardly be defined as the reception of spiritual gifts after baptism. If we understand the verb *potizo* as "effusion," then the difference between being baptized with the Spirit and being "flooded" with the Spirit is slight; in fact, it is quite in keeping with Old Testament imagery in which the Spirit is compared to water which floods the ground.[10] The Spirit penetrates the heart like the water drenching the ground; the believer is saturated with the Spirit.

2. The Spirit and Water-Baptism

Although there is only one passage in the Epistles which speaks of the baptism with the Spirit into the body of Christ, there are several passages in which the Spirit is related to water-baptism. One of the important Pauline texts which brings baptism and the Spirit together is 1 Corinthians 6:11: "But you were washed, you were sanctified, you were justified in the name of the Lord Jesus Christ and in the Spirit of our God." It may be said immediately that we should not make too much of the sequence of the three verbs, as if the apostles were outlining for us an order of salvation, for then we would expect "justified" to stand first.

A question that is often asked of this passage is: Does "washed" mean baptism? Schnackenburg argues that the verb refers to baptism on the grounds that (a) a comparison with Acts 22:16—where baptism and washing are mentioned together— shows that this picture does relate to baptism, even though "washing" is not a synonym for baptism; (b) the middle voice with a causative meaning (as in Acts 22:16) suggests that the individual was responsible for "getting himself baptized"; (c) the aorist tenses support a once-for-all foundation act in the past.[11] Most exegetes agree with Schnackenburg that Paul has baptism in mind. Perhaps the reasons Paul used "washed" instead of "baptized" is the appropriateness of the former in relation to the moral uncleanness which Paul has just mentioned (v. 10). Paul here views Christian baptism as a cleansing effected by the Spirit of God. This cleansing activity of the Spirit in baptism is related to the work of Christ; by the Spirit, Christ's salvatory work is made effective in the believer.

It is not the Spirit who does the baptizing in this passage, but the Spirit effects the cleansing of the heart, expressed by the water bath of the baptism. Since the Spirit is called "God's Spirit," Paul seems to be saying that God is the author of redemption: by his Spirit, on the basis of the work of Christ, God washes away our defilement. C. K. Barrett sums it up in this way:

> Arrested and convinced by the work of the Spirit in Christian preaching, they had expressed in baptism the faith created in them, their sins were washed away, they were brought to God and made members of his people, and became justified believers, living by the power of the Spirit.[12]

Another text in which baptism and the Spirit stand together is Ephesians 4:4, 5: "There is one body and one Spirit, just as you were called to the one hope that belongs to your call, one Lord, one faith, one baptism...." In this seven-member credal statement it is once again suggested that by the Spirit a person becomes a member of the body of Christ through faith and upon confession of Christ's lordship, and that this movement is expressed in water-baptism. The different aspects of a believer's incorporation into the church as the body of Christ are brought together in this confessional formula. F. F. Bruce observes: "Baptism in water continued to be the outward and visible sign by which individuals who believed the gospel, repented of their sins, and acknowledged Jesus as Lord were publicly incorporated into this Spirit-baptized fellowship—'baptized into Christ' (Gal. 3:27)."[13]

Baptism and the Spirit are brought together also in Titus 3:5, where Paul speaks of the "washing of regeneration and renewal in the Holy Spirit." Most commentators agree that the "washing" of which Paul speaks here refers to baptism.[14] Whereas some Christians view faith and baptism as antitheses, the apostles look on them as different aspects of a whole.

B. The Fellowship of the Spirit

All believers are baptized by the Spirit into the body of Christ. This body of Christ found visible expression in apostolic times in the many Christian congregations scattered all over the empire. To become a member of any one of them it was required that one receive the gift of the Spirit and be baptized with water (water-baptism signifying what the Spirit had done). The members of the local congregations, and the church as a whole, thought of themselves as a "fellowship of the Spirit."

This phrase, like "the body of Christ," has both a divine-related and a human-related aspect. The divine dimension is seen in that the believer is said to share in God's or Christ's Spirit; the human aspect is seen in that this common participation in the Spirit brings about a new relationship among persons, a relationship established and directed by the Spirit. Vidler points out that "in the New Testament the presence and life of the Spirit are a corporate experience, a shared experience. No individual can recapture that experience by himself or for himself." [15]

That there is a close correlation between the "fellowship with Christ" and the "fellowship of the Spirit" is obvious. The writer to the Hebrews speaks of becoming partakers of Christ (2:14) and "partakers of the Holy Spirit" (6:4). Paul also speaks both of "partaking of Christ" and of "partaking of the Spirit."

Turning our attention now to the expression "the fellowship of the Spirit," we notice that it occurs only twice in Paul's writings, though the idea may be latent in a number of passages. The phrase occurs once in the triadic closing salutation of the second letter to the Corinthians: "The grace of the Lord Jesus Christ and the love of God and the fellowship of the Holy Spirit be with you all" (2 Cor. 13:14).

There has been much dispute on what precisely Paul meant when he wished the Corinthians "the fellowship of the Spirit." The genitive (*pneumatos*) may be either subjective or objective. If subjective, the meaning is: the fellowship which the Spirit effects, creates, or establishes. If objective, Paul is wishing that his readers might participate or share more deeply in the Holy Spirit. Since, however, the other two members of this triad (the grace of our Lord Jesus Christ and the love of God) are clearly subjective genitives it may be assumed that the third member also represents this usage.[16] It is the grace which comes from Christ, the love which God gives, and the fellowship which the Spirit creates.[17] Not all scholars agree, however, and we may have to admit that no amount of exegetical dexterity will give us the precise thought of Paul at this point. He may even have been deliberately ambiguous in order that both aspects be taken into account: a fellowship created by the Spirit and a sharing in the Spirit.

The only other explicit reference to "the fellowship of the Spirit" is Philippians 2:1. "If there is any encouragement in Christ, any incentive of love, any participation in the Spirit, any affection and sympathy. . . ." In this case the two nouns have no articles in Greek, which opens up another possible meaning of the phrase, namely that the genitive *(pneumatos)* is descriptive or qualitative: "spiritual fellowship." That, however, is not generally accepted as the meaning, and so again it is a choice between the objective and subjective genitive. If subjective, the meaning is that the church is a fellowship which is created by the Holy Spirit; if objective, then the church shares in the Holy Spirit.

We have already pointed out that it is not always necessary to come down clearly on one side or the other. One suspects that the desire for such precision goes beyond Paul's interests. We need not doubt, however, that Paul maintained that all believers participated in the Holy Spirit. Ralph Martin observes that "the surrounding context of the verse (2:1) clinches the point that it is the objective reality of the Holy Spirit in whom the church lives in communion and provides the solid basis for Paul's apostolic directive which follows in 2:2-4."[18] On the other hand, it is clear also that only the Spirit of God can create a fellowship in which people can be exhorted to have "the same mind, having the same love, being in full accord and of one mind. Do nothing from selfishness or conceit, but in humility count others better than yourselves" (vv. 2, 3).

The church is not a club of like-minded people who have

common interests and share a common background. It is a fellowship brought into being by the Holy Spirit. This is the "given," the indicative, if you will. But there is an imperative that goes with this indicative, for this fellowship of the Spirit is realized in practice only if certain conditions are met. After mentioning a number of graces that make for unity among the saints, Paul exhorts the Ephesians to "maintain the unity of the Spirit in the bond of peace" (Eph. 4:3). This means that there is a unity in the community which was created by the Holy Spirit, but this unity must be guarded, watched over. By the exercise of love for one another, the believers keep intact this unity that has been created by the Spirit. Immediately following this exhortation we have the confession: "There is one body and one Spirit" (4:4). Here Paul seems to remind the readers of what was given, of the fact; on the basis of this fact he can exhort them to keep the unity which the Spirit has created.

But not only does the Holy Spirit create and animate the church, and not only do the members share in the Spirit, but the Spirit also lives in the church and finds its dwelling place in the new people of God. This is true both of the individual members and of the church as a whole.

C. The Habitation of the Spirit
1. The Indwelling of the Spirit

The indwelling of the church by the Spirit recalls the dwelling of God in the midst of his people in the Old Testament. Although Israel was reminded repeatedly that God could not be contained in a building, there was no doubt in Israel's mind that God had chosen to dwell in a sanctuary in the midst of Israel. And when God's glory departed from Israel, the prophets expressed the hope that in the age to come God would once again live among his people (Ezek. 37:27; Rev. 21:3). This hope of the prophets was fulfilled when "the Word became flesh and dwelt among us" (Jn. 1:14). After completing the work of redemption, Christ lives in and among his people by his Spirit.

In Romans 8:9 Paul says, "But you are not in the flesh, you

are in the Spirit, if in fact the Spirit of God dwells in you." Again, "if the Spirit of him who raised Jesus from the dead dwells in you, he who raised Christ Jesus from the dead will give life to your mortal bodies also through his Spirit which dwells in you" (Rom. 8:11). In these two verses it is stated three times that the Spirit dwells in the believer.[19] The Spirit assures the believer that he is no longer in the flesh (v. 9); the Spirit is the ground for hope in the resurrection (v. 11). There is no great difference between the indwelling of the Spirit and the indwelling of Christ. Whereas Romans 8:9 and 11 speak of the indwelling of the Spirit, the verse in between (v. 10) speaks of Christ's indwelling ("But if Christ is in you . . ."). This leads Bruce to observe:

> It appears, then, that there is no difference between the indwelling of the Spirit and the indwelling of the risen Christ, so far as the believer's experience is concerned, although this does not mean that Paul identified the risen Christ and the Spirit outright. There is a dynamic equivalence between them, but they are nevertheless distinguished.[20]

Parenthetically, Romans 8:9 speaks not only of the Spirit, but it is the only passage in the New Testament where the believer is said "to be" in the Spirit. (The experience of John of being in the Spirit on Patmos, [Rev. 1:10; 4:1] has a different meaning; it refers to divine revelation and inspiration.) We should not make too much of a distinction, however, between the Spirit's dwelling in the believer and the believer being in the Spirit. Leenhardt points out that "both expressions have a common meaning, namely, the Spirit of God governs our existence."[21] Moreover, the formula *en pneumati* (in the Spirit) is a correlate of *en Christo* (in Christ). If we were to distinguish between these two expressions, we might say that the latter summarizes a believer's relationship to Christ and his finished work on the cross, whereas the former points to the power by which Christ's redemptive work is made real in our lives.[22] While the two formulas are not completely interchangeable, they are parallels. From this C. H. Dodd concludes that to be in the Spirit is to be guided and determined by the example and the teachings of Christ.[23]

The indwelling of the Spirit is not to be understood as an ecstatic experience. It speaks rather of that which is constant and permanent, something not dependent on the fluctuating moods of the believer. More than any other figure of speech which is used to describe the work of the Spirit, it stresses the abiding presence of Christ in the life of the believer. Yet it is a presence of one who is absent. Christ comes to us not directly, but his presence is mediated by the Spirit. The Spirit is the connecting link between Christ and the believer. The Spirit is the Spirit of Christ because he relates us to Christ.[24]

Since God had chosen to live in a sanctuary in the midst of his people Israel (the tent was later replaced with the temple), we are not surprised to find Paul speak both of the individual believer and of the church corporately as the temple of the Spirit, for it is by the Spirit that Christ now lives in us.

2. The Temple of the Spirit

In 2 Corinthians 6:16 Paul explicitly says: "For we are the temple of the living God." The Spirit is not mentioned in this passage, but Stalder may be right in suggesting that if Paul had not been so strongly influenced by Old Testament language at this point, he would have spoken of the indwelling of the Holy Spirit.[25] This we cannot prove, but certainly God's dwelling in the midst of his covenant people is the background for Paul's concept of the church as the temple of the Holy Spirit.

In two passages (1 Cor. 3:16; 6:19) Paul speaks of the church and the believer, respectively, as the temple of God in which the Spirit dwells. It is quite possible that Paul knew the saying of Jesus about destroying the temple made with hands and building up another without hands (Mk. 14:58), and that he is here alluding to that tradition in which a glorious temple was anticipated in the days of Messiah. That Messiah would come to his temple was common knowledge. The Qumran community also looked upon itself as a living temple with the membership being the holy place and the inner council the holy of holies (1 QS viii. 2:5f.).[26]

This hope of a new temple was fulfilled when the Spirit was

poured out. The coming of the Spirit made a temple made with hands obsolete; it belonged to an age that was past; with the coming of the Spirit a new age began. "Do you not know that you are God's temple and that God's Spirit dwells in you?" writes Paul in 1 Corinthians 3:16. The church is God's "shrine" *(naos)* in which the Spirit dwells.[27] Whereas in pagan shrines the image of the god is set up, the Jewish sanctuary had no image, for Yahweh could not be likened to anything. Nevertheless God was present in the sanctuary. In the New Testament, in keeping with what Jesus told the Samaritan woman regarding the proper place of worship (Jn. 4:21), God does not dwell in houses, but among his people; the people of God themselves are the temple.

Peter calls the church a "spiritual house" (1 Pet. 2:5). In this house Christ is the living stone, the cornerstone, the stone which the builders rejected, the stone of stumbling and rock of offense. The members of the community are the living stones in this spiritual house.[28]

Paul introduces 1 Corinthians 3:16 and 6:19 with the rhetorical question "Do you not know?" as if to remind his readers of the dwelling of God among men about which they were well-informed. On the other hand, Paul may be employing a pedagogical device, suggesting to his readers that they should live up to what they in fact were: a temple of God in which the Spirit lives. Sins against the temple were punished very severely (Stephen lost his life because he spoke against the temple), and so Paul warned those who would foment divisions in Corinth of the heinousness of ruining God's temple.

Although the Spirit dwells within the church as God's new temple, one cannot equate every institutional church today with the temple of the Holy Spirit. The Spirit remains free; it is not bound by ecclesiastical structures and human traditions. The Spirit also works outside the institutional church. But even when the institutional church is full of imperfections, the Spirit keeps on speaking to the church, as John reminds us in the seven letters to the churches of Asia (Rev. 2 and 3).

In 1 Corinthians 6:19 Paul says that the body of every believer is a temple of the Holy Spirit. "Do you not know that your body is a temple of the Holy Spirit within you, which you have from God?" Even though Paul has the individual in mind in this passage, he is not thinking "individualistically"; the corporate community is always in the background. But the corporate "temple of the Spirit" is made up of individuals who are also described as sacred shrines where the Spirit lives.

In this context Paul is warning the Corinthians against licentious living. But by underscoring the sanctity of the body of the believer, he is arguing for sexual purity. If the body of the believer is united with Christ through the Holy Spirit, then he cannot unite that body with a harlot. In fact the body has been redeemed and no longer belongs to the believer himself; it belongs to God. He purchased it at the cost of the blood of Christ (v. 20). The body is now indwelt by the Holy Spirit and is an instrument in the service of God. Moreover, because the Spirit indwells the believer, the body has a high destiny; "God will raise us up through his power" (1 Cor. 6:14). In contrast to Gnosticism, where the "spirit" is valued so highly in comparison to the body, the coming of the Holy Spirit to dwell in a believer's body makes it a holy shrine.[29]

In Ephesians 2:20-22 the figure of the "temple of the Spirit" is expanded and related to the old traditions of the "chief stone" of the building of God. The stone oracle in Isaiah 28:16 speaks of the precious cornerstone which God is laying in Zion. This dwelling place of God, in which Christ is the chief stone, was established by the apostles and prophets (Eph. 2:20). The building is held together by Christ, the chief stone, who also gives the building life and strength. Every believer has a place in this building, which is growing into a "holy temple" (v. 21), into a dwelling place of God—and all of this "by the Spirit."

It is the Spirit of God who establishes and sustains this spiritual building, the church. The Spirit is not an appendage of the church, added after its founding; it is the power by which the church emerges,[30] built at its deepest level on the foundation which is Jesus Christ (1 Cor. 3:11).

J. G. Davies suggests that from the Christological point of view the church is static, built on an unshakable foundation, but from a pneumatological point of view it is dynamic.[31] The temple of the Holy Spirit is a present reality, and yet it still needs to be built. The church lives in this kind of polarity, in a tension between present reality and its complete realization at the end when "the Lord God the Almighty and the Lamb" are the temple (Rev. 21:22).

That the image of the church as a temple is not an idealized picture can be seen from Paul's application of the figure to a far-from-perfect community. The rather unsaintly saints of Corinth were reminded that they were a temple of the Spirit. But in spite of all the weaknesses of the flesh, and in spite of the church's many failings, God's Spirit has taken possession of the new people of God; through his Spirit the exalted Lord is effectively present in the community of mortal human beings who confess his name here on earth.

Perhaps we can sum this up with some comments of T. W. Manson:

> The Church is a special creation by God in Christ within which the Holy Spirit—the Spirit of God and the Spirit of Christ—is the ruling power. As such it is the body of Christ because it is the place where God's will is accepted and obeyed; it is the family of God because in it God is really known as Father and the members as brethren.[32]

We need to say more about the Spirit with reference to the family of God.

D. The Spirit and the Family of God

In 2 Corinthians 6:16-18, where Paul calls the church God's temple (v. 16), he concludes with Old Testament covenant formulas reminiscent of Isaiah 43:6 and Jeremiah 31:9: "And I will be a Father to you, and you shall be my sons and daughters" (v. 18). Together with other New Testament writers Paul thought of the Christian community as a family of God. Repeatedly he calls the church a "house" or "household," believers are called "children" or "sons," and they look upon each other as "brothers." If we ask what connection there is between the Holy Spirit and the family of God, we notice that Paul relates the Spirit to adoption and to open access to God our Father.

1. The Spirit and Adoption

The idea of adoption (*huiothesia*—the installation as a son or daughter) has deep roots in salvation history. Israel was God's chosen son (Ex. 4:22; Deut. 14:2; Hos. 11:1). This implied that God had chosen Israel by his free grace and Israel had both privileges and responsibilities as heir of God's promises. Paul on one occasion used the term "adoption" (*huiothesia*) for Israel's privileges as a nation (Rom. 9:4); in the remaining four passages (Rom. 8:15, 23; Gal. 4:5; Eph. 1:5) it is used to describe the privileges and responsibilities of the members of the New Testament church who have entered into the spiritual inheritance of Old Testament Israel. In most instances "sonship" is a satisfactory translation, although "adoption" may be preferable when it is stressed that the sons of God have been given a place in God's family by the unmerited favor of God.

Twice Paul relates "adoption" to the Holy Spirit (Rom. 8:15, 23; Gal. 4:5). Stanley probably overstates the case, but he does underscore the importance of the work of the Spirit in this area of thought when he says that "the most characteristically Pauline view of the work of the Spirit is that which presents him as the Spirit of our adoptive filiation."[33] Similarly Dunn: "A primary element in the experience of the Spirit is awareness and assurance of sonship which he brings."[34]

In Galatians 4 we are informed that Christ came to redeem us "so that we might receive adoption" (vv. 4, 5). And Paul continues, "Because you are sons, God has sent the Spirit of his Son into our hearts, crying 'Abba! Father!' So through God you are no longer a slave but a son, and if a son then an heir" (vv. 6, 7). The Holy Spirit is here called "the Spirit of his Son."

We should not try to make too much of the distinction between Christ's Spirit and God's Spirit, for the Holy Spirit is

God's Spirit which has been sent by the risen Christ. In fact our text says that the same God who sent his Son also sent the Spirit of his Son into our hearts. That God sent the Spirit of his Son into our hearts is a way of saying that what happened at Calvary, Easter, and Pentecost is now made real in human experience. It is through the Spirit that the effects of Christ's work are mediated. Hamilton puts it this way: "The Spirit provides subjective evidence ... to the believer of his objective sonship."[35] And how does this assurance of membership in God's family express itself? By the cry "Abba!" God not only makes us sons through Jesus Christ but he verifies this privileged standing through his Spirit, who moves the believer to express this new relationship by the filial cry of "Father!" The word "cry" *(krazo)* is a forceful word, indicating that this is not a vague conviction but an awareness of no little intensity.

With membership in God's family comes the added blessing of heirship (Gal. 4:7). To call believers "heirs" indicates that all the gifts of salvation which the Holy Spirit assures us are experienced in this life only as a foretaste; the fulfillment is still to come. Indeed, from Romans 8:14-23 it becomes clear that even "sonship" is enjoyed only in a small measure compared to that full standing as sons and daughters in the age to come. Paul begins by declaring that those who are led by the Spirit of God are true sons of God (Rom. 8:14). He goes on to say: "For you did not receive the spirit of slavery to fall back into fear, but you have received the spirit of sonship. When we cry, 'Abba! Father!' ..." (There is some question of punctuation in this verse.) Barrett says, "The very fact that you can address God as Abba proves that the Spirit is at work among you and that you are God's children."[36]

One might say that when a believer is adopted into the family of God, the first word he articulates is "Father." It is the Holy Spirit who teaches us to recognize God as Father. In contrast to Galatians 4:6, where the Spirit makes our adoption real, here the Spirit makes people to be sons and daughters of God and enables them to call God their Father. This same Spirit who makes us God's sons, also assures us that we are God's children ("sons" and "children" are used interchangeably by Paul). The Spirit attests and certifies to us *(summarturei)* that we belong to God's family. "In other words, the relationship of the believer to God, which it was the purpose of the Incarnation to establish, is made an experienced fact by the presence of the Spirit."[37]

In spite of all the blessings of sonship enjoyed in the present, we still wait anxiously *(apekdechomai)* for "adoption" (Rom. 8:23), which is defined as the redemption of the body. At the moment we live in the twilight of the old age and the age to come, but the Spirit who assures us of our sonship also gives us the hope of its complete fulfillment in the age to come. In that day we shall see God; but while we wait we have the assurance by his Spirit that we can approach him freely in our prayers.

2. The Spirit and Access to God

The free access to God which the Holy Spirit opens up to the believer is a gift that Jews and Gentiles have alike (Eph. 2:11ff.). By his blood Christ (2:13) has made those who were once "far off" (Gentiles) to be "near" (i.e., members of the people of God). By the cross these two factions in humankind have been reconciled "in one body" (2:16). The "one" body seems to have a dual meaning: it is Christ's body which hung on the cross by which peace was made; but it is also the "body of Christ," the church, in which this reconciliation is experienced. "For through him we both have access in one Spirit to the Father" (2:18).

The word "access" *(prosagoge)* is used in a variety of ways: for bringing a sacrifice to God, for consecrating people to God, but above all, for introducing a person into the presence of a king. Therefore, the word may be appropriately translated "introduction."[38] Both Jew and Gentile can now come into God's presence "in one Spirit." It is through the work of the Spirit of God that Christ's act of reconciliation becomes effective and fruitful, by breaking down the barriers of hatred and prejudice.

Because Gentiles now also have access to the Father by the Spirit of God, they are no longer aliens and foreigners but citizens like all the "saints and members of the household of God" (v. 19).

Here the image of the church as a family quickly changes to that of a building which grows into a holy temple and this takes place "in the Spirit" (v. 22).

By the Holy Spirit the reconciling work of Christ is made effective and the family of God emerges whose membership is no longer limited by race, culture, or social standing. The Spirit unites believers of diverse backgrounds into one family in which all members have the same privilege of access to the Father. They can all worship him without restrictions "in Spirit and in truth."

We have seen, then, that the Holy Spirit is the author of the Christian community. He baptizes individual believers into Christ's body and binds them together into a fellowship of the Spirit. The Holy Spirit comes to dwell in the hearts of individual believers; likewise, the church may be described as a habitation of the Spirit. Moreover, since all of God's children have the same Spirit by which they call God their Father, and all have the freedom of access into his presence, the church is viewed as God's family.

Up to this point we have focused on the gracious work of the Spirit in creating a new people of God and initiating individual members into this new community. We must now pay attention to the new way of life that springs from such beginnings. In the words of F. F. Bruce:

> The prime function of the indwelling Spirit in the believing community, as in the individual believer, is for Paul the reproduction of the Christ-likeness in his people, until the whole body corporate attains "the measure of the stature of the fulness of Christ" (Ephesians 4:13).[39]

CHAPTER 12

The Spirit and the Christian Life

The restoration of humankind to a new way of life is the work of God the Father, the Son, and the Holy Spirit. Peter puts it thus: "Chosen and destined by God the Father and sanctified by the Spirit for obedience to Jesus Christ and for sprinkling with his blood" (1 Pet. 1:2). The early Christians thought of themselves as the people of God and for that reason spoke of themselves as chosen, selected, or elected by God, as Israel was chosen in the Old Testament. And just as obedience lay at the heart of the Old Testament covenant (Ex. 19:5), so the new people of God have been chosen and destined for "obedience to Jesus Christ." But all of this is made possible by the work of the Holy Spirit. "The choice and purpose of God takes effect through the activity of the Spirit who deals with men in sanctification to set them apart and make them fit for this heavenly calling."[1] When the gospel is heard the Spirit applies God's saving work to the heart of the obedient hearer, convinces him of the trustworthiness of Christ's work on the cross, and makes him obedient to the gospel. Whereas Peter seems to have the initial response of obedience to the gospel in mind, the implication is that this act of obedience will lead to obedience to Christ in daily life.

This work of the Spirit in the human heart, enabling persons to respond to the gospel in which God's election grace is proclaimed, is based on the work of Jesus Christ—"the sprinkling with his blood." Such terminology finds its background in the covenant-making ceremony at Sinai (Ex. 24:3-8) when the altar and the people were sprinkled with blood after Israel promised to obey the words of the covenant. God's saving purposes were carried out by the death of Jesus, by his blood, and the Holy Spirit makes that which happened at the cross, nearly two thousand years ago, a reality in our lives by setting us apart from evil and enabling us to live in obedience to Jesus.

One cannot separate the beginning of the new life in Christ with its continuation. "As therefore you received Christ Jesus the Lord, so live in him (Col. 2:6). While the Spirit, like the wind, is not visible, the coming of the Spirit into a person's life will be visible from its effects on him or her. Where there are no sound effects, one concludes that there is no wind. So, too, when a person does not bow visibly in some way before the wind of the Spirit, one must conclude there is no Spirit. To the Galatians Paul writes: "If we live by the Spirit, let us also walk by the Spirit" (Gal. 5:25). What does it mean to walk in the Spirit?

A. Walking in the Spirit

"Walking" is one of the most common metaphors in the New Testament to describe the life of the Christian. It is a Hebraic concept. Of the great saints of the Old Testament, such as Enoch, it was said that they walked with God. A person's walk comes to stand for his outlook on life, his spiritual and ethical orientation, his behavior. To be a Christian means not only to believe certain things, but also to live a certain way. In fact early Christians were called the people of "the Way" (Acts 19:9, 23). In the Old Testament "God's ways" is an equivalent of "God's commandments." When Paul calls on his converts to remember his "ways in Christ" (1 Cor. 4:17), he is exhorting them to obey his teaching on how to "walk" as Christians.

Paul uses several different Greek words, all of which are

translated into English as "walk." There is the simple *peripateo*, to patter about (our "peripatetic" is derived from it). It is found more than 30 times in Paul alone, with the meaning of living in a certain way.[2] "But I say, walk [*peripateo*] by the Spirit" (Gal. 5:16). At the end of the passage that begins with this exhortation Paul changes words: "If we live by the Spirit, let us also walk [*stoicheo*] by the Spirit" (v. 25). *Stoicheo* means to walk in a straight line, to walk in step; perhaps we could render it: "keep in step with the Spirit." There are other words for walk, but these two are found in a key passage that deals with a believer's walk in the Spirit and we want to restrict ourselves to Galatians 5:16-26.

This passage stands in a broader context in which the apostle warns his readers against legalism, on the one hand, and against license, on the other. These two dangers have attended the church's existence all through the centuries, and Paul offers the life in the Spirit as the antidote to both of these errors. The Spirit delivers the believer from bondage, yet binds him to Christ in such a way that he is careful to do his bidding. In Galatians 5, Paul first exhorted Christians to walk in (or by) the Spirit.

1. The Apostolic Exhortation

"But I say, walk by the Spirit, and do not gratify the desires of the flesh" (Gal. 5:16). Grammatically the command could be rendered either as walk "in" the Spirit or "by" the Spirit. The meaning is not too different, for quite clearly Paul has in mind the power of the Spirit by which the believer can overcome the dominion of the flesh.

To walk in the Spirit does not mean that the believer is engaged exclusively in so-called spiritual activities: praying, singing, reading the Bible, and going to church—although these may very well be part of walking in the Spirit. If this were the meaning, however, Christians could obviously not walk in the Spirit all the time. The apostle wants the entire life of the readers to be a walk in the Spirit, even in earthly or mundane activities, including family life, business ventures, daily work, eating and drinking, and so forth.

The imperative implies that the life in the Spirit does not happen mechanically or automatically. It speaks of human responsibility. Not that we can walk in the Spirit by our own strength, but we must yield ourselves in obedience so that the Spirit can enable us to live a God-pleasing life. Moreover, the imperative is in the present tense and could be rendered "keeping on walking in the Spirit," all the time, day by day.

This walk in the Spirit should not be understood as a series of spiritual "highs" followed by spiritual "lows." Emotionally we may have "highs" and "lows," but the life of the Spirit is not determined by our nervous system; it is not a matter of "mood." It is possible to walk in the Spirit in joy and in sorrow, on dark days and bright, in success and disappointment. To walk in the Spirit is to trust in God's power which is given to us by his Spirit.

We have noticed earlier that to be in the Spirit is not different from being in Christ, although there may be different nuances in these two expressions. To walk in the Spirit is to live a Christlike life, for the Spirit, as Jesus promised, was to glorify him. This means that a life in the Spirit is a life lived in keeping with the teachings of Jesus. So often enthusiasts have felt "led" by the Spirit without regard for Jesus' commandments; that always leads to chaos.

Paul does not address his command to walk in the Spirit to some spiritually superior group in the church, the spiritual athletes or the church's spiritual leaders. Paul does not have a double standard of holiness for clergy and laity. In the early period of the church all members were called "saints," not just the martyrs or those who outdid others in sacred duties. All those who come to life in the Spirit must and can walk in the Spirit. That does not mean, however, that there are no conflicts in such a life.

2. The Moral Conflict

"For the desires of the flesh are against the Spirit, and the desires of the Spirit are against the flesh; for these are opposed to each other, to prevent you from doing what you would." The believer, who has the Spirit of God, still is in conflict with the flesh;

that is, he is still in this age when the flesh exercises its power. At the same time, however, the believer tastes of the powers of the age to come by the indwelling Spirit. This ambiguous situation leads to conflict.

The conflict Paul has in mind here is not a struggle between physical weakness and mental strength, the human spirit. If we think of the conflict in these terms we can easily fall into the error of Gnosticism in which the body was looked upon as evil and only the spirit was good. Rather, Paul has a moral conflict in mind, in which the Spirit of God stands over against the power of the flesh. "Flesh" must not be understood simply as sensuality; it covers the whole scope of evil in our lives. Nor should "flesh" be equated with "body," for by confusing the two, some have tried to attain to greater holiness by suppressing all bodily desires. Indeed, some have mutilated their bodies in the interests of greater holiness.

Nor should we think of the conflict between Spirit and flesh as a conflict of two persons, as if we were divided personalities. Then we could attribute our misdeeds to the flesh and our good deeds to the Spirit and assume no responsibility for either; but we are held responsible for all that we do. It has often been suggested that Paul has the rabbinic concept of the two impulses (the *yetzer ha tob* and *yetzer ha ra'*) in mind. Some rabbis even localized these impulses, the good impulse in the right and the bad impulse in the left kidney, and prescribed all kinds of ways for keeping the evil impulse under control.[3] This was, in fact, a somewhat idealistic view of humanity for it was thought that persons had it within their power to keep the evil impulse under control. But Paul seems to think of the power of evil, the flesh, as an occupation army that has invaded our lives, and without the help of the Spirit of God we are defeated. These two, says Paul, "lie over against each other," like two armies locked in deadly combat.

There is victory, to be sure, but there is no escape from the conflict. Those who teach that the flesh can be eradicated, perhaps by some second work of grace, have not grasped the power of evil nor understood the meaning of Scripture on this point. There is no once-for-all escape from the flesh, this gravitational pull in our lives. Indeed, some of the saintliest Christians have the most acute struggles with the power of evil in their lives. By the Spirit, however, it is possible for an impatient person to become long-suffering, a person with a fiery temper to become meek, a stingy person to become generous.

Paul's understanding of salvation implies that the gracious gifts of God impose obligations upon the believer.[4] They summon the believer to moral action; but this moral endeavor is based on God's saving power which is made real to the believer by the Holy Spirit. The Holy Spirit represents both the demand and supply— demand, in that it calls us to a holy life; supply, in that it makes available the power of Christ's resurrection. The Spirit gives the believer the assurance that Christ has broken the power of sin. This becomes for him the imperative to walk in the Spirit. As he yields his life to the Spirit, he discovers a potential that lies outside himself by which he is enabled to please God.

To indicate clearly what Paul means by the flesh, against which the Spirit has taken up warfare, Paul gives us a long list of works of the flesh (Gal. 5:19, 20). The list begins with sexual aberrations, then goes on to the sins of idolatry and black magic. The works of the flesh include also the sins of the mind and the human spirit: enmity, strife, jealousy, anger, selfishness, dissension, party strife, envy. Even God-given healthy appetites such as eating and drinking can become works of the flesh through overindulgence. Paul does not suggest that all these evil things are always present in the believer's life, but certainly the believer is capable of falling into any of these sins and many more, for the apostle makes it plain that he is giving only samples ("and the like," v. 21). Paul does not have to list all the possible "works" of the flesh, for the believer has the Spirit of God and the Spirit instructs him on what is of the flesh and what is of God. Over against this dark list of "works" of the flesh Paul sets the "fruit" of the Spirit, of which we shall have more to say later. He adds that where love, joy, peace, and other Christian graces grow the law has to keep silent: "Against such there is no law" (Gal. 5:23). There cannot be a restraining law against them when they are exactly the kind of behavior and attitudes God is looking for. The life in the Spirit begins with a "crucifixion" of the flesh; it continues day by day with the Spirit of Christ creating in us a rich harvest of Christian graces. Thus we live victoriously by the power of the Spirit.

B. Led by the Spirit

In the passage we have just discussed Paul speaks also of the "guidance" of the Spirit. "If you are led by the Spirit you are not under the law" (Gal. 5:18). This makes the "walk" in the Spirit much more personal; it emphasizes the voluntary subjection of the will of the believer to the Holy Spirit. Moreover, the distinction here is not between "flesh" and "Spirit," but between "Spirit" and "law." The Spirit is, of course, antithetical to both "flesh" and "law" (when law is understood as legalism; for legalism is just another expression of the flesh). Legalism and a life under the direction of the Spirit are opposites. To be guided by the Spirit does not mean enslavement to legalism on the one hand, nor does it mean license, on the other. The Spirit, however, never leads the believer to act contrary to God's holy law. In fact, the Spirit supplies him with the strength to fulfill God's law, and that explains why Paul can say that the one led by the Spirit is not under law; the law is silenced by obedience.

The guidance of the Spirit must not be understood as some kind of compulsion which the believer can do nothing about. The passive voice of the verb "to lead" *(agesthe)* suggests that the believer yields to the leading of the Spirit. Perhaps one could compare this kind of leading to that of the gentle guidance of a shepherd who leads his flock, in contrast to a driver of cattle who cracks the whip over them and forces them ahead.

A question that naturally arises is: How does the Spirit guide the believer? Sometimes, no doubt, the Spirit nudges us on by inner monitions. The Spirit's voice may come to us through outward circumstances—perhaps the closing of one door and the opening of another. At other times the Spirit may guide us through the words or the example of another believer. One might even submit a matter to the discernment of a group of Christians. Or some godly person may have a "word of wisdom" for us. Then, too, the Lord often guides us through the Scriptures. This approach is open to abuse when, for example, a verse is picked out at random and the will of the Lord discerned by it. Yet a passage of Scripture may well be God's voice saying, "This is the way, walk in it." One cannot very well conceive of the Spirit's guidance apart from prayer, either. In any case, there is no one way in which the Spirit guides all the time. Moreover, we should not think of the Spirit's guidance only when we have decisions to make with regard to our career, family matters, and the many other decisions we face in the course of our daily calling. We need to discern the Spirit's guidance particularly in ethical decision making, in matters of right and wrong. That is the primary concern of our text. Similarly, in Ephesians 5, a "careful walk" is one in which the believer discerns what the will of the Lord is, and that kind of walk is closely tied to the fullness of the Spirit (vv. 15-18).

The believer is called upon to "learn what is pleasing to the Lord" (Eph. 5:10), or to "approve what is excellent" (Phil. 1:10). In a great number of cases he has a clear word of God to guide him. One might think of the Ten Commandments or the many ethical instructions we have in the New Testament, both in the teachings of Jesus and of his apostles. But there are numerous life situations in which no specific word of Scripture can be quoted when ethical decisions have to be made. This is where the Holy Spirit steps into the picture. The Spirit's guidance will not be contrary to Scripture, but he will bring the broader principles of Scripture to bear on our particular problem. It is as Klaus Bockmühl writes: "Fletcher's new morality abolished the law in favor of the situation. Biblical situation ethics is convinced that the Spirit will meet the righteous demands of the law (Rom. 8:4). Law and the Spirit fit together: they are the word of the same God."[5] David Watson, in a striking aphorism, says essentially the same thing: "All word and no Spirit, we dry up; all Spirit and no word, we blow up; both word and Spirit, we grow up."[6]

Another passage in which Paul speaks of the guidance of the Spirit is Romans 8:14. "For all who are led by the Spirit of God are sons of God." One should not read this passage as if Paul were making sonship dependent on the degree to which a believer is under the guidance of the Spirit. What Paul means is that all of God's sons experience the guidance of the Spirit. It is a word of assurance, that those who are led by God's Spirit are members in the family of God.

Precisely what Paul means by "led" (*ago* in the passive) is not easily established. Perhaps the difference between "being led" and "walking" in the Spirit is not all that great. *The New English Bible* translates *ago* (lead) in our text by "moved." Since the Spirit is the Spirit of Christ (Rom. 8:9, 10), perhaps the leading of the Spirit should again be related to Christlike behavior. C. H. Dodd suggests: "To have the Spirit does not mean, as it used to mean, that some mysterious stream of divine essence is passing into the human organism. It means being in the most intimate conceivable touch with a Person."[7] The leading of the Spirit seems to embrace both insight into God's will and an urge to do it. Paul gave the churches ethical guidelines, but there still remained a great many situations in which the individual would have difficulty in applying them, and for this he needed the guidance of the Spirit.

That the Spirit plays a part in sensitizing the Christian's conscience can be seen from Romans 9:1. Here Paul insists that his love for Israel is genuine and points to the witness of the Holy Spirit in his conscience. "My conscience bears me witness in the Holy Spirit." The apostle appeals to his conscience as a trustworthy witness to his love for Israel on the ground that his conscience is formed by the Spirit. That conscience is not the highest court of appeal can be seen from 1 Corinthians 4:4, but the believer must have a good conscience (1 Tim. 1:5). As he submits to the Spirit of God, his conscience is conformed to the will of God.[8] The Holy Spirit "is the Spirit of truth and He brings the truth to shine upon the conscience. When He does so, the conscience becomes a fully informed conscience."[9] In the matter of guidance, then, conscience plays an important role if it is enlightened by Christ and sensitized by the Spirit of God.

C. Strengthened by the Spirit

Writing from prison Paul expressed confidence in his letter to the Philippians that his trials would result in deliverance (1:19). Just what he means by that is not quite certain. It could mean physical deliverance, or that God will not permit him to be put to shame (v. 20), or that he will be saved in the day of Christ, or, quite generally, that all will be well in the end. In any case, he has two good reasons for being confident: the prayers of the Philippians and the Spirit of Jesus Christ. The intercession of his friends and the rich supply of the Spirit of Christ are the two sources which inspire Paul's confidence that Christ will be made great, whether by life or death (v. 20). The noun "supply" (*epichoregia*) is found only here and in Ephesians 4:16 (the verb is more common), and indicates abundant supply.

Bonnard thinks this expression is an allusion to the promise of Jesus to his disciples that the Spirit would come to their aid when they had to face human tribunals (Mk. 13:11; Lk. 12:12).[10] Lohmeyer suggests that it is the help of the Spirit in special need—help in a moment of crisis.[11] In the face of martyrdom Paul looked to the Holy Spirit to give him the strength he needed to remain true to Jesus and to be a good witness to his Lord.

Ephesians speaks more generally of the strengthening of the Spirit. In his second prayer in that letter Paul asks that the readers "be strengthened with might through his Spirit in the inner man" (Eph. 3:16). The "inner man" is not the "new nature" (Eph. 4:24), but a kind of synonym for the "I" (Rom. 7:17, 20), the heart, the real person. Masson points out that there is little difference between the work of the Spirit in the "inner man" and the expression "that Christ dwell through faith in your hearts."[12] "To have Christ dwelling in us and to have the Spirit dwelling in us are the same thing. Indeed, it is precisely by the Spirit that Christ dwells in our hearts."[13] The strengthening in the inner man which the Spirit effects is generous, "according to the riches of his glory." The end result of the strengthening by the Spirit is the knowledge of the love of Christ (vv. 18, 19)—a knowledge unattainable by the person ouside of Christ (1 Cor. 2:14).

When we speak of being strengthened by the Spirit we should remember that God's power is made manifest in weakness (2 Cor. 12:10). The quest for spiritual power can be quite irreligious if one seeks it for one's own gratification. It induces precisely that self-centeredness which the whole experience of religion is designed to annihilate.[14]

> It is not power promised for power's sake, or power for our sake. It is not influence promised for the sake of influence. It is not power to bolster our image or our ego. It is not power so that we can dominate other people's lives or manipulate and control their thinking, their emotions, or their wills. It is not our power in place of our weakness. It is God's power manifest in our weakness. It is God's power using our human weakness as a platform on which it can be seen to be God's power; God's power using our frail storm lamp as a holder from which to shine into the hearts of men; God's power is a tent surrounding us, supporting the framework of the weakness of our human nature. The weakness remains—the power transcends it.[15]

Such observations are in line with what Paul wrote to the Romans: "Likewise the Spirit helps us in our weakness" (8:26a). "Weakness" is a comprehensive term and covers the whole range of human infirmities that characterize our life here on earth. But we are not left to ourselves; the Spirit comes to our aid and strengthens us.

D. Transformed by the Spirit

A fundamental motif of all New Testament ethical teachings is that by faith in Jesus Christ and the presence of the Spirit the believer has a foretaste of what he will become in the future. He is already holy, but he will become so fully only in the end. The new life which the Spirit inaugurated has not yet been completed; the Christian is in the process of transformation—of sanctification— and the Spirit plays an active role in this process. Of course we must not view sanctification individualistically; this transformation of character takes place within the community of the saints. In the interim, between the cross and the parousia, the Holy Spirit is at work transforming the church into the image of Christ.

This is expressed nowhere so vividly as in 2 Corinthians 3:18.

"And we all, with unveiled face, beholding the glory of the Lord, are being changed into his likeness from one degree of glory to another; for this comes from the Lord who is the Spirit." Whereas Paul speaks repeatedly of the final transformation of the believer into the image of Christ (1 Cor. 15:49; Rom. 8:29; Phil. 3:21), here the emphasis lies on the process of transformation that goes on daily.[16]

In a sense 2 Corinthians 3:18 is the high point of the argument of the entire chapter. In contrast to the old order, where Moses alone stood before God "with unveiled face" (Ex. 34:29ff.), this is now the privilege of all the saints. The attempt to restrict the "all" to ministers of the gospel and not to Christians generally is misdirected.[17] The verb *katoptrizo* generally means "to behold oneself in a mirror." Some versions prefer to render it as "reflecting as a mirror"; while this would suit the context quite well in the sense that the Christian reflects the glory which he has seen, it is more natural to suppose it is by "beholding" the image of Christ, rather than by reflecting it, that the Christian becomes changed. Whatever may be the exact significance of this difficult word, the main emphasis of the verse is on the transformation into the image of Christ as he contemplates the glory of the Lord.

"From glory to glory" may mean that the glory which the believer sees in Christ creates a similar glory in him; or that the believer reflects the glory which comes from Christ; or that the Christian advances from one stage of glory to another as he is transformed by God's Spirit.[18] If the latter, then this process of transformation is in anticipation of future glory. By the Spirit's work in transforming the saints the future glory seems to be experienced proleptically.

This reproduction of the image of Christ in the lives of his people is the Spirit's most congenial ministry, and forms a preparation for that day when Christ, their true life, will be manifested, and they too "will be manifested with him in glory" (Colossians 3:4), wearing in its perfection "the image of the man of heaven" (1 Corinthians 15:49).[19]

The general thrust of the passage seems to be that the Spirit, who is the power of the exalted Lord, transforms the believer into the image of Christ. This process of transformation into the image of Christ is elsewhere called "sanctification."[20] "That the work of the Spirit in the Church is primarily that of sanctification is emphasized by the application to Him of the epithet Holy," says J. G. Davies.[21]

    We have already mentioned the passage from 1 Peter where the believers are said to be "sanctified by the Spirit for obedience to Jesus Christ" (1:2). When the gospel is proclaimed the Holy Spirit lays hold of those who respond in obedience, plucks them out of the realm of the profane, and puts them into the sphere of the sacred.[22] In 1 Corinthians 6:11, the Spirit is related to the washing, sanctification, and justification of the believer. Also, we are reminded of the passage in 2 Thessalonians where Paul says that the salvation of the readers occurred "through sanctification by the Spirit and belief in the truth" (2:13). All these passages, however, refer to the principal "setting apart" of the believer for God and his service which takes place at conversion. This is true also of Romans 15:16, where Paul claims that his Gentile converts (who were regarded by some Jewish Christians as unclean because they were not circumcised) were in fact "sanctified by the Holy Spirit."

    Sanctification, however, is not only an initial act but a process; holiness must be "perfected" (2 Cor. 7:1). This aspect of the Spirit's activity is portrayed quite realistically in 1 Thessalonians 4:1-8. Before exhorting his readers to sexual purity, Paul puts the whole matter on a high plane by saying: "This is the will of God, your sanctification" (v. 3). He then touches upon a particular area of sanctification, namely, sexual morality. Very likely he is repeating at this point what he had given his converts orally.[23] Christian missionaries in that early period seem to have had a common core of ethical teachings, as may be seen by comparing Paul's instructions with those of Peter (e.g., 1 Pet. 1:13-22).

    Not only are the Thessalonians to strive after holiness because it is God's will and God is an avenger of evil, but also because they are called to holiness (v. 7). What is more, those who treat the question of sanctification lightly despise God, "who gives his Holy Spirit to you" (v. 8). The implication is that the one who treats sexual aberrations lightly sins against the continuing presence of the Holy Spirit.

Usually Paul speaks of the Spirit as having been given, but here the Spirit is a gift of God which comes to man continuously. The one who carries on in his pagan ways with impunity is not simply breaking a human code, he is sinning against both God and his gift, the Holy Spirit, by which he is present with his people. We have mentioned earlier the references to the indwelling of the Spirit in the believer's life, obligating him to holy living (1 Cor. 3:16; 6:19). Also, we have mentioned the power of the Spirit in overcoming the flesh in the Christian's daily walk (Gal. 5:16-26). "The Spirit is the sanctifying agency in the lives of believers; he wages perpetual warfare against the flesh, but he is more powerful than the flesh, and can put the flesh progressively out of action in those lives which are yielded to his control."[24]

Sanctification is both a present possession as well as an ongoing process effected by God's Spirit. And while the believer cannot change himself, the transformation of his life does not happen automatically. All of God's gifts demand a response, and the writer to the Hebrews can exhort his readers to strive after holiness "without which no one will see the Lord" (Heb. 12:14). Sanctification is not an option for the one who has been saved by God's grace; the desire to be transformed into the image of Christ arises out of the initial sanctification by the Spirit by which we are set apart for God and which calls for separation from the evil and the profane. While striving for perfection, however, the believer recognizes that perfect holiness is a state to which he will attain only in glory. Like Paul, he must forever forget what is behind and strain forward, pressing on toward the goal for the prize of the upward call of God in Christ Jesus (Phil. 3:12-14).

For those who have grown weary in their struggle against the evil of their hearts and the weakness of their human nature, it comes as a great relief to know that God's Spirit is at work in their lives seeking constantly to transform them into Christ's image.

E. Filled with the Spirit

There is only one reference in all the epistolary literature of the New Testament to the filling with the Spirit and that passage is in an ethical context. We have already noticed that several fullness passages in Acts also speak of the deportment of the members of the early church. The chief evidence of the fullness of the Spirit is to be found not in the miraculous, but in the ethical, dimension of the Christian life. Nowhere else in the New Testament are believers commanded to be filled with the Spirit except in Ephesians 5. "And do not get drunk with wine, for that is debauchery; but be filled with the Spirit, addressing one another in psalms and hymns and spiritual songs, singing and making melody to the Lord with all your heart, always and for everything giving thanks in the name of our Lord Jesus Christ to God the Father. Be subject to one another out of reverence for Christ" (5:18-21).

The command to be filled with the Spirit implies that not all believers are so filled. That all Christians have the Spirit of God is clearly taught (Rom. 8:9), but not all have the Spirit's fullness in their lives. The Corinthians, who apparently were richly endowed with spiritual gifts, are called "fleshly" (1 Cor. 3:3), because of their lack of love. It would be hazardous if we attempted to categorize God's people by placing some into the ranks of the "spiritual" and others into the ranks of the "unspiritual," but we all know that Christians are not all equally full of the Spirit. (Paul's exhortation to those "who are spiritual" in Galatians 6:1 probably includes the entire congregation, since all have the Spirit of God.) Moreover, someone who is known to be full of the Spirit may upon occasion fail and act unspiritually. Christians, of course, don't always agree on the marks of spirituality. From the passage just quoted, however, we can see how the fullness of the Spirit in the life of the believer expresses itself.

1. The Apostolic Command

This is not a polite piece of advice. Paul is not simply expressing a pious wish; he is not dreaming of an impossible ideal; but he commands his readers: "Be filled with the Spirit" (v. 18b). Paul's command must not be understood as if the apostle wanted to force people to do something they did not like. He's not cracking the whip over their heads. His concern is that the readers of his epistle experience all that is available to them in Christ.

Moreover, God does not demand where he has not first given. It is often said that the imperatives of the New Testament (the demands) are based on indicatives (the given). Surely, when Paul, God's servant, commands us to be filled with the Spirit, he has no intention of putting a heavy yoke around our necks. On the contrary, he is concerned with our growth and maturity—our health in Christ. It's a command at which we balk only to our own loss and impoverishment. A command given by God for our enrichment calls for our response. There is, however, nothing automatic about the filling with the Spirit. Without our response to God's gift, it cannot be received. The verb is the passive voice ("be filled") suggesting that only as we yield to God will the Spirit fill us. Moreover, the command to be filled with the Spirit is addressed to every member of the church.

The very idea of being filled with the Spirit of God is so overwhelming that some may in fact wonder whether this is not a privilege which God grants only to certain people. Does not the desire to be full of the Spirit itself reek of spiritual arrogance and pride? No, every follower of Christ, no matter how humble, must come to terms with this command. There is no escape from this imperative. The command to be filled with the Spirit is not something we can take or leave. We are obligated to be filled with the Spirit.

A question that naturally arises is whether the filling with the Spirit is a single, unique, post-conversion experience. The verb "to be filled" *(plerousthe)* is in the present tense and this normally means continuous action, although the action may be iterative in the sense that something happens again and again. Michael Green writes:

> To be filled with the Spirit means to allow Jesus to have the fullest control in our lives that we are conscious of. In so far as we do that we will always be finding new areas of self-centeredness to surrender as the Lord who is

Spirit possesses us more and more fully. To such submission all Christians are called. And it is no once and for all transaction: "go on being filled with the Spirit" is the meaning of the original.[25]

John R. Stott agrees: "The present imperative 'be filled with the Spirit' . . . indicates not some dramatic or decisive experience which will settle the issue for good, but a continuous appropriation."[26] Twice in Ephesians Paul says that the believers have been "sealed" with the Spirit; in both instances he uses the aorist tense (punctiliar action), indicating that this happened once and for all when they believed in Christ; but the command to be filled indicates that this must remain the constant concern of the believer. H. C. G. Moule, in an older English work on the Spirit, says that Ephesians 5:18 is not an invitation to spasmodic and tempestuous enthusiasm. He points out that verse 18 deals with spiritual growth and consecration.[27] The filling with the Spirit is related to walking carefully (v. 15) in the midst of evil days, a walk which demands special wisdom.

Since believers experience God in different ways in their Christian pilgrimage, it may well happen that individual saints can point to moments when God worked in a special way in their lives through his Spirit. On one point, however, we must insist, namely that the New Testament nowhere teaches that being filled with the Spirit is a second stage in our salvation experience.

It should be mentioned, perhaps, that nowhere in the New Testament are Christians commanded to be baptized with the Spirit (they are commanded to be baptized with water); the reason is that the baptism with the Spirit is initiatory in character. Believers are commanded, however, to be filled with the Spirit, and the implication is that those who have been baptized with the Spirit are not necessarily filled with the Spirit when they are baptized. All the Corinthians had been baptized with the Spirit (1 Cor. 12:13), but they gave little evidence of the fullness of the Spirit.

Preceding the command to be filled with the Spirit is the prohibition "And do not get drunk with wine" (5:18a). That warning suggests that there may be things in our lives which prevent God from filling us with his Spirit.

2. Human Obstacles to Fullness

Some Bible readers have wrongly inferred from this passage that to be full of the Spirit is a kind of inebriation, such as is brought about by strong drink. It is true that the apostles who spoke with tongues on the day of Pentecost were accused of being drunk with wine (Acts 2:13), but that was because these critics were puzzled by the speaking in tongues. Peter quickly dispelled such charges as ridiculous. To be full of the Spirit does not mean that the believer is lifted up into a state of ecstasy as if he were in a drunken stupor. Clearly in our text drunkenness is the opposite of the fullness of the Spirit.

Whereas the New Testament nowhere forbids the drinking of wine outright (only overindulgence is condemned), the evils that stem from strong drink in our society are so monstrous that we are well-advised to refrain from intoxicating drink altogether, both as a witness against this evil and for our good. Drunkenness, says Paul, leads to debauchery (*asotia*—a word which literally means "irredeemable"; *Heillosigkeit* is the term for it in German).

But having said that, surely we are not to think that avoidance of intoxicating drink will assure us of the Spirit's fullness. There are obviously many other things that can fill our lives (if not our stomachs) in such a way that the Spirit of God is crowded out. Legitimate and innocent practices can also push God's Spirit into a corner. Might not an obsession with sports that fills the lives of some adult members of the church also be a kind of drunkenness? How can people who spend most of their off-hours watching television be full of the Spirit of Jesus? And if our minds are occupied day and night with one question—How can I make an extra dollar?—one cannot help but think that the Spirit must be grieved. We need to examine ourselves again and again to see whether there is something in our lives that blocks the fullness of the Spirit.

But how does the fullness of the Spirit express itself? Paul suggests several marks of this fullness. Following the command to be filled with the Spirit there are five participles which interpret for us the meaning of the fullness of the Spirit.

3. Practical Expressions of the Fullness of the Spirit (vv. 19-21)

First of all, the fullness of the Spirit expresses itself in "joyful song" (v. 19). Schlier thinks that the four participles following the command to be filled with the Spirit are the means by which the fullness of the Spirit is achieved.[28] "Be filled with the Spirit, addressing one another in psalms and hymns and spiritual songs, singing and making melody to the Lord with all your hearts." The Holy Spirit is a Spirit of joy. Indeed, one of the fruits of the Spirit is joy (Gal. 5:22). This joy expresses itself in song. The New Testament is full of songs, beginning with the birth narratives of Jesus and ending with the shattering music of the Apocalypse.

The word "to sing" (psallo) originally meant to pluck the strings, then to accompany song with an instrument, and finally, simply to sing. And that is how the word is used here. Paul also mentions "hymns." Hymen was the Greek god of song and of marriage. The word had already become a religious word and is used here for songs with a Christian message. The third word (odai) is a secular word for song and for that reason Paul qualifies it with the adjective "spiritual." This would not mean that God's people should never sing nature or folk songs, but in Christian worship spiritual songs are called for. The presence of the Spirit is felt when believers build themselves and others up by singing. To sing "in the heart" does not necessarily mean silent singing, although we may well do that even as we go about our daily work. Paul probably means that our singing should have heart in it. Hearty participation in meaningful fellowship and worship is a sign of the fullness of the Spirit. "The fullness of the Spirit will find manifestation in fellowship whenever Christians are found together, and will be given joyful expression in song and praise."[29]

Another expression of the fullness of the Spirit is gratitude: "Always and for everything giving thanks in the name of our Lord Jesus Christ to God the Father" (v. 20). That sounds impossible!

How can we be thankful at all times for everything? Paul knew only too well the dark valleys of suffering through which God had led him. He had his disappointments, his sorrows, his losses. His experiences in Asia were so heavy that, as he said, "We despaired of life itself" (2 Cor. 1:8). On the other hand, when he was beaten and bleeding with his feet in the stocks he and Silas sang praises to God together in a Philippian jail.

Paul is not asking us to become hypocrites and to thank God for evils that strike our lives. Often when we are in the midst of trials the best we can do is to say with the psalmist: "For I will yet thank him." But even in the dark moments of our lives we have the assurance that we are being led by the hand of our heavenly Father. And when the enigmas of life seem insoluble, we can be grateful that in the end he receives us into glory where all mysteries will be plain. However, when our lives are filled with grumbling and complaining, we can be sure that the Spirit does not have full sway in our hearts. Being filled with the Spirit makes us truly grateful.

To show that the fullness of the Spirit has little to do with ecstasy or exuberance, note that another expression of this fullness is submission to one another. "Be subject to one another out of reverence for Christ" (v. 21). In order to live joyfully and gratefully we must do away with all strife. Strife is often caused by arrogance and pride, by exalting ourselves and denigrating others. When God's Spirit fills people's lives they seek to serve one another and treat each other respectfully. We all know that the church is to respect its leaders; wives are to respect their husbands, children their parents. Paul, however, asks every believer to be subject to his brothers and sisters in Christ.

Will such an attitude not undermine all social structure and lead to utter chaos? Surely some must lead and others follow; some instruct and others learn. Yes, indeed, but leadership, too, must be carried out in a spirit of humility; a leader in the church is also subject to his brothers and sisters. In fact, only when leaders treat their "followers" with respect, can they lead. That may not be the world's pattern, but Jesus taught us to be different from the world. "Sometimes a person who claims to be filled with the Spirit becomes aggressive, self-assertive and brash. But the Holy Spirit is a humble Spirit, and those who are truly filled with him always display the meekness and gentleness of Christ."[30]

In sum, then, the expressions of the Spirit's fullness are to be found in our relationship to God and others. "The Holy Spirit puts us in a right relationship with both God and man. It is in these spiritual qualities and activities, not in supernatural phenomena, that we should look for the primary evidence of the Holy Spirit's fullness."[31]

Whereas we are all commanded to seek the fullness of the Spirit, we should be very cautious about making claims about our own spiritual attainments. If we make exclusive individual claims to possess the fullness of the Holy Spirit, we run into serious dangers—the kind for which the Corinthians were known. People who claim such fullness are often distressingly defective in Christian behavior. Green says,

> It is still an observable fact that those who speak most of being full of the Holy Spirit are often governed by other spirits, such as arrogance, divisiveness and party spirit, disorder, lack of love and criticism. It is hard to see how a man can be full of the Spirit if these glaring failures of character persist.[32]

He goes on to warn against putting the emphasis on experience, for the New Testament emphasis is on Christian graces, shown in our relationship to others. The fullness of the Spirit is not a personal quality which one can have independent of the other members of the Christian community. "The fulness of the Holy Spirit, like salvation itself, is corporate no less than individual."[33]

From what has just been said about the fullness of the Spirit we can see that the Spirit is primarily concerned about producing in the followers of Christ those Christian graces which honor their Lord. In other words, a major concern of the apostles in their teaching is that believers bear a rich harvest of the Spirit, "fruit of the Spirit." "It is from the Spirit-filled life that the fruit of the Spirit comes."[34]

F. Bearing the Fruit of the Spirit

1. *The Concept of "Fruit"*

The phrase "fruit of the Spirit" occurs only once in the New Testament. In Galatians 5:22 the "fruit" of the Spirit is placed over against the "works" of the flesh.[35] We must not conclude from this antithesis, however, that the works of the flesh are outward and the fruit of the Spirit is inward and invisible. The Spirit's fruit expresses itself in daily life. Although the expression "fruit of the Spirit" occurs only once (the Byzantine Text has it also in Ephesians 5:9, but the better reading there is "fruit of light"), this does not mean that the concept as such is rare. Everywhere in the Epistles the importance of Christian graces is stressed, and even though we may not find such a large number of them strung together elsewhere in one sentence, the apostles never tire of reminding their readers of what Paul calls the "fruit" of the Spirit.

Why he should use "fruit," when referring to virtues, rather than "works" of the Spirit, is hard to say. It may be only for stylistic reasons. However, the word "works" already had an opprobrious meaning in Galatians because of the constant warning against the "works of law"; perhaps it was not appropriate to use it for the product of the Spirit.[36] Moreover, "fruit" suggests the natural product, the expected harvest of a life lived by the power of the Spirit. The change from *erga* (works) to *karpos* (fruit) may, therefore, be designed to bring out the spontaneity of the Christian life in which the graces listed are the product of the presence of the Spirit in the hearts of the believers.[37] In any case, fruit is not what a person can produce by his own strength. F. F. Bruce writes:

> As an apple-tree does not produce apples by an act of Parliament, but because it is by its nature so to do, so the character of Christ cannot be produced in his people by rules and regulations; it must be the fruit of his Spirit within them.[38]

The change from the plural *erga* (5:19) to the singular *karpos* (5:22) may be purely coincidental, but it may also suggest the harmony and unity of the Christian way of life. This is the view of

J. G. Davies: "The use of the singular . . . points to the unity of the character which the Spirit creates."[39] It is also to be observed that whereas the works of the flesh are said to be "open" (*phanera*), this is not said of the fruit of the Spirit. Again this may be stylistic, but Schlier thinks it is because of the "inwardness" of the Spirit's working.[40] This may be so, as long as the working of the Spirit is not understood as something that happens only in the heart and remains invisible in daily life.

Whether Paul took over pre-Christian lists of virtues from Greek ethicists is a question that has often been debated by scholars. If he took over the vocabulary, he certainly transformed its meaning. There is reason to believe that lists of virtues and vices were part of the moral instruction given to converts to the Christian faith—particularly those from Gentile background—for they reflect common themes of early Christian catechetical teaching.[41]

It is quite possible that the relationship of the Spirit to "fruit," which is here clearly seen as Christian character, goes back to the Old Testament anticipations of the messianic age in which God will pour out his Spirit and all nature will be rejuvenated and the earth become fruitful. In Ezekiel 36:26, where the Spirit is promised, the writer describes the fruitfulness of the trees and the field (v. 30). Again, in Isaiah 32:15, where the Spirit is promised, the wilderness is to become a fruitful field. According to Paul this new age has come and the Spirit is creating a rich harvest of Christian graces, a sign that the church has entered upon the age to come.

2. The Ninefold Fruit of the Spirit

Various attempts have been made to classify the ninefold fruit listed in Galatians 5:22. Whatever arrangement is made it should be observed that the individual fruits overlap in meaning and cannot always be easily distinguished one from another. Most of them have to do with the relationship of the believer to other Christians—a clear indication that what the Spirit works in the heart is expressed concretely in human relations.

Perhaps some of the moral qualities listed by Paul were not considered to be the most popular virtues in Greek ethics; and certainly not one of them is of the spectacular kind. Clearly for Paul the ecstatic expressions of the fullness of the Spirit are no greater evidence of the Spirit's presence in the church than those qualities which make it possible for people to become a "fellowship of the Spirit."[42]

Whereas a threefold division of the nine graces listed is quite popular, there is something artificial about such an arrangement. Yet it serves as a useful order in which to survey this cluster of Christian graces. The first three "fruits" seem to put the emphasis on the believer's relationship to God: love, joy, peace.[43] Love *(agape)* stands at the head of the list, and in one sense all the others could be viewed as expressions of this basic virtue. Moreover, Galatians 5:22 is not the only text that brings love and the Holy Spirit together in close relationship. Paul writes to the Romans that the love of God is poured out into the hearts of the readers by the Holy Spirit (Rom. 5:5). The reference there is not to the Christian's love for God, but to God's love for people. The Christian's love for God would be a rather insecure foundation upon which to build the hope of glory. The hearts of the saints have been suffused with the love of God and this was effected by the Spirit. Again, in Romans 15:30 we hear Paul beseeching his correspondents "through the love of the Spirit" to strive with him in prayer. Here clearly it is a love which the Spirit produces, rather than a love for the Spirit, which would make little sense. It is a love which the Spirit imparts and maintains. The love which the Spirit bestows on the Christian gives him a concern for the welfare of his neighbor to the extent that he can be called upon to "wrestle" in prayer for the needs of others.

In 1 Corinthians 12—14, where the gifts of the Spirit are dealt with, the great hymn of love stands squarely in the center, raising its head above the two chapters like a mighty mountain peak. And in the list of the qualities of "love" (1 Cor. 13:4-8), a number of the "fruits" of Galatians 5:22 are to be found. In 2 Corinthians 6:6, the Holy Spirit stands next to "unfeigned love."

Of Epaphras it is said that he "has made known to us your love in the Spirit" (Col. 1:8). Could it be that he brought Paul some concrete token of their affection? It is a question as to whether the word "spirit" here refers to the Holy Spirit or not, but it is not unlikely. T. K. Abbott suggests that "in the Spirit" "expresses the ground of their love, which . . . belongs to the sphere of the Holy Spirit's influence."[44]

The love which the Spirit evokes in the lives of his own is nothing else than the love of Christ. In Romans 15:30 we notice that Paul made his plea "by our Lord" and "by the love of the Spirit." In other words, the Spirit makes real the love of Christ; the Spirit is the power of the Lord at work. To live a life of love is nothing other than a life in the Spirit. Paul writes to Timothy that "God did not give us a spirit of timidity but a spirit of power and love and self-control" (2 Tim. 1:7). It is worth noticing that two of the virtues mentioned here (love and self-control) are found in Paul's cluster of nine graces in Galatians 5:22.

Another fruit of the Spirit is joy. Not only does Galatians 5:22 say this, but we find a close connection between joy and the Holy Spirit in other passages (we have already observed this connection in Acts). "For the kingdom of God is not food and drink but righteousness and peace and joy in the Holy Spirit" (Rom. 14:17). Joy is one of the qualities of the life to come; it describes the life in the kingdom; it is an eschatological concept. By the Holy Spirit the believer has a foretaste of the eternal joy that awaits him in the kingdom of God at the end of the age. That joy does not mean euphoria and feelings of exhilaration can be seen from 1 Thessalonians, where Paul recalls the conversion of the Thessalonians: "You received the word in much affliction, with joy inspired by the Holy Spirit" (1 Thes. 1:6). Here we see that joy can be experienced amidst pain and distress. It is a joy from a deeper source than the human situation; it comes from the Holy Spirit.

It would take us too far afield to offer here a detailed study of each manifestation of the fruit of the Spirit mentioned in Galatians 5:22. In short, patience, kindness, goodness (the second triad) seem to find expression particularly in our relations with

other people. Finally there are three virtues which have to do
more directly with the believer as an individual: faithfulness,
gentleness, and self-control.

Just as "the desires of the flesh" were but a sample listing, as
Paul says (Gal. 5:16-21), so it is with the nine fruits of the Spirit.
Paul could have added others, but the sampling is sufficient to in-
dicate clearly what the Spirit aims to produce in the believer's life.
Obviously we are to be transformed into the image of Christ.

3. Implications of the Metaphor, "Fruit of the Spirit"

All the Christian virtues listed by Paul in Galatians 5:22 were
to be found in Jesus Christ as he walked on earth; from that it can
be observed that to bear the fruit of the Spirit is to live a Christlike
life. "Fruit of the Spirit" must be read as subjective genitive; it is
fruit which comes from the Spirit of God. This means that it is not
the product of our own attainment. If others see in us characteris-
tics which remind them of Christ, then we give all the credit to
the Spirit of God.

In contrast to the works of the flesh, which we do quite
naturally when left to ourselves, the fruit of the Spirit is something
that lies beyond our strength to attain. John R. Stott writes:

> This fruit (the sum total of these Christian qualities) is the best available evi-
> dence—because it is solidly objective—of the indwelling fullness of the
> Holy Spirit. The real proof of a deep work of the Holy Spirit of God in any
> human being is neither subjective, emotional experiences, nor spectacular
> signs, but moral, Christlike qualities. Here is a Christian who makes great
> claims in the realm of experience, but lacks love, joy, peace, kindness and
> self-control: I think all of us will say that there is something wrong with his
> claims.[45]

Whereas the "fruit of the Spirit" is supernatural in origin in
the sense that we ourselves cannot produce this fruit, it should not
be understood as being unnatural. Nor should the supernatural
source of this fruit absolve us from all responsibility in bearing the
fruit of the Spirit. "The fact that holy living is a product of the
Holy Spirit might easily lead people to suppose that they have

nothing to contribute to the process themselves."[46] There are certain conditions that have to be met if the Spirit is to produce a rich harvest of Christian graces in our life. As in other areas, so also here, we reap what we sow. We cannot sow to the flesh (Gal. 6:7, 8) and expect to reap the fruit of the Spirit. How we live, what we read, the friendships we cultivate, the films we watch, the interests that absorb our time and energy, the way we spend our money—all these things must be considered when we look for a harvest of Christian grace.

Another inference can be made from the metaphor of fruit-bearing: that is, it takes time for fruit to ripen. One cannot expect a Christian character to develop overnight. Whereas the Holy Spirit comes into our lives at conversion, we must allow time for the maturation of the fruit which the Spirit seeks to produce in us. This should not be understood to mean that the believer will produce a rich harvest of Christian graces simply by aging. But as he is filled again and again with God's Spirit, and as he opens up his life to the Spirit's guidance and discipline, others will see in him a growth in Christlikeness. This is not different from what Paul describes as a transformation "from one degree of glory to another" (2 Cor. 3:18).

G. Sinning Against the Spirit

James wrote that God "yearns jealously over the spirit which he has made to dwell in us" (4:5). Whereas the translation of this verse is as problematic as its interpretation,[47] the context suggests that a divided heart stands in contradiction to the Spirit which God has made to dwell in the heart of the believer. One cannot be both a friend of the world and a friend of God, as the apostle has just stated (4:4). The Old Testament speaks of God as a jealous God (Ex. 20:5), meaning that he will tolerate no rival. The Spirit which he has put into our hearts yearns for wholehearted devotion and loyalty to God. Tasker writes: "It is His Spirit that has been given to the Christian, and He cannot view with anything but jealousy the harbouring by the Christian within his soul of any rival spirit such as the spirit of the world."[48]

Fortunately James does not stop there, but goes on to say: "But he gives more grace" (4:6). All believers fail; no one is perfect; they all sin, but God's grace does not cast us away, if otherwise we cling to him with a sincere heart. God's demand for undivided allegiance goes hand in hand with his supply of grace.

If then God's Spirit yearns or longs for our wholehearted love with an intensity of desire or jealous envy, when a believer sins, the Spirit is grieved. Paul warns against this. "And do not grieve the Holy Spirit of God, in whom you were sealed for the day of redemption" (Eph. 4:30).

The Spirit of God is a person capable of being grieved. The context makes it rather explicit how this can be done. Immediately preceding this warning Paul exhorted his readers against unedifying speech which does not build up but which breaks down community relations. Following the warning not to grieve the Spirit, he begged the Ephesians to let all bitterness, wrath, anger, clamor, and slander be put away (4:31); this suggests that anything which ruins the fellowship of the believers with one another grieves the Spirit. However, if we see the warning against hurting the Spirit in the somewhat wider context of Ephesians 4, we would have to mention falsehood, anger, thievery, and other sins as sources of grief for the Spirit of God. The Spirit creates fellowship and loving relations between members of Christ's body; anything that destroys these creations of the Spirit hurts him.

Paul had already said earlier in the letter that the Spirit is the believer's seal, a kind of pledge of the inheritance into which he will enter in the age to come (Eph. 1:13f.); and he reminded his readers then that the Holy Spirit—God's pledge of their final redemption when Christ returns, his assurance that he will know us and accept us when he comes for us—is grieved when their relationship with other believers is broken through sin. "Since he is the 'holy Spirit,' he is always grieved by unholiness, and since he is 'one Spirit' (2:18; 4:4), disunity will also cause him grief."[49]

The writer of the epistle to the Hebrews took this warning a step further. He made it very clear that those who repent and put their trust in Christ become partakers of this Spirit (6:4). However, the danger of hardening one's heart by sin (3:12ff.) is as real for the believer as it was for Israel of old. In spite of the voice of the Spirit speaking to them through the Prophets, Israel fell away from God. Therefore, the author of the epistle to the Hebrews repeatedly warned against the awful sin of apostasy (see 6:6) which is a sin against the Holy Spirit, of which Jesus spoke. "How much worse punishment," he asked, "do you think will be served by the man who has spurned the Son of God, and profaned the blood of the covenant by which he was sanctified, and outraged the Spirit of grace?" (10:29). The context makes it clear that something much more serious is meant than being overtaken in a trespass, as Paul speaks of it (Gal. 6:1). What is meant is "falling away from the living God," of which the writer spoke in Hebrews 3:12. Clearly our text has deliberate apostasy in mind. To bring out the gravity of the sin, the author spoke of willful rebellion against the Father, the Son, and the Holy Spirit. A believer who apostatizes treats the Spirit of grace with scorn and so sins against the Holy Spirit, which makes him, in the words of Jesus, "guilty of an eternal sin" (Mk. 3:29). When the Spirit—by which the sinner is enlightened, God's grace is revealed to him, and Christ's work of redemption is applied to his heart—is insulted and treated with contumely (*enubrizo* is used only here in the New Testament and is a powerful word for insulting the Spirit), God's judgment is sure and severe.

Whereas the sin of apostasy is almost too frightening to contemplate, there is one sin against the Spirit of which many Christians are only too often guilty, the sin of "quenching" the Spirit. "Do not quench the Spirit" is Paul's warning to the Thessalonians (1 Thes. 5:19).

The verb "quench" *(sbennumi)*[50] is used with reference to putting out fire in five of its six occurrences in the New Testament.[51] In 1 Thessalonians 5:19 it is used in a metaphorical sense to signify that the work of the Spirit can be suppressed and restrained in the congregation. A modern equivalent would be "to pour cold water" on the Spirit's activity.[52] Perhaps the fiery tongues that attended the coming of the Spirit at Pentecost suggested this figure of speech to Paul.[53]

Since the following verse (v. 20) warns against despising prophecy, it may be that Paul in his exhortation not to quench the Spirit had in mind particularly the danger of suppressing prophecy in the worship services of the church. However, Paul may have had the gift of tongues or the gifts of the Spirit generally in view. Lang writes: "Paul is rather warning against a deliberate suppression of the extraordinary operations of the Spirit in the congregation."[54] Perhaps an overemphasis on sobriety may have led to a cold disapproval of fervor.[55] The Thessalonians may have tended to lean in the opposite direction from those in Corinth who overrated the ecstatic manifestations of the Spirit. Van Unnik suggests that the Thessalonians, out of fear of being looked down upon as crazy, were hesitant to let the Spirit work in them and express itself in gifts.[56] We should, however, not rule out the possibility that Paul had ethical failures in mind, also. Loafing, immorality, and other evils, which Paul had mentioned earlier in this epistle, also quench the fire of the Spirit. Some Thessalonians evidently were quenching the Spirit and Paul wanted them to stop.[57]

David Watson suggests that we are in danger of quenching the Spirit in our day by putting a premium upon tidiness in Christian fellowship which leads to death. He also mentions bitter spirit, ungodly behavior, and party strife as evils that quench the Spirit.[58] The positive side of the coin is to "be aglow with the Spirit" (Rom. 12:11). "If we neglect the gift of God's Spirit in our lives, if the fire is quenched, there will be a chilling coldness and carelessness which will effectively keep others away from the Savior we are trying to proclaim."[59]

CHAPTER 13

The Spirit and the Worship
of God

In his dialogue with the Samaritan woman, Jesus said: "The hour is coming, and now is, when the true worshipers will worship the Father in spirit and truth, for such the Father seeks to worship him. God is spirit and those who worship him must worship in spirit and truth" (Jn. 4:23, 24). Whereas the coming hour points to Pentecost and the age of the church, Jesus can say the hour is now because he is the bearer of the Spirit and the bringer of salvation. Jesus' words anticipated the day when the worship of God would not be tied necessarily to any particular place, but also that the Spirit which would be poured out would enable the people of God to worship God the way he desires to be worshiped.

Luke concluded his account of the Pentecostal outpouring of the Spirit with a brief description of the worship of the early church as it gathered for instruction, fellowship, the breaking of bread, and prayers (Acts 2:42). Although the New Testament nowhere says that the church gathered for "worship" *(latreia),*[1] the inner strength of the early church lay in its cultic life. Their meetings are simply called a "coming together in assembly" (1 Cor. 11:18; 14:23), and we have warnings not to neglect "to meet together, as is the habit of some" (Heb. 10:25).

It may be that the apostles avoided cultic terms for the worship services of the church to keep it from being identified with cult meetings in Jewish and Greek temples.[2] The practical, everyday services which the members of the church performed, however, were described in cultic terms not only by Paul (Rom. 12:1f.; 15:16; Phil. 2:30; 4:18), but also by Peter (e.g., 1 Pet. 2:4, 5, 9, 10), and especially by the writer to the Hebrews (e.g., 9:14; 12:28). Therefore, when we speak of the "worship" of the early church in this chapter, we are using that word in the loose sense to include those activities which characterized the assemblies of the early church.

There was considerable diversity and freedom in early Christian worship. This is to be expected, particularly since they met in homes. There were prayers, spiritual songs, and confessions of faith. There was the ministry of the word, the collecting of monies, and the celebration of the Lord's supper. These devotional exercises were not simply the product of human endeavor and exertion. "No amount of reflection and energy could have conjured up the presence of Christ if the assembling of Christians had not been directed by the Holy Spirit."[3]

Whereas all aspects of the early church's worship were undergirded by the presence of the Holy Spirit, we want to single out only those elements which are specifically linked with the Holy Spirit in the letters of the New Testament. We begin with a passage in which "worship in the Spirit" is said to be a clear mark of a Christian believer.

A. Worship in the Spirit

Paul claimed that the new people of God "are the true circumcision, who worship God in spirit" (Phil. 3:3). The sacred covenant sign is here spiritualized and carried over to the new people of God. The thought is more fully expressed in Romans 2:25-29, where Paul argued that a true Jew is one who is circumcised in heart. Those who are circumcised in the Spirit, and not in letter (Rom. 2:29), worship God in the Spirit.

When Paul said that the distinguishing mark of the believer is that he worships in the Spirit, it is not at all certain that he had the assembled congregation in mind.[4] The word "worship" *(latreuo)* in Philippians 3:3 will probably have to be understood in a broad sense, embracing also the private life of the Christian.[5] Bonnard suggests that "worship" here must be taken in the wider sense of both the individual's and the community's service to God.[6]

Because of the textual variants in this passage, we face several translation problems. The oldest Greek witness (Chester Beatty Papyrus) omits the word "God" and a number of manuscripts and versions have "God" in the genitive. Either reading leaves the verb "worship" without an object.[7] The problem is augmented by the fact that *pneumati* (spirit) can be understood in different ways. It could mean that the true worshiper dispenses with all external forms of worship and worships God only in his mind; but this simply does not square with what we know of early Christian worship. The view that Christians worship God "in spirit," in the sense that their worship is spiritual, in contrast to Israel's external rites, has some support among exegetes.[8] One might think of Paul's exhortation to the Romans to present their bodies as living sacrifices, which he calls their "spiritual worship" (Rom. 12:1).

Obviously Paul, like Jesus, is an enemy of all worship that is simply external, formal, and routine. But there is another meaning in our passage which seems more central: any worship of God that is genuine, calls for the help of the Spirit of God. The word *pneuma* (spirit) without the article usually means the Holy Spirit, and it is more likely that here it refers not to the human spirit but the Holy Spirit. Since the word "God" is in the genitive in a good many manuscripts and versions, we may have to translate it: "who worship by the Spirit of God." Then there is no doubt about the meaning of "Spirit." The Holy Spirit is the dynamic source of the Christian life and that includes his worship. While it is also true that Christian worship is spiritual in nature (in contrast to animal sacrifices, for example), to worship God in the Spirit does not mean that worship has no external forms. What is important is that Christian worship, whatever form it takes, is inspired and governed by the Spirit of God. In a very expressive manner Professor van Unnik says: "New Testament worship stands within 'the magnetic field of the Holy Spirit.' "[9] Real worship is never easy; indeed it is quite impossible without the help of the Spirit.[10]

We must now look at several of the ingredients of Christian "worship" which are directly linked with the Holy Spirit.

B. The Spirit and Confessions

Vernon Neufeld has scrutinized all the New Testament confessions of faith; he concludes that the earliest creed of the church was simply "Jesus is the Christ" (Mk. 8:29).[11] The messiahship of Jesus was a live issue in the Christian mission to the Jews and the confession "Jesus is Messiah" is found as a major theme in the early parts of the New Testament (e.g., Acts 9:22). As the church moved out into a Gentile environment, the debate about Jesus' messiahship was less an issue. The question was not whether Jesus was the Christ (about that the Gentiles knew very little), but whether Jesus was Lord. "If you confess with your lips that Jesus is Lord . . . you will be saved" (Rom. 10:9). The confessions of the New Testament extend from the simple statement "Jesus is Lord" to detailed summaries of the gospel (e.g., 1 Cor. 15:3-5). F. F. Bruce writes:

> It is evident from the New Testament that the earliest Christian creed, or profession of belief, was one of few words: "Jesus is Lord." But the simplicity and brevity of the statement need not imply a "simple" Christology. When the earliest Christians gave Jesus the title "Lord," they used it as a divine title.[12]

We cannot survey all the confessional formulations in the New Testament, yet we must elaborate a bit on the confession that Jesus is Lord. Paul says that this confession cannot be made without the help of the Spirit. "Therefore I want you to understand that no one speaking by the Spirit of God ever says 'Jesus be cursed!' and no one can say 'Jesus is Lord' except by the Holy Spirit" (1 Cor. 12:3).

Evidently the Corinthians were finding it hard to distinguish between the genuine and the spurious, because they were caught up in emotional ecstasy in their worship services. The criterion of true spirituality, Paul seems to be saying, is not ecstasy or excitement, but rather the confession that is made. It's not known whether any of the Corinthians had ever cursed Jesus when beside themselves; but the apostle made it explicitly clear that should such a thing ever happen, it would obviously not be of the Spirit of God. "Ecstatic utterance can be produced by a variety of stimuli, and the character of the stimulus must be inferred from the substance of the utterance, but the confession of Jesus as Lord ... whether in ecstasy or not, is an unmistakable sign of the Holy Spirit's working."[13]

It is not certain what precisely may have been the background for Paul's instruction on this point. Paul himself, when he was still a persecutor of Christians, tried to induce them to curse Jesus (Acts 26:11). In times of persecution Christians were often put to the test by asking them to confess Caesar as lord, and often when they confessed Jesus as Lord, they lost their lives;[14] but there is nothing in the context of our passage to suggest this meaning.

It has been suggested that some Corinthians in their excitement had forgotten the difference between "cursed be Jesus" and "Jesus is Lord," or that unbelievers who witnessed such enthusiasm were led to curse Jesus, or even that Christians resisted ecstasy by saying, "*Anathema Iesous.*"[15] Another possibility is that hyper-spiritual Corinthians put such a strong emphasis on the glorified Christ that the earthly Jesus was denigrated, even cursed. It may also be a reference to baptism, when the baptismal candidate would confess before the congregation that Jesus was Lord.[16]

This confession, says Paul, cannot be made without the help of the Holy Spirit. Not that a person cannot say these words without the help of the Spirit, but to pledge one's loyalty to Jesus as Lord meant that he had prior claim on the believer (prior to Caesar, also). It signified also that the believer had passed from the domain of the spirit-powers, by which his old life was controlled (Gal. 4:3-9), into the liberty and joy of the gospel. By confessing Christ as Lord the believer submitted himself to his guidance and authority. Such a confession was possible only by the help of the Spirit of God.

We should not overlook the fact that our passage forms the introduction to the long discussion on spiritual gifts. To those Corinthians who prided themselves with having outstanding gifts of the Spirit, Paul seems to be saying: the real test of spirituality is rather the acknowledgment of Christ's lordship in daily life. Such a confession is possible only by the help of the Holy Spirit.

C. The Spirit and Prayer

Much of what the New Testament has to say about prayer deals with prayer as private communion between the believer and his Lord. In addition to private prayers, however, there are records of the corporate praying of the church. In fact several prayers of the church are recorded in the New Testament (e.g., Acts 4:24ff.).

The letters of the New Testament themselves were written in a spirit of prayer. Not only are the readers called to the practice of prayer, but we have a goodly number of prayers right within the letters (e.g., Eph. 1:16-20; 3:14-19). What is of interest to us at the moment is that the Spirit of God inspires and sustains the praying of the saints. The assistance of the Spirit in the Christian prayer life is of paramount importance. There is something new in this, for in rabbinic literature no passage can be found in which prayer is connected with the Spirit of God.[17] By contrast, for Paul "the assistance of the Spirit in the Christian prayer-life is of paramount importance."[18]

Perhaps the most striking aspect of the Christian's prayer is that the Spirit does the praying in him. "And because you are sons, God has sent the Spirit of his Son into our hearts, crying 'Abba! Father!' " (Gal. 4:6). The Spirit cries "Abba!" in our hearts, in the center of our personalities. Bonnard points out that this cry is not the cry of surprise but the cry inspired by the Spirit; the prayer is the work of the Spirit in man.[19]

"Abba" reflects the primitive church's Aramaic background.

The word passed into the prayer life of the church even where the language used was Greek. The opening words of the Lord's prayer may have had something to do with the sacredness of the form *Abba* (although this is not certain).[20] Paul explains that the cry "Abba" is brought forth by the Holy Spirit, and this is no doubt an echo of Jesus' own praying (e.g., Mk. 14:36). There is really no analogous invocation found in Jewish prayers.[21] When a believer says "Abba," he expresses a father-child relationship with an intimacy not known in Judaism.[22] The recognition of God as Father in Christ Jesus is the distinguishing mark of the filial relationship which the Spirit establishes between the believer and God. The word "cry" *(krazo)* emphasizes the earnestness and intensity of the utterance of the Spirit within us; although the verb itself does not suggest an utterance of joy, the freedom enjoyed by God's children would make such a prayer a joyous outcry. His Spirit moves his children, in spite of fears and doubts, to pray to him who is now their Father. "It is only the Spirit within us that can genuinely cry out 'Abba! Father!' "[23]

Romans 8:15 is related to Galatians 4:6. Here again Paul speaks of the freedom which we have as God's sons. We have received a "Spirit that makes us sons, enabling us to cry 'Abba! Father!' " It is in (or by) the Spirit that we cry out to God as Father. The fact that we can address God as Father proves that the Spirit is at work in us assuring us of our sonship. The Spirit of adoption, the Spirit which makes us sons and daughters of God, is the one who creates in God's people that filial love and confidence by which they cry "Abba" and exercise the rights and privileges of God's children. In Romans 8:15 the believers cry "Abba," whereas in Galatians 4:6 the Spirit cries "Abba" in the believer. But there is no essential difference between the two.[24]

There is another important passage in which the Spirit and prayer are related.

Likewise the Spirit helps us in our weakness; for we do not know how to pray as we ought, but the Spirit himself intercedes for us with sighs too deep for words. And he who searches the hearts of men knows what is the mind of the Spirit, because the Spirit intercedes for the saints according to the will of God. Rom. 8:26, 27.

According to Romans 8:22 all of creation is in birth pangs, awaiting the birth of the new aeon, groaning for the unveiling of the glory of God's children (v. 21). The groaning of the sons of God for the redemption of the body joins in with this voice of creation (8:23). Added to this there is the groaning of the Spirit (8:26)—creation, the church, and the Spirit sigh for the age to come.[25] It is in this context that we must understand the prayer of the Spirit.

First we are told that the Spirit helps our weakness (v. 26a). Our weakness is due to the flesh, and when we pray our creaturely weakness comes to the fore. The distance between us and God is so vast that we need a "go-between." We do not know God's will perfectly, nor do we have the strength in ourselves to do it. We do not even know our deepest needs. We do not know how to pray "as we ought" (v. 26b).[26] In Hellenism the one who prayed felt insecure because he did not know whether he had named all the gods; with Paul it is not God (as Father) who makes the one who prays insecure, but the one who prays feels his own weakness only too keenly. The Spirit, then, comes to his aid and overcomes his weakness.[27]

Our weakness is overcome not simply by "learning" how to pray, by being instructed in the proper forms. It is not that the Spirit helps us out by teaching us the correct formulae, gestures, or patterns. No, he does the praying for us "with sighs too deep for words." That expression is difficult. Does Paul mean that the Spirit inspires prayers in our hearts which cannot be expressed in words, or that the Spirit prays for us in a language we cannot understand? If that were so, what do we make of the fact that God, who knows the mind of the Spirit, searches our hearts (v. 27)? The work of the Spirit as intercessor does not annul the activity of the one who prays; the believer does not become merely a channel for the prayer of the Spirit;[28] rather, the believer is raised to full personal dignity in that the Spirit assists him in his feeble efforts to pray. "Sighs too deep for words" are not necessarily inaudible sighs or improper words, but the sighs cover "those longings and aspirations which well up from the spiritual depths and cannot be imprisoned within the confines of everyday words. . . . In such prayer it is the indwelling Spirit who prays, and His mind is immediately read by the Father to whom the prayer is addressed."[29]

The sighs of the heart can hardly be equated with glossolalia, although Käsemann thinks that makes good sense here, for that too is a sign of the believer's weakness.[30] While that kind of praying may be included, we should not restrict this passage to glossolalia. The sighs of the heart are inspired by the Spirit and are carried to the throne of grace by the Spirit; God, who searches the hearts and knows the mind of the Spirit, consequently knows the content and intent of the Spirit's intercession. Moreover, since the Spirit knows God's will, he prays for us "according to God's will" (v. 27b). Bruce writes:

> At a certain stage of religious life the accurate form of words is regarded as essential to the efficacy of prayer; when the spirit of man is in closest harmony with the Spirit of God words may not only prove inadequate; they may even hinder prayer. But God, before whom the thoughts of all men are like an open book, recognizes in those unspoken "groanings" deep in His people's hearts the voice of the Spirit interceding for them in tune with His own will, and answers them accordingly.[31]

And Michael Green reminds us that

> there are some profound depths here for the Christian to ponder. For many of us, prayer in the Holy Spirit is something about which we know very little. Our prayers tend to be mechanical or at best self-centered, and prayer in the Holy Spirit means allowing the Spirit of Christ to pray in us, to pour into our souls his overflowing life of intercession.[32]

Obviously what Paul has to say about the Spirit's help in prayer makes sense only when viewed as an account of deep religious experience, not as a piece of theoretical analysis.[33]

In Ephesians 2:18 there is an allusion to prayer in connection with the Spirit. "Through him we both have access in one Spirit to the Father." "Access" no doubt means the freedom to pray to the

Father, and we have discussed the fuller meaning of this passage earlier (pp. 241ff.); but certainly "access . . . to the Father" would include the idea of coming "with confidence . . . to the throne of grace," to use the words of the writer to the Hebrews (4:16). The Spirit gives Jews and Gentiles the assurance that they can come to God as children come to their father; and this they do when they pray and worship. Thornton says, "Fellowship with man involves and implies fellowship with God, and both depend upon participation in the gift of the Spirit."[34] To have access to the Father "in one Spirit" is not a reference to ecstatic prayer; nor does it mean to pray "in the spirit" (i.e., mentally), in contrast to praying with the lips (i.e., audibly). The meaning seems rather to be that, in virtue of the reconciliation which Christ has made at the cross, God's Spirit not only bridges the gulf between us and God so that we can come into his presence as children come to their father, but by God's Spirit the walls separating people are broken down so that they can worship God together.

We have already mentioned Ephesians 5:20, where thanksgiving (a prominent feature of Christian prayer) is evidence of the fullness of the Spirit (v. 18, see p. 267ff.). The Spirit fills the hearts of the believers with eschatological joy, and this joy expresses itself in thanksgiving in both private and public worship.

In Ephesians 6:18 we read: "Pray at all times in the Spirit, with all prayer and supplication. To that end keep alert with all perseverance, making supplication for all the saints. . . ." Although prayer can hardly be considered as part of the Christian's armor which the writer has just described, the Christian soldier is obviously not well-equipped if he fails in prayer. Every situation in life is an occasion for prayer. Prayer in the Spirit in this passage does not mean glossolalia as in 1 Corinthians 14:15. Nor is it a prayer "in spirit" in the sense of the mind or heart over against audible prayer. The meaning is rather that the Holy Spirit inspires the prayers of the believers. Without the Spirit the prayer of the saints is of no effect. It is also the Spirit that helps the believer to remain alert and to persevere in prayer.[35] Green, however, is of the opinion that Paul had in mind "a deep, free, and intensive time of prayer, when the Spirit takes over and controls and leads in prayer."[36] But Paul's exhortation could just as well apply to all the praying of God's people, for without the Spirit's help they cannot pray. Moreover, it is only by the Spirit of God that Christians can have genuine concern for others so that they make "supplication for all saints."

In 1 Corinthians 14, where Paul discusses the relative importance of tongues over against prophecy, he says: "For if I pray in a tongue, my spirit prays but my mind is unfruitful. What am I to do? I will pray with the spirit and I will pray with the mind also" (vv. 14, 15). Here Paul contrasts praying in the "mind" with praying in the "spirit." Both kinds of prayer are inspired by the Spirit of God. The difference between prayer with the mind and prayer with the Spirit lies rather in the fact that prayer in the Spirit calls for the gift of glossolalia, a gift which not all believers have. It does not follow that one is more spiritual than the other for, as Paul explains, he would rather speak a few intelligible words in public than a torrent of syllables that no one can understand. Prayer with the mind can be understood by others and they can enter into it; prayer in the Spirit should be reserved for private devotions, unless some interpreter can make it meaningful for those present.

Quite clearly here Paul has the charisma of tongues in mind, whereby the believer who possesses this gift can commune with God in praise, prayer, and thanksgiving. This kind of praying builds up the individual but, as Paul says, his mind is unfruitful (v. 14), i.e., it produces nothing or contributes nothing, because no one understands. Since glossolalia is a gift of the Spirit one can say that praying "in the spirit" is a kind of praying that is inspired and sustained and made meaningful by the Holy Spirit.

In the epistle of Jude there is another reference to prayer in the Spirit. "But you, beloved, build yourselves up on your most holy faith; pray in the Holy Spirit" (v. 20). It is sometimes suggested that Jude had prayer in "tongues" in mind;[37] that is doubtful, although we need not exclude that kind of praying from this passage. If glossolalia is meant it is suggested here only

obliquely.[38] The believer, as Jude clearly indicates, is dependent
on the Spirit of God for his prayer life, just as he depends on the
Spirit in other areas of his Christian life. Our prayers are at times
very selfish and the Spirit cleanses and purifies them by his re-
proofs. The Spirit reminds us to pray for others. And when we get
weary of praying the Spirit renews our spiritual strength. In fact it
is only because of the Spirit's presence in our hearts that we pray
at all.[39]

D. The Spirit and Song

The topic of charismatic prayer, which we have just dealt
with, touches also upon the matter of song. Paul says that he will
sing with the Spirit and mind (1 Cor. 14:15). Presumably the singing with the mind is the kind of singing by which the church is
built up, for the members understand what is being sung as they
join together in spiritual hymns. The ecstatic kind of singing, for
which only certain people have the gift (but after which some
Corinthians hankered), edified the one who engaged in it, but it
was of little meaning for others present. Perhaps ecstatic prayer
expressed itself in a hymnic way and so we should not make too
much of a distinction between praying and singing in the Spirit.
There would be a greater difference between praying and singing
with the mind.

Singing in the Christian assembly in general is related to the
Spirit as well. With the outpouring of the Spirit at Pentecost there
seems to have come an outburst of song in the early church; that
is, of course, what we should have expected. We have noticed
earlier (pp. 267ff.) that the fullness of the Spirit, according to
Ephesians 5:18-20, expressed itself in song. "Be filled with the
Spirit, addressing one another in psalms and hymns and spiritual
songs, singing and making melody to the Lord with all your heart,
always and for everything giving thanks in the name of our Lord
Jesus Christ to God the Father." Most commentators seem to
favor the view that spiritual fullness comes to expression in joyful
fellowship, in song, and in perpetual thanksgiving.[40] To speak "to
one another" may have reference to antiphonal singing in the

worship of the church. The same idea is expressed in Colossians 3:16, where it is added that the singing of the congregation is didactic—teaching and admonishing one another in all wisdom in psalms, hymns, and spiritual songs." This would take place in the assembly of the believers, where songs uttered by one believer under the inspiration of the Spirit, would be answered by another. It reflects the spontaneous element in early assemblies.

The three different types of songs mentioned here (psalms, hymns, spiritual songs) are not easily distinguished from one another; and the terms may be used loosely to cover every form of musical composition (see p. 267). It was natural for them to sing Old Testament psalms, but there were very likely new creations as well.[41] If we can distinguish between hymns and psalms in our text, then hymns are probably the Christian creations, although Old Testament psalms were sometimes called hymns also. "Songs" is a neutral word, but with the adjective "spiritual" we clearly have a Christian creation, inspired by the Spirit.

The singing is to be done "to the Lord." This points up the dual aspect of Christian music: "to one another" and "to the Lord." Moreover, the singing is to be done "in the heart." This has little to do with silent singing; it means rather that the singing touches the believer in the depth of his person. It means that the singer is sincerely open before God, turned toward the Lord. This kind of attitude is possible only by the work of the Spirit. In song inspired by the Spirit the church expressed its gratitude and praise to God for redemption in Christ. The rich hymnody that developed in the history of the church is a witness to the activity of the Spirit. "It would have been strange indeed if the Church had remained songless in that first glorious dawn when the light from Christ came breaking across the horizons, making all things new."[42]

When the early Christians assembled for instruction, prayer, song, and fellowship, it was "to equip the saints for the work of ministry" (Eph. 4:12). The church gathered for "worship" so that it might be a true and faithful church when scattered. That included witness, evangelism, and mission. Whether the gospel was proclaimed by the rank-and-file members of the church, or by those who were set apart by the church for this ministry, always it had to be done in the power of the Holy Spirit if the good news was to fall on fertile soil. The apostles in their letters witness to the total dependence of the preacher of the gospel on the help supplied by the Spirit of God.

CHAPTER 14

The Spirit and His Gifts

God did not establish the church and then leave it to its own resources. By his Spirit he equips his children to fulfill their calling in the home, in the gathered Christian community, and in the world. Since the Spirit bestows gifts upon God's people, the gifts are called *pneumatika* (spiritual gifts). A synonymous term is *charismata* (gifts of grace).[1] The word *charisma* is used in both a general sense (e.g., Rom. 1:11; 6:23; 1 Cor. 1:7) and in the more technical sense (e.g., 1 Cor. 12:8-10; 28-30; Rom. 12:6-8) to describe the special endowments which God gives his children. Whereas *pneumatika* occurs more frequently in Paul than *charismata*, it is used rarely in the sense of "spiritual gifts." *Charisma* is a peculiarly Pauline term (used 16 times); it is found only once in non-Pauline writings (1 Pet. 4:10). While some writers seek to make a distinction between *pneumatika* and *charismata*,[2] the difference should not be overstressed. There may be distinct nuances in the two terms, but essentially they mean the same thing when they refer to the gifts of the Spirit. Both terms are found in 1 Corinthians 12:1, 4, in which Paul introduced the topic of spiritual gifts, to which he devotes three chapters of the epistle, as the letter came to be divided. We begin by inquiring into the nature of these gifts.

A. The Nature of the Gifts

Something of the nature of spiritual gifts can be gathered from the very names for the gifts. *Charismata* means that these are gifts which come to us by God's grace *(charis); pneumatika* suggests that they are supplied by the Spirit *(pneuma)*. In fact these gifts come from the triune God. "There are varieties of gifts, but the same Spirit; and there are varieties of service, but the same Lord; and there are varieties of working, but it is the same God who inspires them all in every one" (1 Cor. 12:4-6). The gifts of the Spirit are so diverse because there is a diversity of services *(diakoniai)* and these services cannot be performed without God's energy *(energemata)* in our lives. Putting the three words *(charismata, diakoniai, energemata)* together we might define spiritual gifts, in the words of John R. Stott, "as certain capacities, bestowed by God's grace and power, which fit people for specific and corresponding service."[3] More simply, he suggests a *charisma* "may be regarded either as a gift and the job in which to exercise it, or a job and the gift with which to do it."[4]

A question that naturally comes up when we inquire into the nature of the *charismata* is how they relate to what we call our natural endowments, the development of natural talent, our training, and the like. It's a question Paul does not bother to entertain. In fact the question is misdirected, for it reflects a Gnostic tendency to elevate the "spiritual" over the "natural." The incarnation of Jesus, his willingness to take on human flesh, should keep us from despising what is human. We need not trouble ourselves about discerning which of our gifts (or parts of them) are special endowments by the Spirit and which gifts we have inherited. In fact when a natural gift is put into the service of God it becomes a spiritual gift. "In the New Testament," says David Watson, "there is no sharp distinction between 'natural' and 'supernatural' gifts, even if some . . . demonstrate a more unusual manifestation of the Spirit."[5] He goes on to say:

If any gift or ability, therefore, is used to glorify Christ and to edify his body, it becomes a gift of the Holy Spirit. Of course there must be some conscious dependence on God, together with the inspiration of the Holy Spirit, before a natural ability becomes a true spiritual gift. Without this, the gift can all too easily become an occasion for self-display.... Our attitudes to these natural talents are important. Do I see my talent as *"my* gift," so that I am looking for personal fulfillment for *my* gift? Or do I see it as entirely a gift from God, which he could remove at any moment...?[6]

The same God who made the world and who made us is the one who poured out his Spirit at Pentecost. He is the God of nature and of grace. Moreover, when we look at some of the so-called spiritual gifts they look very mundane, even material. For example, "he who contributes, in liberality; he who gives aid, with zeal; he who does acts of mercy, with cheerfulness" (Rom. 12:8). The Spirit may well take natural endowments and heighten or intensify them so that they can be put into the service of the church.

Another question that is related to the nature of spiritual gifts is: How does one obtain such gifts? Paul's answer is: "All these are inspired by one and the same Spirit, who apportions to each one individually as he wills" (1 Cor. 12:11). The writer to the Hebrews agrees with Paul: "While God also bore witness . . . by gifts of the Holy Spirit distributed according to his own will" (Heb. 2:4). There is, then, a sovereign element in the distribution of spiritual gifts; to rebel against God out of dissatisfaction with one's gifts would be like the vessel asking the maker, "Why did you make me this way?"

What we should caution against is the thinking that certain spiritual gifts are given to people as a reward for their spirituality. If that were so, then we should not have expected spiritual gifts to flourish so richly in Corinth, where there was a lot of carnality.

On the other hand, where there is no interest in spiritual things and in serving the Lord, it is not likely that spiritual gifts will be found very richly. Paul does in fact suggest that there is a human aspect to the receipt of *charismata*. First of all, he encourages his readers to strive particularly for those gifts which help to build up the church (1 Cor. 12:31; 14:1). Also, he suggests the possibility of receiving spiritual gifts through prayer (14:13). But Bruce may be right when he says that these "injunctions seem to be directed to the church rather than to the individual member."[7]

It should not be overlooked, however, that when God gives gifts to his people, no one is overlooked. There is no member of the body of Christ who is not, in the biblical sense of the word, a charismatic. Much would be gained if we recognized this, for today when charismatic is pitted against non-charismatic we create divisions in the body of Christ quite unnecessarily. The gift of leadership makes a Christian just as much a charismatic as the gift of tongues.

Not every person has the same gifts. Paul plainly stated this (1 Cor. 12:29, 30), but it is also borne out in Christian experience. If, however, we recognize the sovereignty of the Spirit in the distribution of gifts, we shall not be unduly perturbed about the fact that others have gifts that we do not have.

Moreover, it will keep us from dictating to others which gifts they ought to have, and prevent us from looking with pride and disdain upon others who lack certain gifts. Human nature is naturally inclined toward feelings of inferiority and superiority. When one person has a particular gift which another does not possess, it is easy to forget that every gift comes only by the grace and sovereignty of God. It was because the Corinthians lost sight of this that Paul had to deal with feelings of inferiority and superiority among them.[8]

But we ask: What are spiritual gifts for?

B. The Purpose of the Gifts

Spiritual gifts are not given to build up our egos or to give us inflated views of ourselves. They are not even given primarily to build us up personally, although that in itself is a legitimate purpose. The real purpose of the gifts is to serve others. The members of our body serve each other by fulfilling their specific function in the place where God has put them, "that the members may have the same care for one another" (1 Cor. 12:25). In similar fashion (and Paul draws out the analogies in great detail in 1 Corinthians 12:12-26), God equips the individual members of Christ's body to serve that body.

Paul teaches this not only by illustration but says so explicitly: "To each is given the manifestation of the Spirit for the common good" (1 Cor. 12:7). The Greek word for "common good" is *sumphoros*, and means "profit."[9] Paul does not mean the profit of the person who has the gift, but that of others. "These *charismata* are not for self-glorification, nor merely for the spiritual benefit of the recipient, but for that of the whole Church."[10]

We notice again that Paul has no doubts that every believer has received some gift or gifts. These gifts are not to make the possessors proud, but to enable them to help others.

That the gifts are given for service is underscored in 1 Corinthians 14, where Paul encourages the Corinthians to strive for those gifts which lead to "upbuilding" *(oikodome)*.[11] "So with yourselves; since you are eager for manifestations of the Spirit, strive to excel in building up the church" (1 Cor. 14:12). Since edification is the purpose of the gifts, Paul downgrades the gift of tongues, since that gift builds up the individual who possesses the gift, in contrast to the gift of prophecy which builds up the congregation (1 Cor. 14:3-5). "Let all things be done for edification" (v. 26) is the governing principle in the use of spiritual gifts. "Upbuilding" runs like a thread through 1 Corinthians 14 (vv. 3, 4, 5, 12, 26).

In the one passage outside of Paul in which the word charisma is used, essentially the same purpose of spiritual gifts is intended. "As each has received a gift, employ for one another, as good stewards of God's varied grace" (1 Pet. 4:10). Peter then mentions the two rubrics under which a multitude of spiritual gifts can be grouped: the ministry in word and in deed (v. 11).[12] Gifts are expressions of God's grace and the believer holds them in trust as a steward. As a faithful steward he must put these gifts into the service of others.

The reason for such a multiplicity of gifts lies in the fact that there are so many *diakoniai* (services, 1 Cor. 12:5). No one has all the gifts and, consequently, no one can do all the work of the church. Some gifts may not strike the eye, as do others, but they are no less valuable. David Watson writes,

> Think, too, how many Christians have been encouraged in the fight by loving and generous hospitality, by the ministry of intercession, by wise counsel, by sacrificial service—the "foot-washing" ministries which can be such a blessing within the body of Christ. It is not just the more spectacular gifts that are valuable in this context, but every gift that is edifying for the church. They are all specifically given to strengthen the church in the battle. [13]

If we are to serve one another (1 Pet. 4:10) and build each other up (1 Cor. 14:26); if our gifts are to be used for the advantage of others and for their profit (1 Cor. 12:7), then it is surely an abuse of spiritual gifts when they are self-directed and self-centered. Also, the emphasis is misplaced when Christians are constantly encouraged to "discover" their gifts. That too leads to self-consciousness. The emphasis ought rather to be on service. It is in his effort to serve that the believer discovers where his gifts are; and if his main concern is to serve others, he remains blithely unconscious of his gifts. It helps him to remain humble and discourages others from being envious. Peter concludes his brief comments on the *charismata* with the hope "that in everything God may be glorified through Jesus Christ" (1 Pet. 4:11). "God is thus glorified when the variety and value of the gifts of His grace are openly manifested in their diligent exercise, and when the ministry thus accomplished is plainly due to God's enabling." [14]

C. The Number of Gifts

Much injustice has been done to this topic by some ardent advocates of gifts who insist that there are nine and no more, and these nine are always present when the church meets; if they aren't, it is said, then clearly the church is either apostate or lukewarm. To be sure there are nine mentioned in the first list in 1 Corinthians 12:8-10, but there are more at the end of the same chapter (12:28). Besides, Romans 12 lists prophecy, teaching, exhortation, liberal giving, helping others, and acts of mercy (vv. 6-8). Also, according to Paul's observation in Ephesians 4:11, 22, the gifts of the risen Lord are people, given to build up the saints so that they can perform their ministry in the world. Interestingly, Paul makes the bold claim that even celibacy is a charisma (1 Cor. 7:7).

Whereas Peter mentions only two gifts, one of utterance and the other of service (1 Pet. 4:11), he underscores that the believer is to be a steward of the "variegated" (*poikilos* means "many-colored") grace of God. The implication is that God's grace is so rich and the needs of the church so diverse that God bestows a great variety of gifts. "It is therefore a mistake to talk of 'the nine gifts.' . . . The variety is considerable."[15]

Not only are there more than nine spiritual gifts, but there may in fact be many more than the ones listed in the New Testament texts. Since the needs of the church vary from time to time, God may equip people in his own way to meet these needs. The question is not whether we can identify a certain number of gifts in a given congregation, but whether the needs of the church (and through the church the world) are met by the services which the members perform. Ralph Martin writes:

> The danger in lumping these nine gifts into a single package and treating them as equally intended for all ages is twofold. On the one hand, we may forget that the Spirit is our contemporary and he fashions *new* gifts for the church's ministry in every fresh setting and challenge of its life. On the other side, we fall guilty to the charge of theological anachronism when we suppose that modern-day Christianity in attempting to recapture its early days can reproduce in precise detail the conditions of its pristine life. To recall and re-live the spirit in which the first believers lived and served their generation is one thing, and may be a legitimate concern. But to encapsulate the spirit in the forms that we think we can carry over from the past is a will-o'-the-wisp endeavour beyond our power to command.[16]

D. Examples of Gifts

It would take us too far afield if we were to make a detailed study of all the *charismata* mentioned in the New Testament. Therefore, we limit ourselves to a brief discussion of the nine gifts listed in 1 Corinthians 12:8-10. These nine can be grouped in different ways. Michael Green's threefold division ("gifts of utterance," "gifts of action," and "gifts of knowledge") seems as good as any.[17]

1. Gifts of Utterance

One gift that Paul valued very highly was that of "prophecy." He devotes the entire fourteenth chapter of 1 Corinthians to show the superiority of prophecy to tongues. Prophecy was widely known in the early church. It was a gift bestowed by the Spirit, poured out at Pentecost (Joel 2:29; Acts 2:18). There were prophets in Jerusalem, Caesarea, and Antioch (Acts 11:27; 13:1), Rome (Rom. 12:6), Corinth (1 Cor. 12—14), Thessalonica (1 Thes. 5:19, 20), and the churches of Asia (Rev. 1:3; 2:20). It was a gift given to both men and women (1 Cor. 11:5). Philip had four daughters who had the gift of prophecy (Acts 21:9).

Although widely practiced in the early church, prophecy is not easy to define. Evidently there was considerable variety. Basically it means to speak a word of the Lord to God's people under the impulse of the Holy Spirit. That this impulse was not irresistible can be learned from Paul's observation that "the spirits of prophets are subject to prophets" (1 Cor. 14:32). They played a vital role in the instruction and edification of the church. However, we cannot simply equate the gift of prophecy with preaching and teaching as we think of it today, although Paul does say that the church is taught and strengthened by prophecy (1 Cor. 14:31).

John Taylor writes:

> Perhaps it is significant that in his lists prophets and teachers are several times paired together. This suggests that these men were gifted with an interpretative insight whereby, intuitively rather than logically, they set down the fundamentals of Christian belief and behavior as this emerged from the, as yet, unthought-out experience of Christ and his resurrection.... But together with such an expository ministry, if such was theirs, the prophets of the early church were clearly gifted with powers of prediction also, as we can find on both the occasions when we meet Agabus.[18]

Since prophets are ranked with apostles as founders of the church (Eph. 2:20; 3:5), it may well be that we will have to think of prophets both in the primary sense of the first-century, apostolic church, and in the secondary sense of others who had the prophetic gift, for we find prophets even after the apostles passed off the scene. If we define prophecy broadly as "the declaration of the mind of God in the power of the Spirit," we shall not be too far from the truth.[19]

There may have been some overlap between prophecy and teaching, or between the "word of knowledge" and the "word of wisdom." However, as practiced in the early church prophecy seems rather to have been God's directing, guiding word for various situations in the life of the church. Because prophecy was valued so highly, it was easy enough for false prophets to step in and lead an entire congregation astray (Rev. 2:20). In the days prior to the formation of the New Testament canon it was of utmost importance that the gift of discernment be exercised. John wrote: "Beloved, do not believe every spirit, but test the spirits to see whether they are of God; for many false prophets have gone out into the world" (1 Jn. 4:1). He then proceeded to give some tests by which the false and the genuine prophets may be distinguished.

Whatever the reason, in some circles there was a tendency already in Paul's day to despise prophecy, for we have his admonition to the Thessalonians not to despise prophecy (1 Thes. 5:20). Was it because prophecy had been abused at Thessalonica? Or was it that they had reacted against the gift of tongues and now carried that aversion over to prophecy, thereby quenching the Spirit?[20] The prohibition against treating prophecy lightly was followed by a positive exhortation: "But test everything; hold fast what is good" (1 Thes. 5:20, 21). The words are strangely reminiscent of a saying of Jesus which is frequently quoted in noncanonical literature, known as the Agrapha: "Show yourselves tried money-changers, rejecting much, but retaining the good."[21] Christians, like good money-changers, must be able to distinguish between true and dubious prophesyings.

A. M. Hunter suggests, "Some men, when they got up to prophesy in church meetings (in Thessalonica), uttered Christian truth; others simply vapoured; and there were still others whose pronouncements might be heretical or even dangerous."[22] Perhaps in reaction to all these utterances the Thessalonians were ready to do away with prophecy altogether. Paul says "No," for that would quench the Spirit and impoverish the church. They must rather learn to discern and to hold to that which is good—a task made considerably easier for us because we have the apostolic writings against which we can test prophetic utterances. Needless to say there is a great lack of discernment on the part of many Christians in spite of the possession of many Bibles in numerous translations. Michael Green says perceptively, "If prophecy unregulated by order could dissipate in individualism and end in sectarianism and heresy (as in Montanism); order without prophecy could so easily turn a deaf ear to the leading of God and relapse into the peace of the graveyard."[23]

For some reason or other the gift of tongues and the interpretation of tongues is listed last in both lists of *charismata* in 1 Corinthians 12. It may be that the Corinthians overvalued glossolalia and so Paul deliberately put it down a few notches. It should be noticed that there are "kinds" *(genos)* of tongues (both words are in the plural). This gift, as described in chapter 14, is distinct from the speaking in tongues that took place at Pentecost, when the gospel broke through all language barriers and people heard the message in their own mother tongue. The gift of tongues that Paul discusses in his letter to the Corinthians was one which was not understood, and without interpretation was not to be used in public. Paul compared tongues with musical instruments which are not understood unless a meaningful variation of notes is played on them. Also, he compared tongues to foreign languages which cannot be understood by someone who has not learned these languages.

Paul maintained, rather, that the gift of tongues adds a new dimension to the possessor's prayer life: "For one who speaks in a tongue speaks not to men but to God; for no one understands him, but he utters mysteries in the Spirit" (1 Cor. 14:2). The gift of tongues provides a freedom to praise God (Acts 10:46). It can express itself in joyful song. Paul had the gift of tongues (1 Cor. 14:19), and he knew that it edified the individual who had this gift (14:4). However, if tongues were not understood by others he does not want them to be used in public unless they are interpreted. Moreover, they are quite useless, even a hindrance, in evangelism (1 Cor. 14:23).

The gift of interpretation of tongues is difficult to define. Evidently the interpretation of tongues does not necessarily mean the translation of what was said in an unknown tongue. Since there are no objective criteria for checking whether the interpretation is genuine, this gift is wide open for abuse. Those who have the gift of tongues are exhorted to pray for the gift of interpretation (1 Cor. 14:13) in order to edify the church, for what is not understood does not edify. When speaking in tongues is combined with interpretation we have a phenomenon somewhat like prophecy—a divinely inspired message. In his concern for order in the assemblies, Paul seems to prefer that tongues be used in the private devotional life of the believer and not in public, where he would "rather speak five words with [his] mind, in order to instruct others, than ten thousand words in a tongue" (1 Cor. 14:19).

2. Gifts of Action

First of all there are the "gifts of healings" (again both words are plural, 1 Cor. 12:9). Perhaps the apostle used the plural to suggest the healing of various kinds of diseases, or various kinds of healings. Jesus healed people and the healings in the early church were a kind of afterglow of our Lord's ministry. In both Jesus' ministry and that of the apostles, healings attended the proclamation of the good news; we never read of healing campaigns. No one in the early church had the gift to heal all diseases. Paul himself had to leave his friend Trophimus sick at Miletus (2 Tim. 4:20), and he himself was not healed of his thorn in the flesh (2 Cor. 12:7-9). He could do nothing about the illness of Epaphroditus (Phil. 2:25-27); he even advised Timothy to apply some medicinal remedy to try to alleviate his gastric problems (1 Tim. 5:23).

Suffering, disease, and death are all part of fallen humankind's lot. And if our redemption from sin is experienced only as a foretaste of what awaits us, how much more the redemption of the body. Therefore, while we rejoice to see God heal both with and without the help of medicine, we must learn to accept suffering as part of our life in the present age. John Taylor reminds us that "God is just as much at work, and just as wonderingly to be praised in the techniques which man has 'mastered' as in the processes which remain a mystery to him."[24] Jesus atoned for sin; sickness does not need to be atoned for; it needs to be removed. However, it will not be completely removed until we arrive in glory where pain and death will be banished forever. It is very cruel to suggest to suffering saints (as did the friends of Job) that if only they got right with God they would be healed. Also, it is very cold comfort to say to someone in pain that if only he had faith he could be healed. On the other hand, we should not minimize the importance of the gift of healing. Perhaps this is an area where cerebral Christianity has not taken God and his Word seriously.

What about miracles (*energemata dunameon*—"works of power")? The ministry of Jesus, as well as that of the apostles, was attended by deeds of power. The gift of performing miracles is not further defined. It would probably include such matters as exorcism or the example of smiting Elymas with blindness (Acts 13). Such miracles had great evidentiary significance in the early period of the church's mission.

The promise of Jesus that his disciples would do "greater things" once the Spirit would be given has sometimes been taken to refer to performing greater and more miracles than Jesus did in his ministry, but that seems to be a misreading of the text. The promise of Jesus refers not to the magnitude of the miraculous but to the extent of the church's mission. Jesus restricted himself to a small part of the world, to Israel, for he had come to die and to bring redemption for all humankind. After Pentecost the church took the good news into all the world. That, I think, is the "greater thing."

We may well be advised to be a bit incredulous about some of the fantastic reports about miracles that one hears occasionally today. This is not to question, however, that God can give to one of his children the gift to do the unusual, something that seems to defy the laws of nature. That God is working in mighty power through chosen instruments even today is beyond dispute, and for that we are grateful.

Perhaps if we related the gift of doing the unusual with the gift of faith, we would not be wide of the mark. All commentators agree that Paul does not have saving faith in mind when he speaks of the gift of faith (1 Cor. 12:9). It is rather the gift to trust God against all odds. God may call someone to a task that seems impossible humanly speaking, such as founding a mission, an orphanage, a school, or a church. God may call someone to lead in a great movement of renewal. We might think of Martin Luther in the sixteenth century, who dared to take on princes and popes. We get a clue as to what Paul means by the gift of faith from chapter 13, where he says that if he had all faith "so as to remove mountains" and had not love, he would still be nothing. In the words of Michael Green,

> the gift of faith seems rather to be this clear insight into the will of God, this staking all upon it, this unwavering conviction that God will provide even in the most impossible circumstances, that has marked some Christians in every age who have received that particular gift from the Spirit.[25]

3. Gifts of Knowledge

Paul lists three gifts which have to do with special insights which the Spirit gives to some people in the church. On the one hand, all believers are to grow in the knowledge of God's will and be filled with wisdom and spiritual understanding (Col. 1:9-11); on the other, there are those who have received special gifts of insight.

It is not altogether clear how the "gift of knowledge" should be distinguished from the "gift of wisdom." Both have to do with insight into God's revelation, God's will—a knowledge quite different from book learning, although book learning is not inimical to the knowledge of God which the Spirit gives to people. Perhaps Paul has in mind some special insight for a given occasion. Either in counseling an individual or in giving counsel to the church some members of the church may be given a special gift of insight into the ways of God by which they can be of great help to God's people.

Much of what can be said about the gift of knowledge is applicable also to the gift of wisdom, and one would think that the gift of teaching embraces an element of both of these gifts, if we can distinguish between them. Green suggests that we are likely to be "on the right track if we interpret the gift of wisdom as a settled disposition of mind, illuminated by the Lord the Spirit, which has a broad understanding of the purposes of God, the Scriptures, and supremely of Jesus himself and his cross."[26]

One final gift needs to be mentioned: the gift of discernment, "to distinguish between spirits" (1 Cor. 12:10). With the many gifts that flourished in Corinth, and with a special hankering for the ecstatic (well-known to them from their pagan past), there was a great need for discernment. God's gifts, good and beneficent in themselves, can all be abused. To prevent that, God gives some people in the church a special sense to distinguish between the genuine and the spurious in the area of tongues, words of knowledge, prophecy, and so forth.

Whereas Paul seems to have in mind those who have been equipped by God's Spirit to discern intuitively whether something is from God or from the evil one, Jesus had given another test: the test of life. "You will know them by their fruits" (Mt. 7:20). In the early church the spiritual gift to discern spirits seems to have gone hand in hand with objective tests such as holiness of life and correct doctrine (1 Jn. 4:2). The post-apostolic church worked out a number of these objective tests, as one can see, for example, from the Didache (11-13) and the writings of Hermas (Mand. 11).

We shall not comment on the other gifts mentioned in

Corinthians and in other epistolary literature. It is obvious, however, when such gifts as "helps" and "administration" are included in the gifts of the Spirit, that there is no aspect of the church's life which is not sustained and empowered by the Holy Spirit.[27] Also, it should be observed that there is really no hierarchy of gifts. In Romans 12:7 the deacon comes before the teacher, but in 1 Corinthians 12:28 the deacon follows the teacher (assuming that "helps" refers to the diaconate). "Sometimes one gift is regarded as the greatest or most important and sometimes another, depending on which one God needs at any given time."[28]

The question that often comes up today is: Are these gifts permanent? or were they given for the apostolic age only?

E. The Permanence of the Gifts

If we ask whether all the twenty or more gifts mentioned in the New Testament are available today, the answer will have to be "No," for among the gifts are also the apostles and prophets. In a general sense, we have apostles today, for anyone who is sent on a mission by the church is an *apostolos* (one who is sent). However, in the primary sense of the word, the age of the apostles is limited to the first century; they have no successors. When bishops of churches died they were replaced, but when apostles died they were not replaced. Similarly, the prophet: if we think of prophets as organs of divine revelation, then we have none today. The apostles and prophets founded the church. Their message is found in the books of the New Testament. If we use the word prophet in a general sense as describing someone who has a special message for the church, we can possibly speak of modern-day prophets. That is to say that there may be people in the church who have a prophetic gift and can speak a word of guidance to the church when it faces decisions or when there are special needs.

Aside from such considerations, however, there is no indication in the New Testament that the gifts would ever be withdrawn. A passage that has been used to argue that the *charismata* were for the apostolic period only is 1 Corinthians 13:10, where

Paul stressed the ephemeral nature of all gifts in comparison to love which is eternal. "When the perfect comes," he said, "the imperfect will pass away." The imperfect obviously applies to the gifts, for he has just admitted that our prophesying and our knowledge are far from perfect (v. 9). But what does the perfect mean? Some answer: the New Testament. Once the biblical canon was complete the gifts became superfluous. But the context is clearly against this line of interpretation. The *teleion* (the perfect) toward which Paul looks is the day when we shall see God "face to face" (v. 12).

If the gifts of the Spirit are given by God to the church to do its service during this time of waiting before the perfect comes, then we have no reason to believe that they have been withdrawn. Why certain gifts recede into the background and others come to the fore from time to time is hard to say. Sometimes no doubt it is the church's fault. When the church fails to take its mission in the world seriously, and when it pays little attention to the life of holiness, it may not sense a great need for the gifts of the Spirit. Sometimes spiritual renewal brings dormant gifts to the surface. On the other hand, since the needs of the church vary from time to time, some gifts may recede into the background at times and others come to the fore. Ralph Martin makes the interesting observation that "while proclamation is a perennial need for the communicating of God's message, miracle-working, healing power, glossolalic speech and its interpretation may be gifts that recede for a while and then are renewed according to the needs of the hour."[29] Somewhat in similar vein F. F. Bruce writes:

> Some of the gifts enumerated are exceptional in character, and the course of Christian history suggests that they are manifested more particularly at the beginning of some new advance of the kingdom of Christ. They were manifested supremely in the apostolic age, and they have tended to reappear subsequently where similar conditions to those of the apostolic age have reproduced themselves.[30]

This should not be interpreted to mean that we are satisfied with the status quo. God's children must constantly be open for new

opportunities of service to others, and this calls for spiritual equipment which only the Spirit of God can supply. Donald Bloesch
writes, "A church where the charismatic gifts in all their wonder
and variety are not in evidence is something less than the church
founded at Pentecost."[31] Often the Spirit is stifled in the church in
the name of orderliness. Paul too was concerned about order, but
not the kind that rules out the great diversity which the Spirit
creates by endowing believers with different gifts to serve God.[32]
All gifts, however, are for this age only, and in that sense they are
temporal; they are the church's equipment for the way, a kind of
vade mecum. Once Christ appears in glory we shall no longer
need these aids, for the imperfect and the partial shall disappear
in the light of eternity. What will remain, however, is faith, hope,
and love, "but the greatest of these is love" (1 Cor. 13:13).

> St. Paul was at pains to emphasize that the more unusual *charismata*, or
> grace-gifts, of the Holy Spirit are not themselves of the essence of the Spirit-
> filled life. They are marked by a certain transience; it is inherent in their na-
> ture to "pass away." This does not mean that they are going to disappear
> from the experience of the church after the apostolic age, but that we are
> not to expect of them the same permanence as belongs to the faith, hope
> and love of the Spirit-filled life.[33]

F. The Gifts of the Spirit and Love

Sandwiched in between two long chapters on the gifts of the
Spirit is a hymn in praise of love—a chapter which Paul obviously
did not dash off without much thought and meditation. In this
chapter he argued that where love is absent all *charismata* are
worthless. There is no question in his mind that the fruit of the
Spirit is of much greater significance than the gifts of the Spirit. At
the top of the list of Christian graces is *agape*, a love which is
poured into our hearts by the Holy Spirit (Rom. 5:5).

Paul begins by comparing tongues with love, and concludes
that even if he had the whole gamut of tongues ("of men and of
angels"), his worship would sink to the level of paganism (gongs
and cymbals) without love (1 Cor. 13:1).

Deep insights into God's revelation ("knowledge"), the gift

of proclaiming God's will ("prophecy"), and the faith to do the humanly impossible have little value without love (v. 2). Even a liberality that leads to the sacrifice of all of one's possessions, even martyrdom, are no substitutes for love (v. 3).

Gifts, then, are not the criterion of spirituality. What counts is Christlikeness. In his description of Christian love (vv. 4-8) one cannot help but think that Paul was drawing a portrait of Jesus. The supreme purpose of the Spirit in the believer's life is to conform him to the image of Jesus Christ.

It should be added that while there is a sovereign element in the distribution of spiritual gifts, this is not the case when it comes to the fruit of the Spirit. The Spirit may give to one member of the church the gift of teaching, to another the gift of tongues, but he does not give to one the gift of joy and to another the gift of love. We are not expected to have all of the gifts of the Spirit. but we are expected to grow in Christlikeness in every respect.

It is a pity that precisely in the understanding and the practice of spiritual gifts love often goes begging. There is jealousy, arrogance, selfishness, and other evils—all of them enemies of Christian love. Moreover, love is not only much more important for the life of the church in this age, but also in the age to come. The gifts of the Spirit are given to believers because of their need, because of the imperfections and limitations that characterize life in this age; love, however, abides forever. And so while gifts should be earnestly desired, love should be pursued above all things (14:1).

The reference to the age to come leads us to make some observations on the eschatological significance of the Holy Spirit.

CHAPTER 15

The Spirit and the Blessed Hope

The early Christian community believed that the last days, which according to the prophets were to be characterized by an effusion of God's Spirit, had arrived. The presence of the Spirit, however, was not only an indication that the messianic age had dawned; it was also the ground of a new eschatological outlook. Although believers were experiencing the powers of the age to come (by the work of the Spirit), they realized full well that this age had not yet come in its fullness; evil forces were still active in this interim period between the inauguration and the consummation of the last days.[1] The outpouring of the Spirit marked the community of believers as belonging to the time-span between the resurrection of Jesus and the parousia, of which the Spirit was a token and pledge.[2]

The Jews at the time of Christ divided history into two ages: the present age and the age to come. The present age was understood as the age preceding the coming of Messiah, the age to come began with Messiah's coming. This concept of the two ages is reshaped by Paul in the light of the Christ-event. "This age" has come to an end, and yet it continues; it is the "present evil age" (Gal. 1:14). "The age to come" has arrived, but it has not yet reached its final goal, its consummation, and so far the present two ages overlap as it were. "This mingling of the two ages," says Schoeps, "constitutes the distinctive eschatological standpoint of Pauline theology."[3] Properly speaking, then, there are three ages: between the "present age" and the "age to come" there is an "intermediate age" in which the two ages coexist.[4]

When Paul called the Spirit "the promise of the Spirit" (Gal. 3:14; Eph. 1:13), he suggests that the coming of the Spirit has inaugurated the age of fulfillment—the age which Old Testament prophets, Jewish apocalyptic writers, the sectarians of Qumran, and even rabbis anticipated. But the Spirit is not only the "promised" Spirit; he also holds promise of good things to come (Eph. 1:13). This tension of the "already" and "not yet" is felt in much of the epistolary literature of the New Testament.

In his benediction in Romans 15:13 Paul prayed, "May the God of hope fill you with all joy and peace in believing, so that by the power of the Holy Spirit you may abound in hope." By the Spirit, God's children have a foretaste of the eschatological joy and peace which comes from hope; by the Spirit they have the assurance that what God has begun he will complete in the day of Christ. The hope of the believer is based on God's acts of redemption carried out through Jesus, but made effective by the Spirit.

In another passage in Romans Paul explains that Christian "hope does not disappoint us, because God's love has been poured into our hearts through the Holy Spirit which has been given to us" (Rom. 5:5). The presence of the Spirit in the heart of the believer assures him that God loves him and that he will bring to fulfillment what he has promised. The possession of the Spirit is an unshakable foundation for the blessed hope. Bruce writes: "For the present, then, they (the believers) live in hope, but theirs is a living and certain hope because it rests in the living Christ, dwelling within them as their personal 'hope of glory' (Colossians 1:27), and is sustained by the power of the Spirit."[5]

Let us look at some of the assurances the Spirit gives to us who live by hope.

A. The Spirit and the Assurances of Hope

The Spirit of Christ, given to every member of the church when he or she is initiated into the corporate fellowship of the Spirit, is a mark denoting that he or she belongs to God. It is a sign that God's ownership of the members of Christ's body is genuine, and that they will eventually obtain complete liberation from all that which binds them to this present evil age.[6] One way of expressing the certainty of this hope is to say that the believers are "sealed with the Spirit."

1. The Sealing with the Spirit

The concept of "sealing with the Spirit" is closely related to that of the Spirit as "first fruits" and as "earnest," so that it is somewhat difficult to discuss one without mentioning the others; but we shall try to keep them separate.

In Paul's letters the "sealing" is mentioned only in 2 Corinthians 1:21 and twice in Ephesians (1:13; 4:30). *Sphragizo* (seal) means "to mark with a sign," "to brand," "to set one's seal upon." Cattle, slaves, and prisoners were marked or branded to indicate ownership. We read, for example, of a slave who dreamed he found a cure for the marks on his forehead. Soldiers usually had the number of their legion or the name of their general tatooed on their bodies. In the Old Testament the literal meaning of "sealing" is somewhat more common than in the New Testament, but the metaphorical meaning is found in both: in the sense of "ratify," "confirm," "attest."[7]

Sealing had an extended use in the Near East, especially for legal purposes, to give validity to documents, to guarantee the genuineness of articles, and to confirm that sacks and chests conveyed the specified amount. In the three passages mentioned above, sealing is used as a metaphor for marking the believers as God's property. The mark is the Holy Spirit which he gives to them. In every case, however, this sealing of the believer is with reference to the future, to the end.[8] Those who have the Spirit belong to God and have the deep assurance that when God brings in the final stage of redemption he will acknowledge them.

This concept of sealing may reflect the pagan custom of marking upon the skin of a devotee the symbol of his god as token of entire consecration, of belonging to him. But it is better to look for the background to the idea of sealing in the Old Testament. Perhaps the marking of Cain (Gen. 4:15) as a sign that God would not abandon him forms part of the background. Then there is the marking of the Jewish houses by blood at the first Passover (Ex. 12:13, 22). A more important passage, however, is Ezekiel 9:4-6, where a *tau* (which in its earlier form resembled an "X") is set upon the foreheads of the faithful Jews who had resisted the heathen abominations and who would be spared from judgment.[9]

Most important in this matter is the practice of circumcision, called the seal of the covenant (Gen. 17:11; Rom. 4:11), by which the children of Old Testament Israel were marked as members of the covenant people. And since in the New Testament the members of the church are incorporated into the Christian community by baptism (which, as we have seen, is related to the work of the Spirit), it is not surprising that baptism came to be known as sealing. It does not follow, however, that baptism is meant in the passages which speak of the sealing with the Spirit.[10] To be sealed with the Spirit means, rather, to be made God's inviolate possession.[11] The view that sealing refers to confirmation has no support in the New Testament.[12]

Whether or not Paul had baptism in mind when he spoke of sealing, the fact remains that sealing takes place when God gives the Holy Spirit, thereby marking the members of the people of God as his property. They are marked out from the rest of humankind as those who really belong to him and who are eternally the objects of his loving care.[13] They still live in this age and are subject to the attacks of the evil one, but they are under God's protection and he will see them through until the perfect day.

> The Spirit thus given is the guarantee and security for the full salvation still to come; that God's giving of his guarantee is his side of the "transaction" of salvation; and that possession of the Spirit thus constitutes this salvation in so far as it can be enjoyed now—the first installment, the "down-payment."[14]

In 2 Corinthians 1:21f. Paul wrote: "But it is God who establishes us with you in Christ, and has commissioned us; he has put his seal upon us and given us his Spirit in our hearts as a guarantee." God has anointed the believers, he has sealed them, and he has given them the Spirit as guarantee. We should not apportion these three figures of speech to various acts or steps in Christian experience, but they do refer to different aspects of our Christian life. The anointing refers to divine enablement for service; the sealing with the Spirit means that God knows us and that we are secure in him; what it means to have the Holy Spirit as a guarantee, we shall see presently.

To be sealed with the Spirit may connote also that the believer, who has God's seal—his stamp—upon him, has the divine character imprinted upon his human personality, and that by the Holy Spirit in his life he reflects the image of God which was defaced through the fall.[15]

The eschatological dimension of the concept of sealing is underscored by the writer of Ephesians 1:13, 14. "In him you also, who have heard the word of truth, the gospel of your salvation, and have believed in him, were sealed with the promised Holy Spirit, which is the guarantee of our inheritance until we acquire possession of it." The writer thinks not so much of the Spirit promised by Old Testament prophets, John the Baptist, or Jesus, but of the promise of good things which the gift of the Spirit brings. The sealing with the Spirit of promise is followed by a reference to full possession of the inheritance of the saints in the future, for which the Spirit has been given as down payment. We are also informed on the occasion when the sealing took place: when they heard the word of truth, the gospel of salvation, and believed in Christ. The gift of the Spirit is God's guarantee that he will keep them safe until the day when they will finally be redeemed. When that day comes they will claim their heavenly possession fully; or, to view it differently, God will claim them finally as his own possession.

Whereas Ephesians 1:13 tells us that the believers were sealed with the Spirit when they believed the gospel of salvation,

Ephesians 4:30 informs us that this sealing was "for the day of redemption." This shows the polarity in the eschatological existence of the people of God. The Spirit makes the Christ-event of the past real in the present, and the Spirit prepares believers for the event that still lies ahead, the parousia. The sealing for the day of redemption is mentioned in Ephesians 4 as a motive for holy living, for it stands right in the midst of a paraenetic passage. The prohibition "grieve not the Spirit" is given as a warning to the readers not to take the presence of the Spirit in their lives lightly. Wounding the Spirit by sinful living is a serious matter, for it touches the "seal" which identifies them as God's people when the day of redemption arrives. They must make sure to revere the Spirit as the pledge of their glorious destiny.[16]

Although the statement that the Spirit is the believer's seal for the day of redemption is used as a warning against thinking lightly of sin, there is in it also a note of assurance. All Christians have God's Holy Spirit as a mark which assures them that they will be kept inviolate until the day of redemption. When that great day comes God will acknowledge them as his own special children.

Sealing, as Green points out, is a property word. "It speaks of belonging. The Holy Spirit is given us to identify us as belonging to Jesus, just as a seal on a letter or brand on a sheep identifies it as mine...."[17] There is great comfort here, for the Spirit's presence in our lives is the guarantee that God in the last day will acknowledge us as his own, and that he will preserve us through the trials and vicissitudes of this life until the day of final redemption dawns.

In two of the three passages we have just studied, the concept of sealing with the Spirit is joined with that of the Spirit as "earnest" (*arrabon*). It is to this concept that we turn next.

2. The Earnest of the Spirit

To 2 Corinthians 1:22 and Ephesians 1:14, in which the sealing of the Spirit is mentioned, we now add 2 Corinthians 5:5. In these three passages the Spirit is also called the *arrabon*. The word *arrabon* is a Semitic loanword which probably found its way into the Greek language through the influence of Phoenician traders, who used it in the sense of "surety" or "pledge." In Genesis 38:17, 18, 20, the substantive, written with Hebrew consonants, is used for the pledge which Judah gave to Tamar. As a rule the word occurs as a verb in the Old Testament, but always with the basic idea of "surety" or "guarantee."[18] Nowhere, however, does it signify the partial payment of a money debt. It was as a loanword in Greek that the word took on this meaning. This is borne out by both classical Greek literature and by the papyri.[19]

"Earnest money" is, of course, but a special application of the "pledge" guarantee. The difference is that "earnest money" represents a real part of the object of the contract, given in advance both to insure final and full payment and also to contribute to it.[20] A pledge is taken back when the contract has been fulfilled; earnest money is part of the payment given in advance. But whatever may be the particular nuance of *arrabon* in a given context, it always denotes an action through which the person concerned is obliged to further action in relation to the receiver. F. F. Bruce points out that *arrabon* is used in modern Greek for engagement ring,[21] which is also a kind of "down payment" of what is yet to come. "He is the Heavenly Lover's engagement ring given to us. We shall carry that ring with us into God's future, when we have a full wedding ring of final union with Christ."[22]

In both 2 Corinthians 1:22 and 2 Corinthians 5:5 it is stated that God has given us the *arrabon* of the Spirit. The genitive "Spirit" is an appositive, and further explicates what *arrabon* means: the *arrabon* is the Spirit. It is epexegetical in the sense that the Spirit is the partial payment. In Ephesians 1:14 the Spirit of promise is said to be "the *arrabon* of our inheritance." There is, however, no real difference between Ephesians 1:14 and the Corinthians passages. In every instance the suggestion is that we do not yet enjoy the fullness of Christ's accomplished work of redemption, but that we possess the guarantee of the Spirit, who witnesses in our hearts to the truth of our sonship and to the inheritance that is ours in Christ.[23] However, as Lightfoot says, the actual spiritual life of the Christian is the same in kind as his future glorified life; the kingdom of heaven is a present kingdom; the believer is already seated on the right of God. . . . Nevertheless the present gift of the Spirit is only a *small fraction* of the future endowment. This idea also would be suggested by the usual relation between the earnest-money and the full payment.[24]

Perhaps there is nothing that brings out so clearly the tension between the "already" and "not yet" in Paul as the concept of *arrabon*. The Spirit in the heart of the believer is his assurance that God will fulfill all his promises of salvation in Christ.

This futuristic aspect of *arrabon* comes out very clearly in 2 Corinthians 5:5. Paul is distressed by the idea of being stripped of the body by death. But he overcomes all horror as he faces this eventuality through the awareness that he has possession of the Spirit. The Spirit is his assurance that his connection with Christ will not be severed by death.[25] It is the assurance that a blessed life awaits him after death. Indeed, the Spirit creates the desire for immortality in the hearts of those "absent from the Lord." During this time of their sojourn the Spirit gives them a foretaste and a pledge of the full and perfect life in the eternal kingdom.[26] The Spirit is the guarantee of the resurrection state, the security that their longing for the "heavenly covering" will be satisfied in due time.[27]

The life of the Christian is marked by incompleteness and longing with respect to knowledge, communion with God, and power and freedom in Christian living; the Christian life is also marked by the desire for the fullness of eternal life. It is on these levels that the Spirit gives anticipation of completeness and fullness.[28] The present possession of the Spirit means that part of the future bliss is already attained, and equally, that part still remains future, still unpossessed.[29] The function of the Spirit is to point forward, to make the Christian sure of what awaits him.[30]

From this it becomes apparent that the "earnest of the Spirit" is not a mere static deposit, but the active vivifying operation of the Holy Spirit within the believer, assuring him that the same principle of power which effected the resurrection of Christ Jesus from the dead is also present and at work within him, preparing his mortal body for the consummation of his redemption in the glorification of his body.[31]

The third passage in which the Spirit is called *arrabon* (Eph. 1:14) states explicitly that the Spirit is the "guarantee of our inheritance." The Spirit is the divine surety that the state of filial adoption which the soul now enjoys will one day reach a consummation in the complete inheritance of glory.[32] "The Spirit of promise" is at once the "guarantee" and the "part-payment" of our inheritance. To say that the Spirit is a pledge-guarantee means that God obligates himself to fulfill his promises to us. To call the Spirit a "part-payment" includes the idea of "guarantee," but goes beyond that to include the concept of a "first installment." "Inheritance" stands for all the gifts of redemption. This redemption is a present blessing but will be experienced in all its fullness in the end. By the Spirit we are given a foretaste.[33] The presence of the Spirit in the life of the believer brings him a partial but a real experience of the life of the age to come. In the age to come the acquisition of the full inheritance will include the redemption of the body. If seal is a property word, "earnest" is the prophetic word. It looks forward to a greater gift in the future while stressing a real gift in the present.[34]

Intimately related to the concept of the Spirit as the "seal" and the "earnest" is that of the "firstfruits" of the Spirit.

3. *The Firstfruits of the Spirit*

The firstfruits are a kind of foretaste of the harvest to come. The term *aparche* (firstfruits) is found in Romans 11:16, where the nation of Israel is said to be consecrated because the patriarchs (the firstfruits) were. In 2 Thessalonians 2:13 (assuming that *aparche* is the correct reading), the early church is called the firstfruits chosen for salvation. In Romans 16:5 *aparche* is used for the first converts in Asia—a kind of foretaste of the harvest that followed. Similarly in 1 Corinthians 16:15 the house of Stephanus is called the firstfruits of Achaia. In 1 Corinthians 15:20, 23, Christ is the *aparche* of the dead. His resurrection guarantees the resurrection of all those united to him.

It is Romans 8:23, however, that we are primarily interested in, for in this passage alone the Spirit is called the *aparche*. "But we ourselves, who have the first fruits of the Spirit, groan inwardly as we wait for adoption as sons, the redemption of our bodies." Again the genitive is epexegetical, meaning that the Spirit is the firstfruits. The background for this metaphor is to be found in the Old Testament cult where the firstfruits were offered and consecrated to God (Deut. 26:1-11; Lev. 2:12; Ezek. 45:1, LXX; 48:9 LXX). The idea of offering the firstfruits to God is, however, not the point which Paul wants to emphasize. He wants rather to stress that the firstfruits are a guarantee that the full harvest will follow soon. The Spirit gives the believer the assurance that all the fruits of Christ's redemptive work will be harvested by him in the future. What the first sheaf is to the harvest, the entrance of the Spirit of God into the heart of the believer is to the glory of ultimate salvation.

Firstfruits means more than the promise given by the sprouting of leaves or the bursting of blossoms. Firstfruits is the actual beginning of the harvest, yet it is not identical with it. Through the Spirit the life of the age to come has been made available to us in the present, in the midst of the decay and death of this evil age. We cannot experience its fullness until our bodies are redeemed.[35]

Since the harvest of redemption has only just begun, the sons of God groan with the rest of creation "until now." The "until now" (v. 22) underscores the eschatological import of the passage. The old aeon (that is the present) has not yet come to an end; the new has not yet fully come. We still experience the "birth pangs" (*sunodinei*, v. 22) of the messianic woes which precede the age to come, as this was thought of in Judaism. O. Michel suggests that these present birth pangs are our guarantee of the world to come.[36] The possession of the Spirit not only assures the believer of full and final redemption, but it also creates in him the desire for this redemption. It is not that he groans in spite of his possession of the firstfruits of the Spirit, but because of it. Berkhof says, "Our hope is based not primarily on what we miss but on what we already have."[37] The Spirit, as the already present power of the life in the new aeon, creates in those who have the Spirit a yearning to share that power and life without the encumbrances of the unredeemed body.

Leenhardt suggests that there are at least three ideas in *aparche:* (a) a part of the sum total is already present; (b) there is anticipation; (c) this first installment is the pledge and guarantee of the reward to come.[38] He adds that we should not lay the emphasis on the "partial" receipt of redemption, but on the chronological aspect of the metaphor.[39] The chronological meaning of *aparche* is certainly strong in 1 Corinthians 15:20 and 23, where Christ is the first to be raised in order of time.[40] The life of the Spirit here on earth does not exhaust the fullness of God's redemptive gifts, for we share the bondage to decay which afflicts all creation. God did not create us that we might suffer and succumb to corruption and death, however. He has given us the assurance of the redemption of our bodies. This blessing belongs to the future when the sonship for which we are waiting becomes full and complete. As a guarantee that this day will come, God has given us the Spirit of sonship.

Since we have the Holy Spirit only as the firstfruits, Eduard Schweizer suggests that we should be modest in our claim. "Even the most Spirit-filled community," he points out, "is not yet in heaven but only in a threatened, groaning, and dying world."[41]

4. The Spirit and Sonship

This is another aspect of the activity of the Spirit which adds to the ground of our hope. The Spirit gives us the assurance that we are God's children. We have observed earlier that the Spirit moves the believer to cry "Abba!" This prayer, which speaks of the filial relationship which has been established between the child of God and the Father, is an assurance of an inheritance in the future (Gal. 4:6, 7; Rom. 8:15-17). This gives the "Abba, Father" an eschatological ring. To be God's children means to be heirs of God, and fellow-heirs of Christ (Rom. 8:17). His children will receive what he received; they will be glorified with him. For the present, this glory is veiled, to be sure. The Spirit, nevertheless, assures the believer of his sonship. "It is the Spirit himself bearing witness with our spirit that we are children of God" (Rom. 8:16). "The inner witness of the Spirit corroborates with ever renewed power our own conviction that God has made us his children, and that consequently all the vast implications of this fact for our future destiny are likewise assured."[42]

Because we are children (v. 16), we are also "heirs" (v. 17). With these two terms Paul has described both the present and the future of the believer's life.[43] Because the Spirit assures us that we are God's children, we also have the assurance that when Christ's glory will be revealed (v. 18), we shall fully possess our possessions. "We ourselves, who have the first fruits of the Spirit, groan inwardly as we wait for adoption as sons, the redemption of our bodies" (Rom. 8:23). That sonship which is awaited in the end is already present in the church today.[44] The notion of inheritance with which the concept of sonship is connected, suggests this future dimension. Moreover, Paul says that all creation awaits the "unveiling" of the sons of God. The sonship of the believers is not yet fully revealed. Sonship in the present is a kind of proleptic sonship, experienced by faith and not by sight. The full experience of sonship is impossible as long as Christians are in the body. Hamilton says, "In relation to sonship specifically, believers wait eagerly for adoption, which is then further defined as the redemption of the body."[45] This future redemption of the body is the unfulfilled aspect of sonship. Possession of the Spirit is a great privilege, but it is not God's final gift. Final acceptance into God's family is the Christian's hope. This hope will be realized only when the body is redeemed, when it is raised from the dead, when the physical gives way to the spiritual. The Spirit is the Spirit of adoption "in the sense that he enables believers to realize their privileges and responsibilities as sons of God against the day when they will be publicly revealed as such."[46] Green says, "Even our sonship, mediated to us by the Spirit, has this ambiguity about it. On the one hand, we can be sure that the Spirit makes us sons

(Romans 8:15). On the other, we have still to wait for our final adoption at the Second Coming (Romans 8:23)."[47] This hope has a solid foundation in the love of God manifested in Christ.

5. *The Spirit and the Love of God*

Because the believer has been justified (Rom. 5:1), he has the "hope of sharing the glory of God" (5:2)—a hope which does not disappoint him (5:5). Since Christ has brought in the new aeon, Christians can boast even now in the glory of God. To share in the glory of God is the ultimate and highest that can be affirmed of the Christ-life, but this glory is ours only "in hope." This hope gives strength in tribulation and a new meaning to suffering (5:3, 4). What is it, then, that makes this hope so strong? It is the love of God for humankind—a love manifested in its utmost limits by the sacrifice of God's Son. This, says Paul, has been poured into our hearts by the Holy Spirit (5:5). The Holy Spirit gives the believer the deep assurance that God's love has been demonstrated in all its fullness in Christ. The sequence of thought in verses 5 and 6 is: (a) hope does not disappoint us, because (b) the love of God has been poured out; and this we know because, (c) while we were weak, Christ died for the ungodly. Christ's death for humankind gives the pentecostal outpouring of God's love real significance.[48] This in turn gives ground for hope of ultimate glory and the assurance that this hope will not prove to be an illusion. As a matter of fact, the presence of the Holy Spirit in the heart is already an indication that God has begun to fulfill his promises.

To say that God's love "floods our hearts," in the sense that it gives us an emotional awareness of his love, is to miss the point, for this would make the assurance of hope depend upon subjective awareness. The Holy Spirit convinces people of God's love for them, by making the death and resurrection of Jesus contemporary for them. To state it differently, the Spirit draws people into Christ's dying and rising, so that the demonstration of his love by his death for sinners is not merely a historical event but a living reality.

We see, then, that the hope of the believer in Christ completing what he has begun, has solid foundations. By the Spirit the believer has been marked out as Christ's possession whom he will redeem in the end. The Spirit is Christ's down payment by which he obligates himself to full "payment" in the future. By the Spirit the believer already enjoys the power of the resurrection as "first fruits" of the harvest which will be his in due time. The Spirit assures the believer full standing in God's family as a son or daughter—one who has free access to the Father as an heir of the Father's possessions. By the Spirit God has assured his own of his immeasurable, unchanging love in the sacrifice of his Son.

The writer to the Hebrews expresses essentially the same thought that we find in Paul: the believers have "become partakers of the Holy Spirit" (Heb. 6:4); because they have received the gift of the Spirit, they have tasted "the powers of the age to come" (v. 5). The "powers" is a reference to the mighty works which accompanied the proclamation and reception of the gospel, by which believers were given a foretaste of that age which is yet to come.

With all these assurances of what is yet to come, we must now ask whether there are some specific things that the Spirit assures us of that will be our possession in the future. We have already mentioned the redemption of the body at the coming of Christ. But this resurrection and transformation of the body is but the gateway to the fullness of eternal life, to righteousness, glory, and the eternal kingdom. All these things are assured to us by the Holy Spirit.

B. The Spirit and the Substance of Hope

On the basis of the Spirit's action in the present, the future age is experienced in an anticipatory way by believers. The Spirit fills them with hope (Rom. 15:13)—a hope which is no fiction, for it is already in the process of being realized. The Christian life is suspended as it were between the two poles of deliverance—the one already attained in Christ, and the other still awaited. By the Spirit they are experiencing the destruction of the powers of death in advance, but the final redemption of the body remains a hope.

The resurrection of the body, then, constitutes in part the substance of the believer's hope.

1. The Spirit and the Redemption of the Body

In Ephesians 4:30 we are informed that the Spirit has sealed the members of the people of God "for the day of redemption." Although this day of redemption entails more than the resurrection of the body, Paul informs us that the Spirit gives us the hope of "the redemption of our body" (Rom. 8:23). He is confident that God "will give life to your mortal bodies" (Rom. 8:11). The Spirit is God's guarantee that mortality will "be swallowed up by life" (2 Cor. 5:4, 5). We are not surprised, then, that Paul trusted in the Spirit of Jesus Christ as he stared death in the face (Phil. 1:19).

Nowhere does Paul give us such an elaborate development of the idea of the resurrection of the body as in 1 Corinthians 15. The interpretation of this resurrection chapter often goes awry because Greek notions of immortality are superimposed on Paul's writings.[49] The "immortality of the soul" is one of the great misunderstandings carried over from Greek thought into the New Testament.[50] The body is not the soul's prison, but the "temple of the Holy Spirit" (1 Cor. 6:19). The body is not evil, it is God's creation, although sin has embraced it as it has the "whole person." Paul knows the difference between body and soul, but not as opposites of evil and good. Both are marked by sin, and both can be set free by the power of the Holy Spirit. This spiritual renewal can be experienced in Christ, but the final transformation of the body does not take place until the end. The resurrection is, as Cullmann points out, not the flight of the immortal soul from the body but "the transition from the present age to the future."[51]

The Spirit gives the believer a foretaste of the glorious consummation by raising him to a new life in Christ, and by enabling him to live in the power of the resurrection. The Spirit also assures him that even though his body goes to the dust, death cannot sever his relationship with the risen Lord, with whom he has become one Spirit. The risen Christ, the firstborn from the dead, has become a life-giving Spirit (1 Cor. 15:45), and by his Spirit he gives those who belong to him a "spiritual body" at his parousia.

With the resurrection of the body other hopes of the saints are fulfilled; one of these is the hope of righteousness.

2. The Spirit and Righteousness

In his letter to the Galatians, Paul said: "For through the Spirit, by faith, we wait for the hope of righteousness" (5:5). True believers are set off from those who seek to be justified through circumcision and other religious observances. They differ in the way in which righteousness is obtained. In contrast to self-effort and the observance of external rites and regulations, the true believers wait for righteousness from the Spirit. The legalists also wait for ultimate justification on the basis of external religious observances, but those who live by faith wait for that righteousness which they already enjoy as a foretaste.

To "wait" (*apekdechomai*) speaks of a strong and eager longing. But there is nothing nebulous about this waiting; the believer waits for "righteousness." "Righteousness" has a variety of meanings in Paul, but here it clearly refers to the gift of salvation which the believer experiences by faith here in this life. Final justification and acquittal, however, takes place only when the believer stands before the judgment seat of Christ (2 Cor. 5:10). To wait for "the hope of righteousness," then, is to anticipate this final justification by God. All of Paul's theology is characterized by the "already" and the "not yet"; this applies to righteousness as much as it does to salvation or to sonship. It is a present possession (Rom. 5:1), but it is also a future hope.

In waiting for the complete and final gift of righteousness, the Spirit plays an important role. "By the Spirit" we wait. It is possible to view "Spirit" and "faith" as coordinates, expressing a dual source of the Christian hope: "through the Spirit by faith" we wait—faith the subjective, Spirit the objective power. The meaning would then be: we anticipate the realization of our hope of righteousness not in the law but, on the one side, through the

Spirit of God and, on the other, by faith. Vos says that "these two designate the subjective and objective ground respectively on which the confident expectation is based."[52]

Like everything else given to us in Christ, the gift of righteousness stands in a tension of hope: we are justified and we shall be justified. Hamilton says, "By *dikaiosune* (righteousness) Paul means the final acceptance of God at the end after which there is no possibility of rejection."[53] The end, of course, is the parousia. The thought of final judgment does not rob the believer of the assurance of salvation, but it becomes a motive for obedience.[54] This assurance of justification by faith as a present possession and as a future hope sets Paul's theology off from that of the synagogue. In Judaism justification was thought of as taking place only in the end; it was not viewed as a present gift.[55] Moreover, there was generally a lack of assurance about justification in the end, because of the merit system by which men sought for righteousness. In one respect Paul is in agreement with Judaism, in the conviction that there will be a judgment in the end. Oepke says that Paul shared with Judaism the hope of final justification but, he adds, the difference lies in "by faith" "through the Spirit."[56] In two respects at least Paul differed from Judaism. First, righteousness was for him a possession available in the present to all those who put their trust in Christ; second, in the deep assurance that in the end those who are in Christ will be acquitted. "The Spirit's presence and power is the ground of the Christian's expectation of complete righteousness and final justification."[57]

3. The Spirit and Eternal Life

According to the prophets, the bestowal of life was to be a central function of the Spirit in the new age. For example, Ezekiel, in his vision of the valley of corpses, saw the breath of Yahweh revitalizing the dead (Ezek. 37:14). In contrast to the rabbis who claimed that the Torah gave eternal life (cf. Jn. 5:29), Paul claimed that the law brought death (Rom. 7:10) and that eternal life is the gift of the Spirit (e.g., Rom. 8:2, 9, 10). "Life" represents all the blessings of the messianic kingdom. Eternal life—the life of the age to come—is the life of the risen Lord which all believers enjoy even while they are in this mortal body by virtue of the work of the Spirit; on the other hand, life is still a hope.

The expression "eternal life" occurs rarely in Paul (see, e.g., Rom. 2:7; 5:21; 6:22; Gal. 6:8), but is not sharply distinguished from "life," which is more common. There has been some dispute as to whether "eternal" has a temporal or a qualitative meaning, but it is not an either/or; it is both. It is a particular "kind" of life, but it is also "everlasting" in duration.[58] At the moment we are interested particularly in the temporal aspect of eternal life. Richardson says, "The tension between the 'now' and the 'not yet' which characterizes New Testament eschatology is particularly evident in respect of life."[59] Christians already have eternal life, but it is hidden (Col. 3:3). However, when Christ who is their life shall be manifest, they shall be manifested with him in glory (Col. 3:4). The life in Christ which is experienced here and now by the power of the Spirit is the guarantee that in the future this eternal life will be manifested in all its fullness.

There is one passage in which Paul says explicitly that eternal life is a gift of the Spirit in the future, namely, Galatians 6:8. "For he who sows to his own flesh will from the flesh reap corruption; but he who sows to the Spirit will from the Spirit reap eternal life." Using the figure of the harvest, Paul relates the Spirit directly to the future by picturing it as the source and basis of eternal life. The verse seems to be an application of a folk saying found in the Old Testament (Hos. 8:7; Prov. 22:8; Joel 3:13) as well as in Greco-Roman philosophy,[60] that a person reaps what he sows. One cannot outwit God (*mukterizo* means to turn up one's nose) by reaping a harvest contrary to what one has sown.[61] In verse 7 the correspondence is between the seed and the harvest, while in verse 8 the correspondence is between the soil and the harvest. Instead of two kinds of seed, two kinds of soil are distinguished. The two kinds of soil are the "flesh" and the "Spirit." "Spirit" should not be limited to the human spirit as Burton suggests, for then "sowing to the Spirit" means simply something like enriching one's own inner life. Moreover, if "Spirit" means man's spirit, one is almost bound to equate "flesh" with the body; that kind of dichotomy is more Platonic than Pauline.[62]

Flesh and Spirit are viewed here as the ends and goals of a person's life. The preposition *eis* (unto) is not to be understood in its local but in its telic sense.[63] To sow to the flesh is to live a life that is governed by the power of sin; to sow to the Spirit is to live under the rule of God's Spirit. This life, in the present aeon, is seedtime; the parousia brings the harvest.[64] To live a life dominated by the principle of the flesh is to suffer "corruption" in the end; by contrast, to live a life controlled by the Spirit of God reaps "eternal life" from the Spirit. Eternal life is the portion only of the one who sows to the Spirit, whose whole orientation in life is determined by the Spirit.

To say that this passage contradicts Romans 6:23, where eternal life is the free gift of God's grace, betrays a misunderstanding of the eschatological gifts of salvation. "Eternal life" is not just something added on at death or at the judgment; it is organically related to the actual life lived.[65] Like "redemption" and "justification," "eternal life" is experienced proleptically in the present by the Spirit. "The Spirit . . . enables [us] to appropriate and enjoy in advance the benefits of the age to come."[66] But all of these blessings of redemption find their fulfillment only at the parousia, when this present age gives way to eternity.

Perhaps nowhere is the relationship of the Holy Spirit to the blessed hope of the church expressed so vividly as in the last book of the Bible. John ends the Revelation with the prayer of the Spirit and the church: "The Spirit and the Bride say, 'Come' " (22:17). Since the second half of the verse is an invitation to the thirsty to come and drink of the waters of life, it is held by some commentators that the "come" of the Spirit is the church's invitation to the world to come to Jesus.[67] While such a reading of the text makes good sense, it is more likely that the first part of verse 17 is the maranatha cry of the church. The Holy Spirit and the church pray for the return of the absent bridegroom, Christ.[68]

How are we to understand the prayer of the Holy Spirit for the return of Christ? That the Spirit helps the church to pray, is clearly taught in Romans 8:36ff., for example. However, here it is not prayer in general but a specific prayer that the Spirit and the church utter: the prayer for Christ's return. Since the Spirit is closely identified with prophecy (Rev. 19:10), we might say that the Spirit speaks to the church through the prophetic word, reminding her of Christ's coming. The book of Revelation itself is a prophetic word (22:9, 10), and as this book is read in the churches the Spirit speaks through it to the church and he calls on the church to join him in the prayer "Come!" "Let him who hears say 'Come.' "

The presence of the Spirit in the church keeps her hope of Christ's return alive. Hundreds of years of waiting have not been able to silence the church's prayer of longing. The Spirit does this in different ways. He gives the church a foretaste of what is yet to come and so keeps her hope alive. He reminds the church by the prophetic Word that Christ's promise to return will someday be fulfilled. The Spirit also makes the church aware of its immaturity and lack of completeness and so creates in her the cry for Christ's return when the imperfect will be done away with. He reminds us that we are pilgrims and strangers in this world and creates in us the longing for the world to come. Like the bride who looks forward to her wedding day when she will be united with her bridegroom, the church looks forward to the marriage supper of the lamb. This hope is inspired and kept alive by the Holy Spirit.

This longing for Christ's return fostered by the Spirit in the church does not, however, lead the church to withdraw from the world into inactivity. We must read Revelation 22:17 to the end. After calling on the church to join the Spirit in his prayer for Christ's return, John reminds the church of her mission in the world. "And let him who is thirsty come." Only after the church has completed its mission, only after the Spirit and the Bride have said "Come" for the last time, will Jesus appear again.

We have tried to map out the contours of the activity of the Holy Spirit in the life of the early church, as these are seen in the

documents of the New Testament. What does this mean for us today? It is one thing to describe the functions of the Spirit in the
apostolic church; it is quite another to experience his presence and
power today. We must, therefore, give heed to Christ's sevenfold
exhortation to the churches of Asia: "He who has an ear, let him
hear what the Spirit says to the churches" (Rev. 2:7, 11, 17, 29;
3:6, 13, 22). In every age we must learn to hear what the Spirit is
saying to the church. While it is impossible for the church to turn
back the clock of history and to relive the church's pioneer days, it
must continue to be guided by the Spirit, who speaks to us by the
apostolic Scriptures.

Notes

Author's Preface

1. J. D. G. Dunn, "Rediscovering the Spirit," *Expository Times*, 84 (Oct. 1972), p. 7.
2. J. A. Mackay, *Christian Reality and Appearance* (John Knox Press, 1969), p. 59.
3. W. Barclay, *A Spiritual Autobiography* (Eerdmans, 1975), p. 25.

Chapter 1

1. The "promise of the Father" in the Lucan texts just mentioned is what grammarians call a subjective genitive, for the promise was made by the Father; the "promise of the Holy Spirit," as we find it in Galatians 3:14, however, is objective genitive, since it is the Spirit that was promised.

2. See the survey on the activity of the Spirit in the Old Testament by G. W. H. Lampe, "Holy Spirit," *Interpreter's Dictionary of the Bible* (hereafter *IDB*), ed. G. Buttrick (Abingdon Press, 1962), II, pp. 626-639.

3. S. Mowinckel, "The Spirit and the Word in the Pre-exilic Reforming Prophets," *Journal of Biblical Literature*, 53 (1934), pp. 199-227.

4. Edmond Jacob, *Theology of the Old Testament* (Harper and Row, 1958), p. 125.

5. M. Green, *I Believe in the Holy Spirit* (Eerdmans, 1975), p. 19. The various quotations from this book throughout my work are used by permission of William B. Eerdmans Publishing Co. and Hodder and Stoughton Ltd.

6. J. Bright, *The Kingdom of God* (Abingdon Press, 1953), p. 150.

7. "Von einer kraeftigen Fortentwickelung des Geistgedankens oder gar der Geisterlebnisse in irgend einer Richtung kann also nicht geredet werden, der fruehere Geistgedanke erhaelt sich und unterliegt gewissen Veraenderungen, Beeinflussungen, die aber auch nicht viel besagen," writes F. Buechsel, in *Der Geist Gottes im Neuen Testament* (Guetersloh: C. Bertelsmann, 1926), p. 99; see also pp. 54-135. See also F. Sjoeberg, "Pneuma," *Theological Dictionary of the New Testament* (Eerdmans, 1964, etc.), VI, p. 382 (hereafter *TDNT*).

8. H. L. Strack and P. Billerbeck, *Kommentar zum Neuen Testament aus Talmud und Midrasch*, 4 Bde. 3 Afl. (Muenchen: C. H. Beck'sche Verlagsbuchhandlung, 1961), II, pp. 125f.

9. K. G. Kuhn, *Konkordanz zu den Qumrantexten* (Goettingen: Vandenhoeck und

Ruprecht, 1960), s.v. Kuhn lists at least 100 references from the main documents but some of these do not speak of the Spirit of God or the Holy Spirit specifically.

10. F. F. Bruce, "The Holy Spirit in the Acts of the Apostles," *Interpretation*, XXVII (April 1973), pp. 166-183.

11. R. Brown, *The Birth of the Messiah* (Doubleday, 1977), p. 269.

12. In Ephesians 5:18 Paul contrasts the stimulation caused by wine with that of the fullness of the Spirit.

13. Brown, *op. cit.*, p. 341.

14. L. Morris, *The Gospel According to Luke* (Eerdmans, 1974), p. 79.

Chapter 2

1. C. H. H. Scobie, *John the Baptist* (Fortress Press, 1964), p. 102.

2. *Ibid.*, p. 113.

3. W. Lane, *The Gospel According to Mark. The New International Commentary of the New Testament* (hereafter *NICNT*) (Eerdmans, 1974), p. 48.

4. In contrast to the Synoptists, who have the promise in the future tense, John has it in the present. One might, however, think of the expression "He who baptizes with the Holy Spirit" (Jn. 3:33) as a futuristic present.

5. A. M. Hunter, *Gleanings from the New Testament* (Westminster Press, 1975), p. 35.

6. J. D. G. Dunn, *Baptism in the Holy Spirit* (Alec R. Allenson, 1970), p. 11.

7. F. D. Bruner, *A Theology of the Holy Spirit* (Eerdmans, 1970), p. 37.

8. D. Lange, *Eine Bewegung Bricht Sich Bahn* (Brunnen Verlag, 1979). Lange reports in great detail how the *Gemeinschaftsbewegung* within the confines of the Lutheran state church wrestled for years with the question of a second work of grace and finally set itself off from it. This double work of grace is reflected in the popular hymn "Rock of Ages," written by Toplady, in which the line "Be of sin the double cure, save from wrath, and make me pure" emphasizes the two stages of the experience of God's grace. Modern American Methodism has changed "double" to "promised cure." See Bruner, *supra*, p. 43.

9. J. R. W. Stott, *Baptism and Fullness* (Inter-Varsity Press, 1976, 2nd ed.), p. 68.

10. J. D. G. Dunn, "Rediscovering the Spirit," *Expository Times*, 84, (Oct. 1972), p. 40.

11. J. D. G. Dunn, "Spirit-Baptism and Pentecostalism," *Scottish Journal of Theology*, 23 (1970), p. 406.

Chapter 3

1. F. F. Bruce, *Paul: Apostle of the Heart Set Free* (Eerdmans, 1977), p. 207.

2. M. Green, *The Truth of God Incarnate* (Eerdmans, 1977), pp. 40f.

3. W. Lane, *The Gospel According to Mark* (Eerdmans, 1974), p. 58.

4. I. H. Marshall, *Commentary on Luke* (Eerdmans, 1978), p. 153.

5. Jerome, quoted in Hennecke-Schneemelcher, *The New Testament Apocrypha* (Westminster Press, 1963), I, p. 163.

6. J. D. G. Dunn, *Baptism in the Holy Spirit* (Alec R. Allenson, 1970), p. 32.

7. L. Morris, *The Gospel According to John* (Eerdmans, 1971), p. 152.

8. R. E. Brown, *The Gospel According to John* (I-XII), *The Anchor Bible* (hereafter *AB*) (Doubleday, 1966), I, p. 158.

9. Dunn, *op. cit.*, p. 24.

10. Lane, *op. cit.*, p. 59.

11. Dunn, *op. cit.*, p. 30.

12. Marshall, *op. cit.*, p. 169.

13. *Ibid.*, p. 171.

14. J. Taylor, *The Go-Between God* (Fortress Press, 1973), p. 20.

15. M. Green, *I Believe in the Holy Spirit* (Eerdmans, 1975), p. 39.

16. Marshall, *op. cit.*, p. 184.

17. Taylor, *op. cit.*, p. 91.

18. M. Green, *op. cit.*, p. 54.

19. Lane, *op. cit.*, p. 146.

20. Green, *op. cit.*, p. 36.

21. R. V. G. Tasker, *The Gospel According to St. Matthew* (Eerdmans, 1961), pp. 128f.

22. H. W. Beyer, "Blasphemia," in *TDNT*, eds. G. Kittel and G. Friedrich (Eerdmans, 1964, etc.), I, p. 624.

23. C. E. B. Cranfield, *The Gospel According to St. Mark*, 2nd ed. (Cambridge, 1963), p. 142.

Chapter 4

1. I. H. Marshall, *Commentary on Luke* (Eerdmans, 1978), p. 470.

2. F. D. Bruner, *A Theology of the Holy Spirit* (Eerdmans, 1970), pp. 170ff.

3. L. Morris, *The Gospel According to St. Luke. Tyndale New Testament Commentaries* (hereafter *Tyndale*) (Eerdmans, 1974), p. 196.

4. J. Taylor, *The Go-Between God* (Fortress Press, 1973), p. 85.

5. See above, p. 35.

6. H. L. Strack and P. Billerbeck, *Kommentar zum Neuen Testament aus Talmud und Midrasch*, 3. Afl. (Muenchen: C. H. Beck'sche Verlagsbuchhandlung, 1961), II, p. 431.

7. *Ibid.*, p. 420.

8. R. E. Brown, *The Gospel According to John. AB* (Doubleday, 1966), I, p. 130.

9. R. Schnackenburg, *The Gospel According to St. John* (Burns and Oates/Herder and Herder, 1968), I, p. 372.

10. L. Morris, *The Gospel According to John. NICNT* (Eerdmans, 1971), p. 216.

11. The *Apostolic Constitutions* of Hippolytus, VI.3.15.

12. H. R. Boer, *Pentecost and Missions* (Eerdmans, 1961), p. 72.

13. F. F. Bruce, *New Testament History* (Doubleday, 1971), pp. 156f.

14. 1QS iv:19-21.

15. The Greek word *pneuma* means both "wind" and "spirit" and the word "blow" comes from the same root.

16. Boer, *op. cit.*, pp. 72f.

17. Brown, *op. cit.*, I, p. 140.

18. F. F. Bruce, "The Holy Spirit in the Acts of the Apostles," *Interpretation, XXVII* (April 1973), p. 166.

19. Morris, *John*, p. 270.

20. Schnackenburg, *op. cit.*, I, p. 437.

21. Brown, *op. cit.*, I, p. 180.

22. *Ibid.*, I, p. 180.

23. Schnackenburg, *op. cit.*, I, p. 437.

24. C. K. Barrett, *The Gospel According to St. John* (Westminster Press, 2nd ed., 1978), p. 238.

25. Brown, *op. cit.*, I, p. 180.

26. Schnackenburg, *op. cit.*, I, p. 435.

27. "Sukkah," in *The Mishnah*, edited by H. Danby (Clarendon Press, 1933), pp. 172-181.

28. J. Marsh, *Saint John. Pelican New Testament Commentaries* (Penguin Books, 1968), p. 340.

29. "Sukkah," 3:8-15; 4:1-10.

30. W. Grundmann, "Krazo," in *TDNT*, II, pp. 898-903. *Krazo* occurs 4 times in John "and denotes a message which is declared in spite of contradiction and opposition." *Ibid.*, p. 901.

31. For a discussion of the variant readings see B. M. Metzger, *A Textual Commentary on the Greek New Testament* (United Bible Societies, 1970), p. 218.

32. Taylor, *op. cit.*, p. 85.

33. R. V. G. Tasker, *The Gospel According to St. John. Tyndale* (Eerdmans, 1960), p. 106.

34. Marsh, *op. cit.*, p. 342.

35. S. H. Hooke, "The Spirit Was Not Yet," *New Testament Studies*, IX (1962-63), pp. 372-380.

36. Brown, *op. cit.*, I, p. 320.

37. J. Behm, "Koilia," in *TDNT*, III, pp. 788f.

38. Morris, *op. cit.*, p. 424.

39. 1 QH 8:16.

40. Brown, *op. cit.*, I, pp. 323f.

41. Behm, *op. cit.*, III, p. 787.

42. See Marsh, *op. cit.*, p. 341; Morris, *op. cit.*, p. 425; Brown, *op. cit.*, I, pp. 323f.

43. J. I. McCord, "Emptying and Filling"; farewell remarks to the 1977 graduating class of Princeton Theological Seminary.

44. C. K. Barrett, *The Gospel According to St. John* (Westminster Press, 2nd ed., 1978), p. 88.

45. I. H. Marshall, *The Epistles of John. NICNT* (Eerdmans, 1978), p. 116.

46. J. Behm, "Parakletos," in *TDNT*, V, p. 801; for scholarly monographs on the Paraclete see O. Betz, *Der Paraklet* (Brill, 1963) and G. Johnston, *The Spirit-Paraclete in the Gospel of John* (Cambridge, 1970).

47. Brown, *op. cit.*, II, p. 1132.

48. Behm, *op. cit.*, II, p. 804.

49. G. Braumann, "Advocate," in *The New International Dictionary of New Testament Theology* (hereafter *NIDNTT*), ed. C. Brown (Zondervan, 1967-71), I, pp. 90f.

50. Brown, *op. cit.*, II, p. 1139.

51. Barrett, *op. cit.*, p. 461.

52. Brown, *op. cit.*, II, p. 1140.

53. Marsh, *op. cit.*, p. 509.

54. Barrett, *op. cit.*, p. 463.

55. Morris, *op. cit.*, p. 656.

56. Barrett, *op. cit.*, p. 467.

57. H. Küng, *The Church* (Sheed and Ward, 1967), pp. 201f.

58. Brown, *op. cit.*, II, p. 689.

59. Morris, *op. cit.*, p. 784.

60. A. M. Hunter, *Probing the New Testament* (John Knox Press, 1971), p. 66.

61. W. F. Arndt and F. W. Gingrich, eds., *A Greek-English Lexicon of the New Testament* (University of Chicago Press, 1957), s.v.

62. Barrett, *op. cit.*, p. 488.

63. Brown, *op. cit.*, II, pp. 712f.

64. D. A. Carson, "The Function of the Paraclete in John 16:7-11," *Journal of Biblical*

Literature, 98/4 (1979), pp. 547-566.

65. M. Green, *I Believe in the Holy Spirit* (Eerdmans, 1975), p. 47. Used by permission.

66. Barrett, *op. cit.*, p. 570.

67. Brown, *op. cit.*, II, p. 1038.

68. J. D. G. Dunn, *Baptism in the Holy Spirit* (Alec R. Allenson, 1970), p. 178.

69. Morris, *op. cit.*, p. 847.

70. Bruce, *The Book of Acts. NICNT* (Eerdmans, 1954), p. 33.

71. Brown, *op. cit.*, II, p. 1038.

72. Dunn, *op. cit.*, p. 178. See also D. Bruner, *A Theology of the Holy Spirit* (Eerdmans, 1970), p. 64.

73. Green, *op. cit.*, pp. 41f.

74. J. D. G. Dunn, *Jesus and the Spirit* (Westminster Press, 1975), p. 144.

75. Marsh, *op. cit.*, p. 643.

76. Brown, *op. cit.*, II, p. 1039.

77. B. Lindars, *The Gospel of John. New Century Bible* (hereafter *NCB*) (Attic Press, 1972), p. 611.

78. W. Barclay, *The Gospel of John* (The Saint Andrew Press, 1955), II, p. 319.

79. Brown, *op. cit.*, II, p. 1043.

Chapter 5

1. J. D. G. Dunn, *Baptism in the Holy Spirit* (Alec R. Allenson, 1970), p. 44.

2. J. D. G. Dunn, *Jesus and the Spirit* (Westminster Press, 1975), p. 141.

3. J. H. E. Hull, *The Holy Spirit in the Acts of the Apostles* (Lutterworth, 1967), pp. 50f.

4. Roland de Vaux, *Ancient Israel: Its Life and Institutions* (McGraw-Hill, 1961), pp. 490f.

5. *Ibid.*, pp. 490f.

6. G. W. H. Lampe, "The Holy Spirit in the Writings of St. Luke," *Studies in the Gospels*, ed. D. E. Nineham, p. 198.

7. Philo, in *De Dec.* 9, 11; *De Spec. Leg.* 31, describes the giving of the law in terms that are strangely parallel to Luke's Pentecost account.

8. Hull, *op. cit.*, p. 53.

9. *Ibid.*, p. 55.

10. G. Vermes, *The Dead Sea Scrolls in English* (Penguin Books, 1962), pp. 31, 44.

11. Philo, *De Dec.*, pp. 33, 46.

12. The filling of the house in which the 120 sat is reminiscent of the temple scene in Isaiah 6.

13. R. F. Zehnle, *Peter's Pentecost Discourse* (S. B. L., 1971), p. 117.

14. Dunn, *Jesus and the Spirit*, p. 148.

15. I. H. Marshall, "The Significance of Pentecost," *Scottish Journal of Theology*, 30/4 (1977), p. 357.

16. F. F. Bruce, "The Holy Spirit in the Acts of the Apostles," *Interpretation, XXVII* (April 1973), p. 171.

17. F. F. Bruce, *Paul: Apostle of the Heart Set Free* (Eerdmans, 1977), p. 281. Used by permission.

18. Hull, *op. cit.*, pp. 95ff.

19. *Ibid.*, p. 99.

20. H. Bietenhard, "Onoma," in *TDNT*, V, p. 274.

21. Bruce, "The Holy Spirit in the Acts of the Apostles," *Interpretation, XXVII* (April 1973), p. 171.

22. Dunn, *Baptism with the Holy Spirit*, p. 53.

23. W. Neil, *The Acts of the Apostles* (Attic Press, 1973), p. 79.

Chapter 6

1. M. Green, *I Believe in the Holy Spirit* (Eerdmans, 1975), p. 137. Italics his.

2. J. D. G. Dunn, *Baptism in the Holy Spirit* (Alec R. Allenson, 1970), p. 65.

3. C. S. C. Williams, *The Acts of the Apostles* (Adam and Charles Black, 2nd ed., 1964), p. 116.

4. W. Neil, *The Acts of the Apostles* (Attic Press, 1973), p. 122.

5. F. F. Bruce, *The Book of Acts* (Eerdmans, 1954), p. 182.

6. G. W. H. Lampe, *Seal of the Spirit* (Longmans, Green and Co., 1951), pp. 70ff.

7. F. D. Bruner, *A Theology of the Holy Spirit* (Eerdmans, 1970), p. 176.

8. Green, *op. cit.*, pp. 138f. Used by permission.

9. *Ibid.*, p. 133.

10. J. R. W. Stott, *Baptism and Fullness* (Inter-Varsity Press, 1976), p. 30.

11. *Ibid.*, p. 34.

12. Bruner, *op. cit.*, p. 193.

13. F. F. Bruce, "The Holy Spirit in the Acts of the Apostles," *Interpretation, XXVII* (April 1973), p. 176.

14. Stott, *op. cit.*, p. 36.

15. J. H. E. Hull, *The Holy Spirit in the Acts of the Apostles* (Lutterworth, 1967), p. 118.

16. I. H. Marshall, "The Significance of Pentecost," *Scottish Journal of Theology*, 30/4 (1977), p. 369.

Chapter 7

1. J. R. W. Stott, *Baptism and Fullness* (Inter-Varsity Press, 1976), pp. 47f.

2. M. Green, *I Believe in the Holy Spirit* (Eerdmans, 1975), p. 153. Used by permission.

3. I. H. Marshall, "The Significance of Pentecost," *Scottish Journal of Theology*, 30/4 (1977), p. 355.

4. J. H. E. Hull, *The Holy Spirit in the Acts of the Apostles* (Lutterworth, 1967), p. 65.

5. Stott, *op. cit.*, p. 48.

6. H. Schlier, "Parrhesia," in *TDNT*, V, pp. 871-886.

7. H. C. Hahn, "Openness," in *NIDNTT*, ed. C. Brown (Zondervan, 1967), II, p. 736.

Chapter 8

1. The "Holy Spirit," with or without the article, is found 42 times; "Spirit," with or without the article, is found 10 times; twice the "Spirit of the Lord" is mentioned, and once "the Spirit of Jesus." It is doubtful whether Luke wanted to make any theological distinction between these different forms.

2. R. P. Martin, *The Family and the Fellowship* (Eerdmans, 1979), p. 23.

3. J. D. G. Dunn, *Baptism in the Holy Spirit* (Alec R. Allenson, 1970), p. 5.

4. J. Taylor, *The Go-Between God* (Fortress Press, 1973), p. 84.

5. F. F. Bruce, *Commentary on the Book of Acts. NICNT* (Eerdmans, 1955), p. 79.

6. Dorothy Sayers, *A Matter of Eternity* (Eerdmans, 1973), p. 23. Used by permission.

7. Martin, *op. cit.*, p. 31.

8. F. F. Bruce, "Lessons from the Early Church," in *In God's Community*, eds. D. J. Ellis and W. W. Gasque (Harold Shaw, 1979), p. 159.

9. F. F. Bruce, *Commentary on the Book of Acts. NICNT* (Eerdmans, 1955), p. 115.

10. *Ibid.*, p. 122.

11. K. Lake and H. J. Cadbury, in *The Beginnings of Christianity*, eds. Jackson and Lake (Baker Book House, reprinted 1965), IV, p. 107.

12. E. Haenchen, *The Acts of the Apostles* (Westminster Press, 1971), p. 333.

13. J. H. E. Hull, *The Holy Spirit in the Acts of the Apostles* (Lutterworth, 1967), p. 158.

14. A. M. Hunter, *Probing the New Testament* (John Knox Press, 1971), p. 69.

15. A. J. Mattill, "The Purpose of Acts: Schneckenburger Reconsidered," in *Apostolic History and the Gospel*, eds. Gasque and Martin (Eerdmans, 1970), pp. 110f.

16. Dunn, *op. cit.*, p. 49.

17. Hull, *op. cit.*, p. 155.

18. O. Betz, "Dunamis," in *TDNT*, II, p. 312.

19. D. Watson, *I Believe in the Church* (Eerdmans, 1978), p. 173. The various quotations from this book are used by permission of William B. Eerdmans Publishing Company and Hodder and Stoughton Ltd.

20. F. W. Dillistone, "The Holy Spirit and Christian Mission," in *The Theology of Christian Mission*, ed. G. Anderson (SCM Press, 1961), p. 279.

21. L. Coenen, "Witness," in *NIDNTT*, ed. C. Brown (Zondervan, 1975), III, p. 1044.

22. M. Green, *I Believe in the Holy Spirit* (Eerdmans, 1975), p. 68.

23. *Ibid.*, p. 69.

24. H. R. Boer, *Pentecost and Missions* (Eerdmans, 1961), p. 213.

25. A. von Harnack, *The Mission and Expansion of Christianity* (Harper and Brothers, 1961), p. 368.

26. Hull, *op. cit.*, p. 142.

27. S. Weinstock, "Geographical Catalogue in Acts 2:9-11," *The Journal of Roman Studies*, 38 (1948), pp. 43-46.

28. E. Schweizer, *Church Order in the New Testament* (SCM Press, 1961), p. 75.

29. Taylor, *op. cit.*, p. 3.

30. Bruce, *Acts*, p. 186.

31. David Watson, *One in the Spirit* (Fleming H. Revell, 1973), pp. 55f.

32. B. M. Metzger, *A Textual Commentary on the Greek New Testament* (United Bible Societies, 1971), p. 360.

33. C. S. C. Williams, *The Acts of the Apostles* (Adam and Charles Black, 1964, 2nd ed.), p. 143.

34. Haenchen, *op. cit.*, p. 396.

35. H. B. Swete, *The Holy Spirit in the New Testament* (Baker Book House, reprinted 1964), p. 106.

36. Williams, *op. cit.*, p. 192.

37. Leslie Newbigin, *The Open Secret* (Eerdmans, 1978), pp. 71f. Used by permission.

38. Bruce, *Acts*, p. 394.

39. J. Dupont, *The Sources of Acts* (Herder and Herder, 1964), p. 90.

40. A. T. Robertson, *Word Pictures in the New Testament* (Broadman Press, 1930), III, p. 360.

41. E. F. Harrison, *Acts: The Expanding Church* (Moody Press, 1975), p. 323.

42. Haenchen, *op. cit.*, pp. 143f., n. 9.

43. F. F. Bruce, "The Holy Spirit in the Acts of the Apostles," *Interpretation, XXVII* (April 1973), p. 183.

Chapter 9

1. Hermann Gunkel, *Die Wirkungen des heiligen Geistes nach der populaeren Anschauung der apostolischen Zeit und der Lehre des Apostels Paulus* (Vandenhoeck und Ruprecht, 1888), p. 11.

2. H. W. Robinson, *The Christian Experience of the Holy Spirit* (Fontana Books, reprinted 1962), p. 20.

3. E. W. Hunt, *Portrait of Paul* (A. R. Mowbray and Co., 1968), p. 111.

4. M. Green, *The Second Epistle General of Peter and the General Epistle of Jude.* Tyndale (Eerdmans, 1968), p. 91. Some commentators read this passage as if it spoke rather of the correct interpretation of prophecy than of its inspiration. See, for example, J. N. D. Kelly, *A Commentary on the Epistles of Peter and of Jude* (Adam and Charles Black, 1969), pp. 323f.

5. D. Bloesch, "The Sword of the Spirit: The Meaning of Inspiration," *Themelios* (May 1980), p. 14.

6. F. F. Bruce, *The Epistle to the Hebrews* (Eerdmans, 1964), p. 241.

7. J. R. W. Stott, *Guard the Gospel* (InterVarsity Press, 1973), p. 101.

8. Bloesch, *op. cit.*, p. 14.

9. E. Best, *1 Peter. NCB* (Attic Press, 1971), p. 81.

10. Kelly, *op. cit.*, pp. 60f. Kelly is of the opinion that Peter did not have the Holy Spirit in mind but rather the preincarnate Christ, whom he thought of as a Spirit-being.

11. A. M. Stibbs, *The First Epistle General of Peter* (Eerdmans, 1959), p. 83.

12. Bloesch, *op. cit.*, p. 14.

13. Justin, *Apology*, pp. i., 61, 65.

14. J. Glöel, *Der Heilige Geist in der Heilsverkündigung des Paulus* (Gotha, 1888), p. 287.

15. E. Staehlin, "Nun," in *TDNT*, IV, p. 1118.

16. M. A. Chevallier, *Esprit de Dieu, Paroles d'hommes* (Delachaux et Niestle, 1966), p. 114.

17. G. Delling, "Ereunao," in *TDNT*, II, pp. 655-657.

18. A. Robertson and A. Plummer, *A Critical and Exegetical Commentary on the First Epistle of St. Paul to the Corinthians* (Charles Scribner's Sons, 1916), p. 44.

19. C. K. Barrett, *A Commentary on the First Epistle to the Corinthians* (Adam and Charles Black, 1968), p. 74.

20. *Ibid.*, p. 75.

21. H. B. Swete, *The Holy Spirit in the New Testament* (Baker Book House, reprinted 1964), p. 234.

22. J. R. W. Stott, *Baptism and Fullness* (Inter-Varsity Press, 1976), pp. 62f.

23. T. K. Abbott, *Critical and Exegetical Commentary on the Epistles to the Ephesians and to the Colossians* (Eerdmans, 1957), p. 28.

24. E. K. Simpson and F. F. Bruce, *Commentary on the Epistles to the Ephesians and Colossians* (Eerdmans, 1957), p. 186.

25. D. Watson, *I Believe in the Church* (Eerdmans, 1978), p. 172.

26. Bloesch, *op. cit.*, p. 25.

27. O. Cullmann, *Christ and Time* (Westminster Press, 1950), p. 157.

28. Chevallier, *op. cit.*, p. 109.

29. G. Delling, "Plerophoria," in *TDNT*, VI, p. 309.

30. C. Masson, *Les Deux Épitres de Saint Paul aux Thessaloniciens* (Delachaux et Niestlé, 1957), p. 20.

31. A. Robertson and A. Plummer, *op. cit.*, p. 33.

32. E. B. Allo, *Seconde Épitre aux Corinthiens* (J. Gabalda et Cie, 1956), p. 25.

33. W. Grundmann, "Dunamis," in *TDNT*, II, p. 312.

34. R. V. G. Tasker, *The Second Epistle of Paul to the Corinthians. Tyndale* (Eerdmans, 1958), p. 92.

35. Robertson and Plummer, *op. cit.*, p. 196.

36. Allo, *op. cit.*, p. 176.

37. Bruce, *1 and 2 Corinthians*, p. 212; Hughes, *The Second Epistle to the Corinthians*, p. 228; Swete, *The Holy Spirit in the NT*, pp. 196f.; Filson, *Second Corinthians. The Interpreter's Bible* (hereafter IB), X, p. 349.

38. G. Johnston, *Ephesians, Philippians, Colossians and Philemon* (Thomas Nelson and Sons, 1967), p. 26.

39. H. L. Strack and P. Billerbeck, *Kommentar zum Neuen Testament aus Talmud und Midrasch* (C. H. Beck'sche Verlagsbuchhandlung, 1961), III, pp. 618, 687f.

40. J. R. W. Stott, *God's New Society* (InterVarsity Press, 1979), p. 282.

41. M. Barth, *Ephesians 4-6. AB* (Doubleday, 1974), p. 777.

42. *Ibid.*, p. 785.

43. D. Watson, *I Believe in the Church* (Eerdmans, 1978), pp. 171f. Used by permission.

44. *Ibid.*, p. 219.

45. L. Goppelt, *Der Erste Petrusbrief* (Vandenhoeck und Ruprecht, 1978), p. 109.

46. J. N. D. Kelly, *A Commentary on the Epistles of Peter and of Jude* (Adam and Charles Black, 1969), p. 63.

Chapter 10

1. J. D. G. Dunn, *Baptism in the Holy Spirit* (Alec R. Allenson, 1970), p. 108.

2. J. Denney, "The Theology of the Epistle to the Romans," *The Expositor*, 3 (1901), p. 423.

3. R. T. Stamm, *The Epistle to the Galatians. IB* (Abingdon Press, 1953), X, p. 498.

4. Fr. Büchsel, *Der Geist Gottes im Neuem Testament* (C. Bertelsmann, 1926), p. 308.

5. J. Glöel, *Der Heilige Geist in der Heilsverkündigung des Paulus* (Gotha, 1888), p. 130.

6. Denney, *op. cit.*, p. 426.

7. Feine says, "Der Glaube an die Sühnkraft Christi ergreift den Geist." P. Feine, *Theologie des Neuen Testaments* (J. C. Hinrichs'sche Buchhandlung, 1922), p. 278.

8. Dunn, *op. cit.*, p. 108.

9. M. Green, *I Believe in the Holy Spirit* (Eerdmans, 1975), p. 76.

10. Dunn, *op. cit.*, pp. 158f.

11. R. Bultmann, *Theology of the New Testament* (Charles Scribner's Sons, 1951), I, p. 332.

12. O. Michel, *Der Brief an die Römer* (Vandenhoeck und Ruprecht, 1963), p. 189.

13. R. T. Fortna, "Romans 8:10 and Paul's Doctrine of the Spirit," *Anglican Theological Review*, XLI (1959), pp. 77f.

14. M. A. Chevallier, *Esprit de Dieu, Paroles d'hommes* (Delachaux et Niestlé, 1966), p. 90.

15. F. V. Filson, *The Second Epistle to the Corinthians.* (Abingdon Press, 1953), X, p. 306.

16. Bultmann, *op. cit.*, I, pp. 262f.

17. P. E. Hughes, *Paul's Second Epistle to the Corinthians. NICNT* (Eerdmans, 1962), p. 101. Used by permission.

18. G. R. Beasley-Murray, *Baptism in the New Testament* (Eerdmans, 1962), p. 210.

19. Dunn, *op. cit.*, p. 168.

20. I. H. Marshall, *The Epistles of John. NICNT* (Eerdmans, 1978), p. 202.

21. *Ibid.*, p. 219.

22. Green, *op. cit.*, p. 78.

23. Hermann Gunkel, *Die Wirkungen des heiligen Geistes nach der populären Anschauung der apostolischen Zeit und der Lehre des Apostels Paulus* (Vandenhoeck und Ruprecht, 1888), p. 106.

24. J. Blunck, "Freedom," in *NIDNTT*, ed. C. Brown (Zondervan, 1967), I, p. 717.

25. R. Schnackenburg, *The Moral Teaching of the New Testament* (Seabury Press, 1965), p. 277.

26. J. Murray, *The Epistle to the Romans. NICNT* (Eerdmans, 1959), p. 276.

27. A. M. Hunter, *Interpreting Paul's Gospel* (SCM Press, 1954), p. 24.

28. J. A. T. Robinson, *The Body* (Regnery, 1952), pp. 17ff.

29. Dunn, *op. cit.*, p. 147.

30. E. D. W. Burton, *A Critical and Exegetical Commentary on the Epistle to the Galatians. International Critical Commentary*, (hereafter ICC) (T. and T. Clark, 1920), p. 302.

31. J. Denney, *op. cit.*, p. 428.

32. C. E. B. Cranfield, "St. Paul and the Law," *Scottish Journal of Theology*, 17 (1964), p. 66.

33. O. Cullmann, *Christ and Time* (Westminster Press, 1966), p. 237.

Chapter 11

1. G. W. H. Lampe, *The Seal of the Spirit* (Longmans, Green and Co., 1951), p. 51.

2. G. Johnston, *The Doctrine of the Church in the NT* (Cambridge University Press, 1943), p. 69.

3. J. G. Davies, *Spirit, Church and Sacraments* (The Faith Press, 1954), p. 45.

4. R. Schnackenburg, *The Church in the New Testament* (Herder and Herder, 1965), p. 17.

5. *Ibid.*, p. 100.

6. D. Watson, *I Believe in the Church* (Eerdmans, 1978), p. 231. Used by permission.

7. Johnston, *op. cit.*, p. 98.

8. J. R. W. Stott, *Baptism and Fullness* (Inter-Varsity Press, 1976), p. 42.

9. M. Green, *I Believe in the Holy Spirit* (Eerdmans, 1975), p. 132. Used by permission.

10. R. Schnackenburg, *Baptism in the Thought of St. Paul* (Blackwells, 1964), p. 85.

11. *Ibid.*, p. 3.

12. C. K. Barrett, *The First Epistle to the Corinthians* (Adam and Charles Black, 1968), p. 143.

13. F. F. Bruce, *The Epistle to the Ephesians* (Pickering and Inglis, 1961), p. 81.

14. D. Guthrie, *The Pastoral Epistles. Tyndale* (Eerdmans, 1957), p. 205.

15. A. R. Vidler, *Christian Belief* (SCM Press, 1950), p. 56.

16. R. V. G. Tasker, *The Second Epistle of Paul to the Corinthians* (Eerdmans, 1958), p. 191.

17. A. Plummer, *A Critical and Exegetical Commentary on the Second Epistle of Paul*

to the Corinthians (Charles Scribner's Sons, 1915), p. 383.

18. R. P. Martin, *The Family and the Fellowship* (Eerdmans, 1979), p. 38.

19. Paul's *oikein* (dwell) is parallel to John's *menein* (remain).

20. F. F. Bruce, *Paul: Apostle of the Heart Set Free* (Eerdmans, 1977), p. 209. Used by permission.

21. F. J. Leenhardt, *The Epistle to the Romans* (Lutterworth, 1961), p. 207.

22. F. Neugebauer, "Das paulinische 'in Christo,' " *New Testament Series*, IV (1957/58), p. 133.

23. C. H. Dodd, *The Meaning of Paul for Today* (Collins, 1957), p. 422.

24. N. Q. Hamilton, *The Holy Spirit and Eschatology in Paul* (Oliver and Boyd, 1957), p. 11.

25. K. Stalder, *Das Werk des Geistes in der Heiligung bei Paulus* (Evz. Verlag, 1962), p. 431.

26. Bruce, *Paul*, p. 211.

27. O. Michael, "Naos," in *TDNT*, IV, pp. 880-890.

28. L. Cerfaux, *The Christian in the Theology of St. Paul* (Herder and Herder, 1967), p. 297.

29. Stalder, *op. cit.*, pp. 431f.

30. H. Schlier, *Der Brief an die Epheser* (Patmos-Verlag, 1957), p. 145.

31. Davies, *op. cit.*, p. 82.

32. T. W. Manson, *On Paul and John* (SCM Press, 1963), p. 72.

33. D. M. Stanley, *Christ's Resurrection in Pauline Soteriology* (Pontifical Biblical Institute, 1961), p. 284.

34. J. D. Dunn, "Rediscovering the Spirit," *Expository Times*, 84 (Oct. 1972), p. 9.

35. Hamilton, *op. cit.*, p. 11.

36. Barrett, *op. cit.*, p. 164.

37. D. Hill, *Greek Words and Hebrew Meanings* (Cambridge University Press, 1967), p. 277.

38. K. L. Schmidt, "Prosagoge," in *TDNT*, I, pp. 133-134.

39. Bruce, *Paul*, pp. 210ff.

Chapter 12

1. A. M. Stibbs, *The First Epistle General of Peter. Tyndale* (Eerdmans, 1959), p. 72.

2. H. Seesemann, "Pateo," in *TDNT*, V, pp. 940-946.

3. P. Billerbeck, "Der gute und der boese Trieb," in *Kommentar zum Neuen Testament aus Talmud und Midrasch*, eds. H. L. Strack and P. Billerbeck, IV, pp. 466-483. See also R. E. Murph, "Yetzer in the Qumran Literature," *Biblica*, XXXLX (1958), pp. 334-344; J. Pryke, " 'Spirit and Flesh' in the Qumran Documents and Some New Testament Texts," *Revue de Qumran*, II (1965), pp. 345-360; O. J. F. Seitz, "Two Spirits in Man: An Essay in Biblical Exegesis," *New Testament Studies*, VI (1959-60), pp. 82-95.

4. H. Schlier, *Der Brief an die Galater* (Vandenhoek und Ruprecht, 1962), p. 264.

5. K. Bockmühl, "Law and the Spirit," *Christianity Today* (Feb. 24, 1978), p. 49.

6. D. Watson, *I Believe in the Church* (Eerdmans, 1978), p. 157.

7. C. H. Dodd, *The Meaning of Paul for Today* (Collins, 1957), p. 140.

8. A. Schlatter, *Gottes Gerechtigkeit, Ein Kommentar zum Roemerbrief* (Calwer Verlag, 1959), p. 293.

9. W. Fitch, *The Ministry of the Holy Spirit* (Zondervan, 1974), p. 130.

10. P. Bonnard, *Le Épitre de Saint Paul aux Galates* (Delachaux et Niestlé, 1953), p. 27.

11. E. Lohmeyer, *Die Briefe an die Philipper, an die Kolosser und an Philemon* (Vandenhoeck und Ruprecht, 1961), p. 52.

12. C. Masson, *Le Épitre de Saint Paul aux Ephésiens* (Delachaux et Niestlé, 1953), p. 180.

13. J. R. W. Stott, *God's New Society* (InterVarsity Press, 1979), p. 135.

14. J. Taylor, *The Go-Between God* (Fortress Press, 1973), p. 220.

15. L. Samuel, "The Spiritual Life No One Is Talking About," *Christianity Today* (Jan. 21, 1977), p. 12.

16. Not only is *metamorphoumetha* (transformed) in the present tense, but "from glory to glory" suggests an ongoing process also.

17. P. E. Hughes, *Paul's Second Epistle to the Corinthians. NICNT* (Eerdmans, 1962), p. 117.

18. R. V. G. Tasker, *The Second Epistle of Paul to the Galatians. Tyndale* (Eerdmans, 1958), p. 68.

19. F. F. Bruce, *Paul: Apostle of the Heart Set Free* (Eerdmans, 1977), p. 210. Used by permission.

20. O. Proksch, "Hagiasmos," in *TDNT*, pp. 113-115.

21. J. G. Davies, *Spirit, Church and Sacraments* (The Faith Press, 1954), p. 221.

22. F. F. Bruce, *1 and 2 Corinthians. NCB* (Attic Press, 1971), p. 62.

23. L. Goppelt, *Der Erste Petrusbrief* (Vandenhoeck und Ruprecht, 1978), p. 86.

24. Bruce, *Paul*, p. 210.

25. M. Green, *I Believe in the Holy Spirit* (Eerdmans, 1975), p. 153.

26. J. R. W. Stott, *Baptism and Fullness* (Inter-Varsity Press, 1976), p. 61.

27. H. C. G. Moule, *Veni Creator* (Hodder and Stoughton, 1892), p. 218.

28. Schlier, *Epheser*, p. 249.

29. F. Foulkes, *The Epistles of Paul to the Ephesians* (Eerdmans, 1963), p. 152.

30. Stott, *God's New Society*, p. 209.

31. Stott, *Baptism and Fullness*, p. 60.

32. Green, *op. cit.*, p. 156.

33. *Ibid.*, p. 157.

34. Fitch, *op. cit.*, p. 191.

35. S. Wibbing, *Die Tugend und Lasterkataloge im Neuen Testament* (Alfred Toepelmann, 1959), p. 75.

36. E. D. W. Burton, *A Critical and Exegetical Commentary on the Epistle to the Galatians* (T. and T. Clark, 1920), p. 313.

37. D. Guthrie, *Galatians. NCB* (Attic Press, 1974), p. 139.

38. Bruce, *op. cit.*, p. 461.

39. Davies, *op. cit.*, p. 6.

40. Schlier, *Galater*, p. 256.

41. A. M. Hunter, *Paul and His Predecessors* (SCM Press, rev. ed., 1961), p. 128.

42. D. Hill, *Greek Words and Hebrew Meanings* (Cambridge University Press, 1967), p. 271.

43. J. R. W. Stott, *Only One Way* (InterVarsity Press, 1968), p. 148.

44. T. K. Abbott, *Epistles to the Ephesians and to the Colossians* (T. and T. Clark, 1897), p. 201.

45. Stott, *Baptism and Fullness*, p. 79.

46. *Ibid.*, p. 80.

47. J. B. Adamson, *The Epistle of Jesus. NICNT* (Eerdmans, 1976), pp. 170ff.

48. R. V. G. Tasker, *The General Epistle of James. Tyndale* (Eerdmans, 1956), p. 91.

49. Stott, *God's New Society*, p. 189.

50. Fr. Lang, "Sbennumi," in *TDNT*, VII, pp. 165-168.

51. L. Morris, *The First and Second Epistles to the Thessalonians. NICNT* (Eerdmans, 1959), p. 175.

52. R. A. Ward, *Commentary on 1 and 2 Thessalonians* (Word Books, 1973), p. 117.

53. R. K. Harrison and C. Brown, "Quench," in *NIDNTT*, III, pp. 109f.

54. Lang, *op. cit.*, p. 168.

55. Ward, *op. cit.*, p. 117.

56. W. C. van Unnik, "Den Geist löscht nicht aus (1 Thes. 5:19)," *Novum Testamentum*, 10 (1968), pp. 255-269.

57. The negative *me* which precedes the present imperative indicates that an action is going on and that it is to cease.

58. D. Watson, *One in the Spirit* (Fleming H. Revell, 1973), pp. 100-112.

59. *Ibid.*, p. 56.

Chapter 13

1. K. Hess, "Serve," in *NIDNTT*, III, pp. 549-550. The word *latreia* is used of the individual Christian's worship and of Jewish and pagan cults, but not of the gathered Christian community. Other cultic terms in the New Testament are *threskeia* and *leitourgia*.

2. E. Schweizer, "The Service of the Church," *Neotestamentica* (1963), p. 333.

3. R. P. Martin, *Worship in the Early Church* (Eerdmans, 1964), p. 131.

4. H. Strathmann, "Latreuo, latreia," in *TDNT*, IV, pp. 58-65.

5. E. Lohmeyer, *Die Briefe an die Philipper, an die Kolosser und an Philemon* (Vandenhoeck and Ruprecht, 1961), p. 127.

6. P. Bonnard, *L'Épitre de Saint Paul aux Philippiens* (Delachaux et Niestlé, 1950), p. 60.

7. B. M. Metzger, *A Textual Commentary on the New Testament* (United Bible Society, 1971), p. 614.

8. F. W. Beare, *A Commentary on the Epistle to the Philippians* (Adam and Charles Black, 1959), p. 105.

9. W. C. van Unnik, quoted in R. P. Martin, *Worship in the New Testament*, p. 131.

10. D. Watson, *I Believe in the Church* (Eerdmans, 1978), p. 168.

11. V. H. Neufeld, *The Earliest Christian Confessions* (E. J. Brill, 1963).

12. F. F. Bruce, *The Spreading Flame* (Eerdmans, 1979), p. 239. Used by permission. The Greek word "Lord" *(kurios)* was used in the Septuagint for the Hebrew "Yahweh" and so New Testament writers transferred *kurios* to Jesus without embarrassment, for they held him to be divine.

13. F. F. Bruce, *1 and 2 Corinthians* (Attic Press, 1971), p. 118.

14. Pliny, *Epistles*, x, p. 96.

15. C. K. Barrett, *A Commentary on the First Epistle to the Corinthians* (Adam and Charles Black, 1968), pp. 279ff.

16. See the baptismal confession in the Byzantine Text of Acts 8:37.

17. H. L. Strack and P. Billerbeck, *Kommentar zum Neuen Testament aus Talmud und Midrasch* (C. H. Beck'sche Verlagsbuchhandlung, 1961), III, p. 243.

18. D. M. Stanley, *Christ's Resurrection in Pauline Soteriology* (Pontifical Biblical Institute, 1961), p. 281.

19. P. Bonnard, *L'Épitre de Saint Paul aux Galates* (Delachaux et Niestlé, 1953), p. 88.

20. D. Guthrie, *Galatians. NCB* (Attic Press, 1977), p. 115.

21. G. Kittel, "Abba," in *TDNT*, I, pp. 5-6.

22. J. Jeremias, *The Central Message of the New Testament* (Charles Scribner's Sons, 1965), p. 18.

23. Watson, *op. cit.*, p. 168.

24. W. Bieder, "Gebetswirklichkeit und Gebetsmoeglichkeit bei Paulus," *Theologische Zeitschrift*, 4 (1948), p. 25.

25. K. Niederwimmer, "Das Gebet des Geistes, Roem, 8:26f.," *Theologische*

Zeitschrift, 20 (1964), p. 253.

26. E. Schweizer, "Pneuma," in *TDNT*, VI, p. 428.

27. Bieder, *op. cit.*, p. 38.

28. *Ibid.*, p. 33.

29. F. F. Bruce, *The Epistle of Paul to the Romans* (Eerdmans, 1963), p. 175.

30. E. Käsemann, *Commentary on Romans* (Eerdmans, 1980), p. 241.

31. Bruce, *op. cit.*, p. 171.

32. M. Green, *I Believe in the Holy Spirit* (Eerdmans, 1975), p. 97. Used by permission.

33. J. Knox, *The Epistle to the Romans. IB* (Abingdon-Cokesbury, 1954), IX, p. 523.

34. L. S. Thornton, *The Common Life in the Body of Christ* (Dacre Press, 1942), p. 94.

35. G. Johnston, *Ephesians, Philippians, Colossians and Philemon* (Thomas Nelson and Sons, 1967), p. 27.

36. Green, *op. cit.*, p. 96.

37. J. D. G. Dunn, *Jesus and the Spirit* (Westminster Press, 1975), p. 246.

38. M. Green, *The Second Epistle General of Peter and the General Epistle of Jude* (Eerdmans, 1968), p. 184.

39. J. N. D. Kelly, *A Commentary on the Epistles of Peter and of Jude* (Adam and Charles Black, 1969), p. 28b.

40. Beare, *op. cit.*, X, p. 714.

41. Martin, *Worship*, p. 43.

42. A. B. Macdonald, quoted in R. P. Martin, *Worship in the New Testament*, p. 40.

Chapter 14

1. H. H. Esser, "Grace," in *NIDNTT*, II, p. 121.

2. M. A. Chevallier, *Esprit de Dieu, Paroles d'homme* (Delachaux et Niestlé, 1966), p. 148.

3. J. R. W. Stott, *Baptism and Fullness* (Inter-Varsity Press, 1976), p. 87.

4. *Ibid.*, p. 87.

5. D. Watson, *I Believe in the Church* (Eerdmans, 1978), p. 104.

6. *Ibid.*, p. 105. Used by permission.

7. F. F. Bruce, *Answers to Questions* (Zondervan, 1973), p. 97.

8. Watson, *op. cit.*, p. 106.

9. K. Weiss, "Sumphero, etc.," in *TDNT*, IX, pp. 69-78.

10. A. Robertson and A. Plummer, *A Critical and Exegetical Commentary of the First Epistle of St. Paul to the Corinthians. ICC* (T. and T. Clark, 1914), p. 264.

11. J. Goetzmann, "House," in *NIDNTT*, II, pp. 251-253.

12. L. Goppelt, *Der erste Petrusbrief* (Vandenhoeck und Ruprecht, 1978), pp. 286-292.

13. Watson, *op. cit.*, p. 161.

14. A. M. Stibbs, *The First Epistle General of Peter. Tyndale* (Eerdmans, 1959), p. 157.

15. Watson, *op. cit.*, p. 104.

16. R. P. Martin, *The Family and the Fellowship* (Eerdmans, 1979), p. 53. Used by permission.

17. M. Green, *I Believe in the Holy Spirit* (Eerdmans, 1975), pp. 161-192.

18. J. Taylor, *The Go-Between God* (SCM Press, 1972), p. 214.

19. Bruce, *Answers*, p. 97.

20. W. Neil *The Epistle of Paul to the Thessalonians* (Hodder and Stoughton, 1950), p. 130.

21. J. Jeremias, *Unknown Sayings of Jesus* (S.P.C.K., 1958), pp. 89ff.

22. A. M. Hunter, *Probing the New Testament* (John Knox Press, 1971), pp. 123-126.

23. Green, *op. cit.*, p. 174.

24. Taylor, *op. cit.*, p. 213.

25. Green, *op. cit.*, p. 181.

26. *Ibid.*, p. 188.

27. Fr. Buechsel, *Der Geist Gottes im Neuen Testament* (C. Bertelsmann, 1926), "Auch Gemeindeleitung, Lehren, usw. sieht Paulus als Charismata" (translation: Church leadership, teaching, etc., Paul views as *charismata*) p. 356.

28. E. Schweizer, *The Holy Spirit* (Fortress Press, 1980), p. 93.

29. Martin, *op. cit.*, p. 53.

30. Bruce, *Answers*, p. 97.

31. D. Bloesch, *Essentials of Evangelical Theology* (Harper and Row, 1979), II, p. 108.

32. J. D. G. Dunn, "Rediscovering the Spirit," *Expository Times*, 84 (Oct. 1972), p. 43.

33. Taylor, *op. cit.*, p. 21.

Chapter 15

1. R. Schnackenburg, *New Testament Theology Today* (Palm Publishers, 1963), p. 87.

2. G. W. H. Lampe, *The Seal of the Spirit* (Longmans, Green and Co., 1951), p. 46.

3. H. J. Schoeps, *Paul* (Lutterworth, 1961), p. 99.

4. M. Goguel, "Pneumatisme et eschatologie dans le Christianisme primitive," *Revue de l'Histoire de Religions*, 134 (1946), p. 161.

5. F. F. Bruce, *Paul: Apostle of the Heart Set Free* (Eerdmans, 1977), p. 210.

6. E. W. Hunt, *Portrait of Paul* (A. R. Mowbray and Co., 1968), p. 125.

7. G. Fitzer, "Sphragis," in *TDNT*, VII, pp. 943ff. Of the 32 occurrences of *sphragis*, *sphragizo*, and *katasphragizo* in the New Testament, 22 are found in the Apocalypse.

8. N. Q. Hamilton, *The Holy Spirit and Eschatology in Paul* (Oliver and Boyd, 1957), p. 28.

9. A. Richardson, *An Introduction to the Theology of the New Testament* (SCM Press, 1958), pp. 350f. This theme is taken up in Revelation 7:3; 9:4 where the tribes of the new Israel are sealed before judgment comes.

10. Contrary to what Kirby says. J. C. Kirby, *Ephesians, Baptism and Pentecost* (McGill University Press, 1968), p. 153.

11. Fitzer, *op. cit.*, VII, p. 950. "Durch den Geist versiegelt heisst zu einem unantastbaren Eigentum gemacht zu sein" (translation: To be sealed by the Spirit means to have been made inviolable possession.)

12. This is the view of G. Dix, *The Theology of Confirmation in Relation to Baptism* (1964) and L. S. Thornton, *Confirmation: Its Place in the Baptismal Mystery* (1954).

13. R. V. G. Tasker, *The Second Epistle of Paul to the Corinthians. Tyndale* (Eerdmans, 1958), p. 48.

14. J. D. G. Dunn, *Baptism in the Holy Spirit* (Alec R. Allenson, 1970), p. 134.

15. P. E. Hughes, *Paul's Second Epistle to the Corinthians. NICNT* (Eerdmans, 1962), p. 41.

16. F. W. Beare, *A Commentary on the Epistle to the Ephesians. IB* (Abingdon-Cokesbury, 1953), X, p. 701.

17. M. Green, *I Believe in the Holy Spirit* (Eerdmans, 1975), p. 81.

18. B. Ahern, "The Indwelling Spirit, Pledge of Our Inheritance," *Catholic Biblical Quarterly*, 9 (1947), p. 180.

19. J. H. Moulton and G. Milligan, *The Vocabulary of the Greek Testament Illustrated from the Papyri and Other Non-Literary Sources* (Hodder and Stoughton, 1954), p. 79.

20. Ahern, *op. cit.*, p. 182.

21. F. F. Bruce, *The Epistle to the Ephesians* (Pickering and Inglis, 1961), p. 37.

22. Green, *op. cit.*, p. 82.

23. Richardson, *op. cit.*, p. 115.

24. J. B. Lightfoot, *Notes on the Epistles of Paul* (London, 1895), p. 324.

25. O. Cullmann, *Christ and Time* (Westminster Press, 1950), p. 239.

26. F. V. Filson, *The Second Epistle to the Corinthians. IB* (Abingdon-Cokesbury, 1953), X, p. 328.

27. J. Behn, "Arrabon," in *TDNT*, I, p. 475.

28. D. Hill, *Greek Words and Hebrew Meanings* (Cambridge University Press, 1967), p. 272.

29. C. K. Barrett, *The Holy Spirit and the Gospel tradition* (Macmillan Co., 1947), pp. 161f.

30. H. A. A. Kennedy, "St. Paul's Conception of the Spirit as Pledge," *The Expositor*, 6th series, 4 (1901), p. 278.

31. Hughes, *op. cit.*, p. 174. Used by permission.

32. Ahern, *op. cit.*, p. 183.

33. *Ibid.*, p. 187. Ahern quotes Theodore of Mospusestia, who called the *arrabon* a "sample taste."

34. Green, *op. cit.*, p. 81.

35. G. E. Ladd, "Eschatology and the Unity of New Testament Theology," *Expository Times*, 68 (1955-57), pp. 273f.

36. O. Michel, *Der Brief an die Roemer* (Muehlenberg Press, 1949), p. 204.

37. H. Berkhof, *The Doctrine of the Holy Spirit* (John Knox Press, 1964), p. 107.

38. F. J. Leenhardt, *The Epistle to the Romans* (Lutterworth, 1961), p. 222.

39. *Ibid.*

40. G. Delling, "Aparche," in *TDNT*, I, pp. 485f.

41. E. Schweizer, *The Holy Spirit* (Fortress Press, 1980), p. 110

42. L. S. Thornton, *The Common Life in the Body of Christ* (Dacre Press, 1942), p. 125.

43. A. N. Nygren, *Commentary on Romans* (Muehlenberg Press, 1949), p. 328.

44. E. Schweizer, "Huiothesia," in *TDNT*, VIII, p. 394.

45. Hamilton, *op. cit.*, p. 32.

46. Bruce, *op. cit.*, p. 428.

47. Green, *op. cit.*, p. 83.

48. Thornton, *op. cit.*, p. 96.

49. N. Dahl, *The Resurrection of the Body* (SCM Press), pp. 37-58.

50. O. Cullmann, *Immortality of the Soul or Resurrection of the Dead?* (The Epworth Press, 1958), p. 15.

51. *Ibid.*, p. 38.

52. G. Vos, "The Eschatological Aspect of the Pauline Conception of the Spirit," in *Biblical and Theological Studies* (1912), p. 238.

53. Hamilton, *op. cit.*, p. 34.

54. G. Schrenk, "Dike, etc.," in *TDNT*, II, p. 208.

55. *Ibid.*, p. 205.

56. A. Oepke, *Der Brief des Paulus an die Galater* (Evangelische Verlangsanstalt, 1957), p. 119.

57. Hill, *op. cit.*, p. 274.

58. *Ibid.*, p. 188.

59. Richardson, *op. cit.*, p. 74.

60. P. Bonnard, *L'Épitre de Saint Paul aux Galates* (Delachaux et Niestlé, 1953), p. 126.

61. E. D. W. Burton, *A Critical and Exegetical Commentary on the Epistle to the Galatians. ICC* (Charles Scribner's Sons, 1920), p. 341.

62. *Ibid.*, p. 342.

63. Oepke, *op. cit.*, p. 154.

64. *Ibid.*, p. 154.

65. Hill, *op. cit.*, p. 189.

66. F. F. Bruce, *Paul*, p. 209.

67. R. H. Mounce, *The Book of Revelation. NICNT* (Eerdmans, 1977), p. 394. Also, G. E. Ladd, *A Commentary on the Revelation of John* (Eerdmans, 1972), p. 294.

68. G. R. Beasley-Murray, *The Book of Revelation. NCB* (Attic Press, rev. ed., 1978), p. 343.

Index of Scriptures

David Ewert was born in the Ukraine and immigrated to Canada with his parents in 1926. He joined the Mennonite Brethren Church in 1939, and spent five years as a student in several Bible institutes. He earned his BA at the University of British Columbia, and his BD at the Baptist Seminary in Toronto. He holds an MA in biblical literature from Wheaton College, and an MTh from Luther Seminary, St. Paul. He earned his PhD in New Testament at McGill University, Montreal.

In 1944 Ewert married Lena Hamm, who had also come with her German-speaking parents from the USSR. They have five children, four of them married. Their eldest daughter and her husband are in medical work in Tanzania; their youngest daughter and her husband are teaching in Warsaw, Poland; one son and a daughter and their spouses are teachers in Vancouver, B.C., and one daughter lives in Fresno.

After teaching in Bible institutes for seven years, Ewert was on the faculty of the Mennonite Brethren Bible College, Winnipeg, for nineteen years. In between he served for short terms as visiting professor at Union Biblical Seminary, Yeotmal, India; Regent College, Vancouver; and Canadian Bible College, Regina. In 1972 the Ewerts moved to Harrisonburg, Virginia, where Ewert taught New Testament for three years at the Eastern Mennonite Seminary. In 1975 he joined the faculty of the Mennonite Brethren Biblical Seminary, Fresno, California, where he has taught Greek language and exegesis, and New Testament theology.

Besides seminary teaching Ewert has served in teaching and

preaching missions to Paraguay, Brazil, India, Austria, Germany, and Switzerland. Ewert is an ordained minister of the Mennonite Brethren Church and has taken an active part in the development of some of its schools and its publications.

He is the author of a biblical study of the Christian hope, *And Then Comes the End* (Herald Press, 1980).